FAITH
IN HISTORY AND SOCIETY

FAITH
IN HISTORY
AND SOCIETY
TOWARD A PRACTICAL
FUNDAMENTAL THEOLOGY

Johann Baptist Metz

TRANSLATED BY DAVID SMITH

A CROSSROAD BOOK
THE SEABURY PRESS · NEW YORK

1980
The Seabury Press
815 Second Avenue
New York, N.Y. 10017

Originally published as *Glaube in Geschichte und Gesellschaft* ©
1977 Matthias-Grünewald-Verlag, Mainz

Printed in the United States of America

Library of Congress Cataloging in Publication Data

Metz, Johann Baptist, 1928–
Faith in history and society.
(A Crossroad book)
Translation of Glaube in Geschichte und Gesellschaft.
Includes index.
1. Apologetics—20th century.   2. Christianity
and politics.   3. Theology, Doctrinal.   I. Title.
BT1102.M4713   239′.094   78-27277
ISBN 0-8164-0426-7

Contents

PART 1
C O N C E P T

PART III:
CATEGORIES

Foreword

This book indicates a way of theology. I have called it a practical work of fundamental theology or a fundamental theology with a practical aim. This subtitle indicates the general direction in which I hoped to travel in the book. I have subdivided the journey into three stages or parts, with the headings Concept—Themes—Categories.

My elaboration of this practical fundamental theology is a critical development of my original approach to a new political theology. Unlike the classical political theology, to which many critics tried to link my new approach in an attempt to ruin its chances before it had been fully developed, the new approach was in no sense intended to give religious height and depth to politics that were already being promulgated, evolved or put into practice elsewhere or simply to make a theological copy of a political model. On the contrary, my intention, in evolving a new political theology, was primarily to go to the roots of and criticize the strange historical and social lack of political consciousness that characterizes Christianity in general and Christian theology in particular. I had this in mind because it is not possible, without self-deceit, to regard Christianity and theology as politically innocent and entirely without intention. My new political theology, then, is predetermined by a need to expose 'pure' Christianity for what it really is—an attempt to protect Christian teaching from the practical demands made by radical Christianity.

In the course of developing this practical fundamental theology, an attempt is made to steer a way between the Scylla of extreme privatization and the Charybdis of strict secularization and in this way to gain access to the practical basis of its real identity. The theological parts of this book have been written explicitly from the point of view that the widely discussed crisis of identity in Christianity is not primarily a crisis of the Christian message, but rather a crisis of its subjects and institutions. These are too remote from the undeniably practical implications of the message and so tend to destroy its power.

I am greatly indebted to my friends and collaborators in Münster for the valuable help that they have given me and the stimulus that they have provided.

It is difficult to express my special thanks to Tiemo R. Peters, who has from the beginning encouraged me to write this book and supported me with his penetrating, precise and critical suggestions. In this, he has done a great deal not only for the letter, but also for the spirit of this book.

The volume is dedicated to all students of political theology. I take the liberty of counting Karl Rahner among those who are well disposed towards the discipline.

Münster, Autumn 1977   *Johann Baptist Metz*

PART I

Concept

1. Between evolution and dialectics
The point of departure for a contemporary fundamental theology

'Always be prepared to make a defence to anyone who calls you to account for the hope that is in you' (1 Pet 3. 15). Any Christian theology, then, can be defined, at least in its task and intention, as a defence of hope.[1] What is the hope that is in question here? It is the solidarity of hope in the God of the living and the dead, who calls all men to be his subjects. In our defense of this hope, we are concerned not with a conflict between ideas unrelated to any subject, but rather with the concrete historical and social situation in which subjects are placed, with their experiences, sufferings, struggles and contradictions.

1. The need to analyze the situation and the special features of this analysis

If we are concerned, then, with the human situation,[2] we have first to analyze this situation, since we cannot expect an analysis to be provided in advance either by theology or by any standardized philosophy. The historical aspect of our analysis is discussed in the following two chapters (2 and 3 below), while the dominant aspects of the necessary point of departure for a contemporary fundamental theology are considered in greater detail in the fourth chapter of Part I. The various concrete aspects of this analysis of the situation are then examined separately in the discussion of different themes in the second part of the book. This is done in order to avoid an artificial separation between characterizing the situation and reflecting upon it theologically.

In this first section, I will confine myself to a brief, general outline of two important features of the analysis of the situation.

1. Any analysis of this situation and of the social point of departure for a Christian defence of hope must nowadays inevitably be made on a world-wide scale. Socio-political and economic relationships are becoming increasingly interdependent and for this reason no situation can be determined in the concrete without considering this global aspect. Any attempt to obtain a practical result without taking the global aspect into consideration will only be dubiously abstract.

It would therefore not be honest to recommend that the Latin American churches and theologians should accept an analysis of the situation that is different from the one that we would evolve for ourselves in the northern regions of the world and which would therefore produce different results. The conflict between North and South that is so extensively discussed nowadays cannot be defined or resolved in regional terms, nor can it be neutralized by the Church and theologians as a purely political and economic event. It is above all a conflict with significant effects on the one Church throughout the world. The detailed implications of this will be examined in the course of this book and especially in Chapter 4 below.

In this context, it would be good for European theologians to take up the challenge with which they have been confronted for some time now by the Latin-American theology of liberation.[3] We can no longer simply go on exporting our western theology to the countries of Latin America, where there are now hardly any customers who are sufficiently interested to buy it. As I see it, it is more important for western theologians to try to see their theology within the context of world-wide processes and to take seriously the fact that it is conditioned by its situation within the particular context of middle-class, Central-European society.

2. It is also important to bear in mind that this world, which we are bound to analyze and which we tend to call the world of our experience, is in fact a secondary or meta-world, in other words, a world which, in itself and in its deepest reality, bears the deep impression of many systems and theories and which can therefore only be experienced and possibly changed in and through these systems and theories. If this fact is forgotten, the result may easily be the acceptance of an uncritical idea of praxis. A praxis which fails to take into account the complex structure of the world or our expe-

rience of it as secondary will therefore inevitably remain sporadic and ineffective. It stands symbolically for a new reality that is sought, but cannot itself bring this reality about, because it is again absorbed by the systems and theories that have become valid.

These systems, theories or interpretations of the world, within which we experience the world itself, will be discussed more fully later on. In the meantime, however, we must content ourselves with a very brief description. On the one hand, there is the system based on an evolutionary interpretation of the world and reality, which has its roots in the Enlightenment on the one hand and our western middle-class society on the other. On the other hand, however, there is also the historical and materialist dialectical system, which can be interpreted historically as a particular way in which the Enlightenment was realized [4] and which is manifested historically and socially above all in the socialist societies of the East.

2. The apologetical and practical character of a contemporary fundamental theology

This formal definition of a situation that is present today and has to be taken into account by theologians has important consequences. In the past, at a time when metaphysical thinking was predominant or when societies were still determined by a religious objective, it might have been possible for the theoretical points of departure that were currently valid to be simply taken over by a fundamental theology that was concerned with the theoretical foundations of Christian faith or used by that theology as a means for clarifying its own problems. This procedure is, however, no longer possible today. Neither of the two theoretical points of departure, to which all the theories that are valid today can be more or less directly traced back, is in any sense innocent or neutral with regard to religion and Christianity and therefore also with regard to theology. They can be regarded, with different degrees of explicitness, as meta-theories with respect to religion and theology. In other words, religion can, for the purpose of these theories, in principle be either reconstructed or abolished and seen as pointing to a more comprehensive theoretical system. [5]

The Christian defence of faith, then, may come into conflict with attempts to reconstruct religion on the basis of an evolutionary theory of the world of the kind that has made a deep impression on all analytical theories of science, action or language, to classify it adequately in accordance with quasi-evolutionary principles and in this way to give its public claim to validity a purely relative value. In this context, evolution should not be seen as a symbol leading to knowledge, but with a relevance that is confined, for example, only to the sphere of natural science. Here at least, it is active as a fundamental symbol of knowledge and logic and has a theoretical status which is not clear as far as its totalizing tendency is concerned. We may, however, say quite explicitly here that evolution should certainly not be understood in this context in the sense in which it is used in everyday parlance. Nor should it be thought of as a teleologically directed development, in the sense of a non-dialectical process in the advance of mankind.

We should regard evolution here rather as a basic acceptance of a technical rationality which can no longer be justified and within which structures and tendencies as well as phenomena of greater or lesser complexity are revealed and can be classified, but which is not, as a whole, capable of being further clarified and which therefore functions as a quasi-religious symbol of scientific knowledge.[6] This evolving consciousness is also active by virtue of the fact that it is already present, as a kind of feeling for life, in man's pre-scientific consciousness and has as such impressed itself on modern man's everyday experience of himself. Man's consciousness of his own identity has become weaker and more damaged in the course of human progress. Man is at the mercy of a darkly speckled universe and enclosed in an endless continuum of time that is no longer capable of surprising him. He feels that he is caught up in the waves of an anonymous process of evolution sweeping pitilessly over everyone. A new culture of apathy and lack of feeling is being prepared for him in view of his experience of fragile identity. It is therefore important to bear in mind the deep effects of this evolving consciousness which bears up a whole theory of the world.

Historical and dialectical materialism also claims to have seen through the strongly religious content of Christianity and to have taken over, more successfully, the liberating tendencies of the Christian religion in a secularized utopian form. This dialectical materialism must, however, become the victim of an evolutionary logic that lacks a subject, if it can only base its intention to set the world free on a teleology of freedom that is perhaps wrongly expected of matter or nature itself. I shall discuss this critical supposition later.[7] We may in any case be sure that religion and dialectics would be close to each other if they had a common opponent in the evolutionary consciousness that ultimately silences history, the subject and liberation as authentic realities. This factor will also be discussed later on in this book. In the meantime, however, I would draw attention to two important aspects in the elaboration of a contemporary fundamental theology.

1. Any fundamental theology, which claims, as it should, to investigate the foundations of theology has an apologetical aspect, not simply incidentally or as a kind of historical survival, but as part of its essential nature. An essential task of fundamental theology, then, is to defend, justify or give an account of the authenticity of religion, in opposition to those systems that claim to be meta-theories of theology. In other words, it must do what is meant by the word 'apologetics'.

2. In view of these very comprehensive theories, fundamental theology of this kind cannot justify itself by developing another and even more comprehensive theory which might be a theological meta-theory of the existing world theories. It must, if it is to avoid a speculative regression into infinity, justify itself as theology by a return—or regression—to subjects and the praxis of subjects. In other words, it has to regard itself as a practical foundation discipline or as practical fundamental theology. As such, its task is to evoke and describe a praxis which will resist all evolutionary attempts at reconstruction and any attempt to do away with religious practice as an independent entity or the religious subject as an authentic element in the process of a historical and materialist dialectical system.

The following conclusion can be drawn from these two statements. A theology which is theoretical because it is interested in justification must be apologetical. It cannot simply subordinate itself to the existing types of theory if it is to function as theology. If it is theoretical because it is interested in justification, then this theology must be practical and guided by a new dialectical tension between theory and praxis. It can only deal effectively with attempts at evolutionary reconstruction or to impose a total social conditioning of religion by adopting a praxis that breaks open these systems of interpretation. As a theology which seeks to justify, then, fundamental theology is essentially apologetical and practical. It is only in this way that it can guarantee the authenticity of faith and make it valid.[8]

3. Biblical defence

We are bound to ask who would really want nowadays to defend Christian hope or the Church. The task has for a long time been regarded with suspicion. Apologetics are thought to be tactically dishonest, dogmatic in the bad sense, tending to take ideological short cuts and formalistic in argument. The apologist is suspected of being incapable of learning and unwilling to learn, with the result that he reacts with astonishment and firmness to the critical questions that arise spontaneously in new situations.

This practical apologetical aspect of fundamental theology does not, however, mean that the fundamental theologian is necessarily uncritical or insensitive to all theory. On the contrary, it is indicative of a very uncritical attitude to insist exclusively on pure theory (this question will be discussed in greater detail later on). To emphasize the practical apologetical aspect of fundamental theology, then, does not lead to a helpless or impotent opening out of theology or an irrational rigidity and dogmatism towards the current theories. Practical fundamental theology has the difficult task of dealing with these theories in an attempt to demonstrate that they cannot validate their meta-theoretical claims to explain away religion or operate with unproved assumptions. The obvious sign of this is the irrational predominance of the symbol of evolution.

The fact that the Christian religion cannot be defended by purely theoretical arguments, but that an apologetical praxis has to be applied in its defence is fully in accordance with the biblical datum of apology. I would therefore draw attention to two fundamental aspects of this apology within the context of the New Testament which are at the same time concepts of practical reason.

1. It is important to remember that the language of the defence of Christianity that is found in the New Testament is legalistic in origin.[9] Not only the biblical language of this defence, but also

such theological concepts as satisfaction, emancipation, autonomy and so on have their origin in the law. This origin in the language of the law shows that, in the New Testament sense, the Christian is again and again on trial and has in practice to justify his hope in this situation. His defence or apology therefore is a kind of public justification of Christian hope. We know from the history of the early Church that being on trial and speaking in defence of the Christian religion could often be a matter of life or death. A clear example of an early Christian who was both an apologist and a martyr is Justin. This may perhaps justify our claim, despite the fact that it cannot be proved conclusively by linguistic arguments, that defence or apology is very close to what is known in the New Testament as the imitation of Christ.[10] Finally, we are bound to point out that Jesus himself is seen by the evangelists as being in a similar situation of trial. They present us with the encounter that took place between Jesus and his witnesses on the one hand and the political authorities of the state on the other. In and through his suffering and death, Jesus defended his hope.[11]

The biblical concept of defence, then, has a legal origin, even though this usage was not current and it cannot be proved beyond all doubt that apology and imitation are synonymous. This can be expressed in Hasidaean terms in the following way. If an old rabbi was, during one of the bloody persecutions of his people, dragged before the court and asked: 'How do you justify your religious praxis?' he would reply: 'How can I convince you, if you are not convinced by the suffering of my people?'[12]

2. The biblical concept of apology also has an eschatological and apocalyptic perspective. In the New Testament, what is ultimately involved in this defence is man's trial before Christ in the court of justice at the end of time: 'We must all appear before the judgment seat of Christ, so that each one may receive good or evil, according to what he has done in the body' (2 Cor 5. 10). It is obvious that, in this context, the word 'apology' can best be translated as 'justification'.[13] This justification at the end of time will clearly not be a purely intellectual defence of hope, but a praxis. This justification or vindication is above all a concept of practical reason.

What, then, does it mean, justification in an eschatological and apocalyptic perspective? Surely any concrete justification is made impossible in advance by the dimensions of this eschatological and apocalyptic perspective, in which the whole of history and human society are visible. Surely too, this gives rise to a dangerous confusion. Is this concept, based as it is on a universal perspective, perhaps not *a priori* unsuitable for the purpose of praxis? Or is it possible, in the present situation in which mankind and the world are placed, for it, because of its universal nature, to be really politically and socially in accordance with that situation? Are there not very many tasks of a universal dimension and on a world-wide scale today which can be described with relative ease, but for which there are apparently no specific subjects of justification, at least not at present?[14]

4. Outside the territory of the system

If we take this practical and apologetical aspect of fundamental theology seriously, then the latter will, precisely as a practical fundamental theology, become a political theology of the subject, with certain clear consequences for the theological self-understanding of this discipline. It cannot simply develop as a system of justification without a subject, nor can it provide its themes of its own accord and calculate in advance the difficulty of the challenges or the tests that may confront it. The field in which it proves its value lies outside the territory of any previously conceived theological system. It is, as it were, defined by the social and historical situation with all its painful contradictions. The fundamental theology that I have in mind will always be closely linked to a praxis that is opposed to any attempt to condition religion socially or to reconstruct it theoretically. It is, in other words, linked to the praxis of faith in its mystical and its political dimension.

In this sense, then, fundamental theology is bound to be systematically interrupted by this praxis. This is why it can and should never be a theology that is purely confined to books or lectures— because of its claim to justification. It has to absorb new praxis and new experiences if it is to prevent itself from reproducing the concepts of earlier praxis and experiences.

This procedure does not lead automatically to theological continuity. This can only be maintained or acquired by practical fundamental theology if the latter is seen as a corrective with regard to existing theological systems and approaches and if it preserves and passes on the substance and intention of those systems in a critical and corrective relationship with them. What is more, the form of this corrective may also be the way which we are given today and are expected to follow, by means of which a purely theological continuity will succeed in theology.[15]

I conclude this chapter with a brief review of the basic subject matter of the remaining three chapters in this first part of the book. In Chapter 2 I shall attempt to show how this practical fundamental theology that I have outlined in the present chapter results from the historical situation in which the Christian Church and its theology are placed. In Chapter 3 I use this fundamental theology as the basis from which to criticize the religion of the privatized middle class that in turn places the religious subject in a situation of crisis. Finally, in Chapter 4, an attempt is made to throw light on the total conception of this practical fundamental theology as a political theology, and to use it as the basis for further theological work.

Notes

1. One of the most important aspects of the task of the explicit Christian today is to make a defence of hope. This is clear from the title given by the synod of German bishops to a 'Confession of faith in our time' ('Our hope') and their introductory statement in this document, describing the 'defence of faith' as 'the Church's task'. The World Council of Churches is also preparing a document on the faith of Christians, in which the key concept is 'defence of hope'.

2. In this, we are omitting another need that inevitably arises from our understanding of defending hope—the need to ask who is to make this defence, who is the most suitable subject of such a work of apologetics and what is the function of the professional theologian in an apologetical process which should not take place in the sphere of pure ideas and in the absence of subjects, but must be deeply involved in the experiences and sufferings of human history.

3. It is obvious that various points of contact and opportunities for a critical exchange of ideas between the political theology and the theology of liberation will arise in the course of our considerations in this book. This applies not only to their mutual insistence on an analysis of the situation on a world-wide scale, but also to many important elements of the theology that is to be developed in this book. These include a concentration on the primacy of praxis, the basic category of solidarity and a theology of the subject based on the idea of the whole of mankind in solidarity and subjection to God. In this sense, my development of a practical political fundamental theology, in which the question not only of the situation and the point of departure, but also of the interests and the bearers of that theology is raised, is in itself an at-

tempt to go beyond the narrow confines of central European theology or at least to define its conditioning factors and limits more clearly. L. Rütti has taken seriously the need to take this world-wide scale in political theology into account: *Zur Theologie der Mission* (Mainz and Munich, 1972). Several authors have, within the framework of political theology, been concerned with the need to interpret and communicate critically the intentions of the theology of liberation. These include the contributors (R. Almeida-Cunha, L. A. De Boni, F. Castillo, G. Süss and others) to F. Castillo, ed., *Theologie aus der Praxis des Volkes* (Mainz and Munich, 1978) and G. Süss, *Volkskatholizismus in Brasilien* (Mainz and Munich, 1978). One article that is important in its treatment of the relationship between the theology of liberation and political theology is F. P. Fiorenza, 'Political Theology and Liberation Theology: An Inquiry into their Fundamental Meaning', T. M. McFadden, ed., *Liberation, Revolution and Freedom. Theological Perspectives* (New York, 1975), pp. 3–29.

4. See L. Goldmann, *Der christliche Bürger und die Aufklärung* (Neuwied, 1968).

5. For a penetrating controversy with (analytical) meta-theories of theology and a continuation of the basic intentions of political theology, see H. Peukert, *Wissenschaftstheorie—Handlungstheorie—Fundamentale Theologie* (Düsseldorf, 1976).

6. A system orientated towards evolution, which in its wider effects can be regarded as a kind of substitute for metaphysics, may be able to classify religion, in its strictly privatized form, quite functionally into the categories of social processes. It may, for example, do this with the aim of absorbing resistance and disappointments that might endanger the course of those social processes (which are, in the last resort, without subjects).

7. For this evolutionary disintegration of the dialectics of liberation, see, for example, J. Habermas' recent attempt to reconstruct historical materialism on the basis of evolution.

8. These ideas did not predominate in my article on 'Apologetics' in *Sacramentum Mundi* I (Freiburg & London, 1967), pp. 266–276. In that article, I maintained that apologetics were neither an adaptation, nor an attempt to fit Christian faith into a ready-made, formal and universal pattern, either of a cosmological and metaphysical or of a transcendental, existential or personal kind. In its justification of faith, it tried to be open to all patterns of faith and to keep what Bonhoeffer had called the 'counterlogos' of the cross and resurrection of Jesus Christ constantly in view; this counter-logos could be proved true not as a pure idea, but only in a (historical) activity that was orientated towards its eschatological promises.

9. See G. Ebeling, 'Erwägungen zu einer evangelischen Fundamentaltheologie', *ZThK* 67 (1970). This article contains some important ideas about the theological development of this concept.

10. For the content and meaning of 'imitation' in the sense of apologetical praxis, see my *Followers of Christ* (London & New York, 1978).

11. See H. Schlier, *Besinnung auf das Neue Testament* (Freiburg, 1964), p. 193.

12. The underlying intention of this particular conception of practical fundamental theology is to give valid expression to the inheritance of the Jewish religion which is so often overlooked and to which justice cannot be done in the pure exegesis of Old Testament texts.

13. See G. Picht, *Wahrheit—Vernunft—Verantwortung* (Stuttgart, 1969), pp. 318–342.

14. See also G. Picht, *op. cit.*

15. I am of the opinion that Karl Rahner's transcendental theology can only be continued without a break if it is criticized and corrected with the help of experiences and a praxis that are not derived from the theological system hitherto in use. Rahner's transcendental theology continued to be dramatic and in that respect free of the suspicion of being tautological, as long as it was a corrective, in other words, as long as it was engaged in controversy with a theological opponent. In the initial stages of Rahner's transcendental theology, that opponent was neoscholasticism. The first crises of identity began to appear in Rahner's theology, however, when this opponent finally collapsed in exhaustion in the strong arms of transcendental theology. We may go further and say that even Karl Barth's early *Deus dixit* theology was also a corrective theology. His uncompromising 'commitment to God'—with which Barth himself insisted every theology should yet cannot begin—was therefore not a badly concealed positivism of revelation, because it criticized and corrected the predominant liberal theology of the period.

2. Roundabout ways to a fundamental theology
An attempt at a historical self-analysis

The apologetical approach forms the basis of all genuine Christian theology. As an attempt to justify or defend Christian hope, it is as old as Christianity itself and the controversy in which the Christian religion has always been engaged.[1] One basic experimental aspect of theological reasoning is clearly visible in fundamental theology, namely that it is concerned with experiences, insights and theories with a theological character that cannot always be ascertained in advance because it has to be rediscovered again and again in a historical, experimental synthesis. It is not purely by chance that nontheological definitions (concepts) are always available in fundamental theology, which is obviously in a permanent state of being systematically reconstructed if this experiment of theological reasoning is found to be present in its structure.

For a long time it has been recognized that the classical division of fundamental theology into three parts (religion, Jesus Christ and the Church) and the inner structure of each of those three parts had been determined by historical factors. The form and content of the treatise on the Church, for example, are still to some extent conditioned by the controversies of the post-Reformation period. Most of the questions in the treatises on religion and Jesus Christ are still reactions to the controversy about the metaphysical and historical foundations of Christianity that was current during the period of the Enlightenment. Indeed, almost the whole repertoire of classical concepts and problems to be found in fundamental theology (or theologies) today can be traced back to precisely that period and its radical self-questioning. The concept of religion and the distinction between religion and revelation and the problem of natural theology that are both connected with it are all questions originally asked during the post-Reformation era. They can all be grouped under the heading of the question of the possibility of and the conditions governing revelation as such that is based on a rationality outside history and independent of subjects. This rationality that is presumably outside or above history is nonetheless conditioned and made relative by history and, although it has always determined and still determines the structure of fundamental theology, it does not necessarily lead directly to the heart of those questions with which contemporary fundamental theology is confronted.

Apologetics did not emerge as an independent theological discipline until the end of the Enlightenment, when it came as a reaction to the problems that had been raised during that period. In the immediately post-Reformation period and the Baroque age, the disputes that took place were almost exclusively interconfessional and concerned with what we now call controversial theology (the period of the great arguments with the *gentes,* as represented, for example, in Thomas Aquinas' *Summa contra gentiles,* had passed long since). These disputes also took place within a cosmos that was recognized on both sides to be Christian.[2] The Enlightenment, however, introduced two important changes in the situation of the Church and its theology. On the one hand, the identity of faith and religious consciousness, which had hitherto been accepted more or less unquestioningly, ceased to exist. Christian faith found itself confronted with a universal critical concept of religion and challenged to justify or defend itself. On the other hand, the unity of religion and society, which had similarly hitherto been accepted without question, also broke up, beginning in France during the early period of the Enlightenment. Christianity began at that time and in that place to appear, in relationship to its social environment, for the first time as a particular aspect of an all-embracing historical and social connection with the world that could determine the universal consciousness of man more and more fully.

It was, at that time and in that way that the requirements for a form of questioning and criticism of religion that is still of great importance today were evolved. This questioning mainly takes the form of a criticism of ideology. In other words, it tries to place the Christian religion in a connection with the social processes of the world that might determine it and to expose religion as a function (or ideological superstructure) of certain relationships or certain subjects in society. The religious subject came therefore to be defined as the conscious social subject that is not yet adequate for itself or as the social subject with a false consciousness.

In what follows, I shall therefore attempt to check theology against its ability to take the so-called Enlightenment as an epochmaking event seriously and to deal with it critically. In the first section below, I shall examine the ways in which such themes as tradition, authority and reason, which were carefully considered by the philosophers of the Enlightenment, were debated (or not debated) by the theologians of the periods preceding, during and following the First Vatican Council. In the second section, I shall look at the attempts made by more recent theologians to overcome the thinking of the Enlightenment in the light of German idealism or the principle of secularization.

In the third part of this chapter, the attempts made firstly by the apologetical approach and secondly by the new theology to break through the influence of Enlightenment thinking are critically considered together with the aim of establishing whether what has taken place politically since the Enlightenment has in fact been realized in theology and the Church of the First and Second Vatican Councils. The aim, in other words, in this third section is to ascertain whether the Church has been able not only to make use of the questions considered by the Enlightenment, but to recognize those questions as rooted in the rise of a new kind of man—the citizen or middle-class subject—and his relationship with religion and faith. This third section is of special importance in connection with my attempt to define a practical fundamental theology today. It is also inevitably bound to lead to certain changes in our attitude towards the apologetics of Vatican I and the new theology of Vatican II. It will also make me correct to some extent the contribution that I have so far made to the formulation of a political theology. Finally, it forms a preparation for a renewal of the debate with the Enlightenment that is undertaken in the third chapter of this part of the book ('Political theology of the subject as a theological criticism of middle-class religion'). Section 3 of this chapter and the third chapter of Part I should therefore be seen as a single argument.

1. The apologetical front

The Tübingen school can certainly be regarded as an exception to the general pattern of apologetics in the Catholic Church during the

nineteenth century.[3] From the end of the eighteenth century onwards, its members (including J. S. Drey, J. B. Hirscher, J. A.
Möhler and J. E. Kuhn) engaged in brilliant theoretical apologetics
which constituted what was in the best sense of the word a theology
of response which was at that time not, as was later the case,
isolated from all other systematic and historical concerns in the
sphere of theology. On the contrary, the apologetics of the Catholic
members of the Tübingen school arose directly out of those other
concerns. As F. A. Staudenmaier has said, 'the only true Christian
apologetics are a direct self-representation of the spirit of Christianity'.

The apologetics of the Catholic Tübingen school were in no
sense isolated from the philosophy and science of the period. Indeed, the weakness of these aggressive and interdisciplinary apologetics was above all to be found in their being based on the conviction of the members of the school, who were fully acquainted with
nineteenth-century scientific progress, that the problems of the Enlightenment had already been overcome, or would soon be overcome by the idealism and romanticism of the age. In so doing, the
Tübingen theologians gave too little attention to the central problem
of the Enlightenment that Kant had approached and Marx had later
explored in depth with important consequences—the primacy of
practical reason.

a. Roundabout the middle of the ninteenth century, however, a
second attack was made against the foundations of Christianity by
thinkers such as Feuerbach, Marx and Nietzsche and religion was
radically criticized under the guise of a criticism of ideology. At the
same time, with rather tragic consequences for the history of theology, the powerful light shed by the apologetics of response of the
Catholic school at Tübingen began to grow dim and was replaced
by another form of pure apologetics which was isolated from contemporary historical and philosophical concerns. This is the period
of what is usually known as neo-scholasticism. This theology pre-
dominated in the Catholic Church during the second half of the
nineteenth century until as late as the nineteen-thirties.

Neo-scholasticism has left a lasting impression on apologetical
theology as a whole and indeed on every attempt that has been
made from the mid-nineteenth century until the present time to provide a theological response to all contemporary questions. Although
they are not at all easy to assess, I shall discuss the achievements

and the important figures of neo-scholastic theology later in this book. In the meantime, however, I am bound to point out that it was in certain clear ways a regressive movement. It retreated from contemporary philosophical and related problems and, at a time when the safe foundations of theology began to shake, sought refuge in the past and revived earlier traditions. Kleutgen, a leading exponent of neo-scholasticism, called his work a 'theology of antiquity' (*Theologie der Vorzeit*) and the title is very revealing.

The cognitive and political isolation of neo-scholasticism is fully in accordance with the spirit of Catholic Christianity at the time when this theology was formulated. During this period, Catholics, rather feebly imitating the great Corpus Christianum of the High Middle Ages, had retreated into a to-some-extent political stronghold which might be called a nineteenth-century *Corpus Catholicum*. Apologetics became polemics in a very far-reaching sense, even embracing social action (Bismarck's *Kulturkampf* is the classical example of this). During the first phase of apologetics, the mutual relationships that existed between Catholicism and Protestantism were very fruitful,[4] but these soon deteriorated into defensive attitudes, isolation and even aggressive denial. The aim was above all to achieve a new stability.

Neo-scholastic apologetics also remained isolated from theology as a whole and moved in the fringe areas of the consciousness of and teaching about faith. It was above all a theory of the *praeambula fidei*. It was a concept not of mediation but of defence. One of the most important consequences of the neo-scholastic approach was that theology was threatened with division into two separate spheres of assertive and defensive thinking. Dogmatic theology and apologetics tended to exist side by side without touching. Theologians specializing in the first discipline were not conscious of any need to justify Christian faith, while apologists lost sight of the living content of faith and were consequently in the long run unable to defend it in accordance with its content and its immanent intelligibility. One result of this attitude was that neo-scholastic theologians often discussed aspects of faith objectively in order to protect them from the critical questions raised by the contemporary world with the inflexible weapons of apologetics.

These apologetics were deeply marked by a defensive attitude and proved to be incapable of constant honest self-criticism and correction of the kind that ought to arise from the very heart of Christianity. As a consequence, the neo-scholastic apologists looked more and more outside Christianity itself for the causes of failure in theology and the Church.

b. Religion and society became more and more radically separated as a result of the Enlightenment and this led to a loss of plausibility, universality and normativity in theology and the Church. The relationship between religion and society, which had, until the Enlightenment, been unquestioningly accepted in dogmatic theology, therefore became a problem, on the assumption that *Doctrina christiana* (or *Doctrina catholica*) could not provide the basis for giving consent to social action. In the course of the nineteenth century, the Church attempted to make up for this loss of universality and normativity by evolving its own social teaching, which is to be found in the papal encyclicals that appeared in the nineteenth century and the Roman pronouncements about social and political questions of the time.[5]

This social teaching of the Church also formed part of the apologetical syndrome. Neo-scholastic apologetics raised a protective wall around Catholic dogmatic theology to defend it against the historical, philosophical and general scientific questions that attacked it. In the same way, a relief attack was made against the political challenge of the times in the social teaching of the ninteenth- and early twentieth-century Church. In other words, the fight against civil democracy, liberalism in the nineteenth century and finally Marxism was carried on just in front of the fortress Church, on the territory of pure social ethics. In this attempt, the theological and dogmatic content of the Christian message was as far as possible kept out of the controversy about social matters. It was therefore an indirect attempt to deal with the basic problems of faith and theology while bypassing the controversies of the period. (Those problems were, of course, always 'political'.)

What is important, however, to bear in mind is that controversy with political and economic ideas and theoretical systems of any period cannot be carried on by means of apologetics or in the fringe areas by means of neo-scholasticism or the Church's social teaching. It has rather to be carried on by using the very substance of Christian faith. This conviction forms the basis of the political theology that is developed in this book.[6]

c. The political phenomenon, which is also concerned with theology and the history of the Church and has usually been known as traditionalism, can be regarded as a prototype of the apologetical front described above.

Traditionalism was a theoretical movement connected with the state and society in France at the end of the eighteenth and the beginning of the nineteenth centuries, that is, immediately following the French Revolution. It took the form of a radical criticism and generally also a rejection of the political form of Enlightenment thought that was current during the Revolution. The most prominent representatives of this movement in France were de Bonald, Lamennais and de Maistre. The movement also had lay exponents in other European countries, notably the political philosopher Burke in England, Donoso Cortez in Spain and three outstanding Germans, J. Görres, F. von Baader and the young Pilgram.

The traditionalists differed from the neo-scholastic theologians or the exponents of the Church's social teaching in that they believed that the identity of the Christian religion could not be considered, let alone saved, outside the social context in which it was placed. For this reason, any attempt to mediate aspects of faith such as original sin, divine authority and providence socially was also regarded by the tradionalists as an attempt to save its substance.

The traditionalists threw doubt on the knowledge gained through natural reason (pointing again and again in this context to the weakening power of original sin) and stressed how unsuitable natural reason was as a means of providing access to the idea of God or revelation (referring repeatedly in this instance to the need for what they called a primitive revelation). In so doing, the traditionalists played the part of adversaries in the theology of the nineteenth century and the Church of the First Vatican Council. The Fathers of that Council were clearly opposed to traditionalism in their teaching about the relationship between *ratio* and *fides* and their pronouncements about revelation and man's knowledge gained through revelation.

Later, in the third chapter of this part of the book, I shall be able, by dealing with a number of questions which will become clear at the end of this examination of the progress of fundamental theology, to recognize what is legitimate and indeed theologically indispensable in traditionalism and to see its achievements in the field of apologetics in a different light. At present, however, I must confine myself to criticizing traditionalism as a social and political aspect of apologetics.

The traditionalists' rejection of reason and the general public use of reason has to be seen as operating within a directly political context. They rejected reason because they wanted to invalidate its claim to criticize the prevailing authority of the state and those who held that authority and to overcome systematically the idea of democratic self-government that was regarded as the capital sin of the French Revolution. This process was very problematical because it contained the danger and clearly recognized fact of making the Christian religion and its dogmas move in the direction of a restoration of an earlier system. The traditionalists' denial of the primacy of reason, then, did not operate within a primarily theological context. It was, on the contrary, almost exclusively interested in making the idea of a powerful monarchy prevail over that of middle-class democracy (the latter was, of course, based on the concept of universal autonomy which had its roots in the primacy of human reason). The traditionalists therefore made use of theological data and gave these a relative value in order to emphasise political ideas and systems and to keep the mass of the people, who were thought to be insufficiently mature to hold political power, in a state of subjection.

An even more basic process, however, can be seen in this aspect of traditionalism—the hypostasization of political power or an attempt to trace political authority back to religious authority with the aim of giving politics the stability and immunity possessed by religion. This is, however, not primarily a theological question concerned with the way in which political authority is related to the authority of God. If authority could be shown to be an expression of God's plan, the traditionalists believed, then the monarchical idea of political authority could be safeguarded and made unassailable.

This theory of sovereignty clearly had an influence on the practical ideas of primacy and infallibility at the First Vatican Council, although the Council in fact condemned traditionalism, or rather those of its teachings which were dogmatically immediately identifiable (the need for a primitive revelation and the denunciation of natural reason). The disastrous aspect of the division between dogmatic theology and social theory as described above is made quite clear here. The dogmatic aspects of traditionalist teaching were condemned by the First Vatican Council, but the social teaching of traditionalism was validated in the practical self-understanding of the highest authority of the Church.

2. The breakthrough of the apologetical front by the new theology

In this section, I shall discuss very briefly and simply the path followed by the new theology in its breakthrough of the apologetical front and its attempt to defend Christian faith by means of a constructive association with recent traditions. In the previous section, I drew attention to the theological movements that were active in and around the First Vatican Council. In this section, I shall be dealing with the theological changes connected with Vatican II.

The new beginning made with Vatican II was preceded by several decades of preparation on the part of French and German theologians especially working in the nineteen twenties and thirties and elaborating their ideas immediately after the Second World War.

a. The neo-scholastic ghetto, with its defensive attitude towards the philosophical and scientific traditions of the modern world, was broken through. Catholic theologians came to understand that this modern consciousness was really representative of the historically mediated totality of the modern world, on the basis of which a critical theological concept had to be elaborated if they were to talk about God and his dealings in history with men. The dialogue conducted in the nineteenth century by the members of the Tübingen school with the great traditional representatives of modern thinking which had been more or less completely broken off was resumed. The dialogue with the world continued, not in a defensive way, but with the aim that had characterized earlier periods of Christian theology, namely of assimilating critically and productively what was of positive value in those great traditions.

Characteristically, the new theology began almost exactly where neo-scholasticism had left off—at the debate with the philosophy of idealism and especially with Kant, who was regarded as the precursor of idealism, and his criticism of pure reason. I am bound to point out in this context that it was the transcendental Kant whose thought was considered by the new theologians working before and after the Second World War, not the Kant of the philosophy of history or the Kant of practical reason. German idealism was therefore considered by the new theologians along the path of certain clear (Hegelian) traditions, embracing phenomenology, existentialism and personalism, to such an extent that present-day systematic theology and apologetics still seem to be determined by the philosophical forms within the tradition of German idealism, even when the latter is not explicitly taken into account.

Not only apologetics in the narrower sense of the word but the whole of systematic theology have been affected by this development in theological thinking. This has not come about purely by chance. It is a remarkable feature of the twentieth-century breakthrough in Catholic theology that apologetics have regained a more genuinely theological character and have come to be a theological discipline in the narrow sense of the word and are no longer used as they were in neo-scholasticism as the front line protective forces of dogmatic theology with certain tasks allocated to them. In other words, one clear result of the new theology has been that apologetics have become fundamental theology and are now concerned not simply with strategic defence, but also with the fundamental problems of Christian faith.

One of the most important elements in this twentieth-century penetration of neo-scholasticism by the new theology was the movement known as immanentist apologetics, which developed as a result of the work of the French philosopher Maurice Blondel and the controversy with various French representatives of the Modernist movement. In the German-speaking countries, on the other hand, the most significant result was that fundamental theology came to be regarded as a kind of investigation of theological principles or simply as a fundamental theological discipline. The leading exponents of this kind of fundamental theology in the German-speaking world are G. Söhngen, B. Welte and H. Fries, each of whom has, of course, a different emphasis. It is, however, Karl Rahner who has been responsible for the clearest and most lasting exposition of this tradition in Catholic theology of apologetics and fundamental theology, in the distinction that he has always made in his dogmatic teaching between formal and fundamental theology. According to Rahner, the formal structures of dogmatic theology are dealt with in fundamental theology, which is to some extent formal dogmatism. Dogmatic theology can also only continue to be meaningful if it is a material fundamental theology, that is, if it expresses the contents of dogmatic theology that it presents in the context of the questions raised by the contemporary world. It is only possible to be a true hearer of the Word in the strictly theological sense if one at the same time hears the objections raised by the world of one's own time and shares the problems of that world. The name of Rahner, who has always insisted on the legitimate function of classical apologetics and the rational and historical apologetical form of argument, is therefore always associated with this new phase in Catholic theology, in which the contents of Christian faith have been mobilized for a critical justification of that faith, in other words, for the apologetical task of theology in the strict sense of the word.

b. I am bound in this context to point to the ecumenical significance of this new beginning in Catholic theology. The reformulation of apologetics and renewed understanding of the part they played in theology as a whole led above all to a marked decrease in polemics and confrontation between the different Christian confessions.[7]

It is also important to mention another development in apologetics. After the penetration of neo-scholasticism by the new theology and the resumption of dialogue with contemporary ideas, the Enlightenment once again came to occupy a central place in the minds of Catholic theologians, who began to suspect that the ideas of the Enlightenment had not been sufficiently well understood by the idealists, the romantics and their successors, the phenomenologists, the existentialists and the personalists. This problem, which had been either forgotten or suppressed by the representatives both of the Tübingen school and of the new theology of the twentieth century, became one of the most important themes in fundamental theology.

This acute and complex problem of a criticism of metaphysics and Christianity that is not based on idealism is still unresolved today. It has not yet been fully understood and many aspects of it have not yet been discussed. Yet this positivistic or Marxist criticism of religion is, in all its contemporary variants, now clearly shaking the very foundations of theology and Christianity as a whole.[8]

To begin with, an attempt was made by the new theologians to do justice to the autonomy of reason and the world, which had become historically conscious of itself in the Englightenment, in the so-called secularization argument. Special attention has to be given to this theology of secularization in any examination of development of fundamental theology. This is important not only because it is something which concerns all the Christian confessions and is therefore a valuable ecumenical aspect of the new apologetics, but also because it is, according to the theological arguments based on the transcendental approach, existentialism or personalism, the theoretical aspect of the new theology that has been most discussed and has in one way or another received the greatest measure of consent.

There is, of course, one version of the theology of secularization in which Christianity appears not as a victim or as an opponent, but rather as the originator of the process of secularization. This is the incarnation, in which God's acceptance of the world in his Son is interpreted as the most radical release of the world to itself, with the result that the principle of incarnation becomes the principle of secularization.[9] In the incarnation, Christian faith sets the world free to itself, releases it from the immediate normative claims of the religious traditions and thus brings about its fundamental secularity.[10] It pays for this by means of a special kind of freedom from the world. At the same time, however, it can only remain closely connected with these processes of secularization by virtue of the fact that it has also constituted them historically.

In my *Theology of the World,* I moved clearly in the direction of a theology of secularization, but at the same time criticized it explicitly in the political theology that I formulated in the book. I asked, for example, whether the secularization argument in the form in which I have described it above could really lead to a constitution of theological reason in the contemporary situation or whether it would not invalidate it or else lead to a purely privatistic choice. I also asked whether, if the pre-condition for secularization was faith's freedom from the world, the critical and liberating power of Christianity with regard to history and society was not forgotten or at least obscured. I came in this way to see the argument of the new political theology as increasingly plausible, namely that the idea of a faith that was quite free from the world could be viewed with suspicion for several reasons. It might, for example, become on the one hand, because of its privatistic isolation, an ideological climax or a symbolic paraphrase of every single historical or social process in the world. On the other hand, its secularity might be basically no more than a novel way of immunizing Christianity and therefore simply a bad form of apologetics in the most sublime sense of the word.[11]

Another form of theology of secularization grew out of the traditions of the liberal theology of the nineteenth century. This liberal theology of the world had an influence on many more Christians than simply the supporters of the nineteenth-century liberal theology and it is still of importance in Protestantism today.[12] It can be summarized in a few words. What was regarded by the thinkers of the critical age of the Enlightenment as rational is, according to this liberal theology of the world, fundamentally Christian. The Christian and theological interest is identified in this movement with such contemporary historical interests as emancipation, freedom and man's coming of age. The Christian element consists in the affirmation of these contemporary processes. Secularization is regarded as Christianization.

In my opinion, this energetic forward-looking form of apologetics leads (and has indeed already led) to the theological reason being absorbed in the abstract emancipative reason of the modern era. Its creed is based on the canonization of developments that have in fact taken place and the tendencies that were in fact manifested during the Enlightenment. Theological understanding of the Enlightenment seems to consist of an ultimate acceptance of the triumph of the Enlightenment over the Christian Church or of the replacement of Christianity by the Enlightenment.

What is hardly recognized at all is that there is an inner dialectical tension in emancipation, Enlightenment and secularization and that the Enlightenment has therefore given rise to problems over and above what it has itself raised to the level of a problem, has put as a question on the order of the day and has enabled to be discussed. This knowledge, it has to be admitted, has not been present from the beginning in the new political theology and one of the most important aims of this book is to formulate it.

3. A Pyrrhic victory over the Enlightenment or the secretly enthroned middle-class subject in theology

a. In the progressive liberal Christian apologetics described at the end of the preceding section, the tables were turned completely against the apologetics which the neo-scholastic theologians, the exponents of the Church's social teaching and the traditionalists used as a defensive front against the Enlightenment and contemporary thought generally. The Enlightenment is no longer regarded as the quintessence of anti-ecclesiastical and anti-theological provocation. It is treated as a *locus theologicus,* a place, in other words, where Christianity becomes universally rational and therefore at the same time historically universal. In one form or another, almost all theologies that have in their own time been regarded as modern or progressive have been filled with satisfaction with regard to this late victory. Whereas the earlier Catholic apologists had defended tradition and authority, the liberal theologians pleaded, with the restrained pathos of the Enlightenment, for democracy, public life, honesty, freedom of conscience, autonomy and freedom to express one's opinion in the Church. Their plea was to a great extent justified, but it should not be forgotten that, when they took up the weapons of the Enlightenment, these liberal apologists also took over the difficulties.

The weapons of the earlier apologetics, with their strong opposition to the Enlightenment, could, of course, obviously be used against the arguments of the liberal and the new theologians, both of whom have emphasized emancipation, freedom and so on. But the latter have not allowed themselves to be defeated or even persuaded to follow the anti-Enlightenment path, which they have recognized as wrong.

It has, however, proved necessary to re-examine the Enlightenment itself and to throw a new and radical light on the Enlightenment in the form of a political and theological enlightenment of the processes of the modern era. These are not simply the same as the new concepts used in contemporary reflection about the Enlightenment and made more precise in the course of time. What is more

27

important than these new concepts themselves is the process by which they become rooted in the new man's understanding of himself. In other words, the subjects who articulate themselves—and assert themselves—in these concepts are more important than the concepts themselves.

I shall discuss this question of the subject in greater detail and in many different contexts in the following chapter. In the meantime, however, I would like to draw attention to a few important aspects of this theme. In the first place, a new man, the citizen, arose in the Enlightenment and came to assert himself in the processes of the modern era, during which he was made absolute. Secondly, this new man or middle-class subject has become established through the liberal and the modern theology, both of which have made use of the ideas of the Enlightenment (though with a different emphasis). Finally, and perhaps most important of all, a middle-class concept of praxis has to a great extent replaced the authentically Christian concept of freedom and praxis that is critical of society. In other words, it has reduced the Christian concept to the level of the private subject existing without problems in society and to that of individual moral righteousness.

It is therefore obvious that there is an urgent need for a practical fundamental theology that will continue along the path of Christian apologetics, restore the radically Christian concept of praxis and place it at the disposal of the subject who is not yet established (as a middle-class citizen), that is, at the disposal of the state of all men as subjects and the process by which they become subjects.

b. A new light is thrown from the vantage point of practical fundamental theology on the work of those apologists who acted with the right conservative instinct in combatting the Enlightenment and the emergent middle class as enemies of Christian faith. Because they did not do this consciously and consistently, however, they were quickly defeated by their middle-class opponents. What is more, the new liberal theologians treated Christian apologetics in their defeated state with a scorn that revealed the naivety of the trifling way in which they had dealt with the inner crisis of identity in Christianity created by the Enlightenment and the middle-class subject.

Christianity has had to face a challenge of enormous proportions in the presence of the middle-class citizen. This new man can be defined as the subject who is in control and at the same time in need in society. His ability to control now has hardly any remaining receptive aspects and he is already able to dominate almost everything in the natural world and in human history. His practical understanding is orientated almost exclusively towards models that are based on this control of nature and on the satisfaction of his own needs. His other practical patterns of behaviour as a subject are disappearing and losing their effectiveness.

The seriousness of this challenge is bound to lead the Christian to respect the attempt made by the neo-scholastic theologians to combat the tendencies outlined in the preceding paragraph, although it has to be admitted that they did not succeed in finding suitable critical means. Their tendency to immunize Christianity is understandable, although it is difficult to understand why they were prepared to risk everything in the Church and theology in the face of middle-class power and to define the essence of Christianity according to the dictates of middle-class plausibility. I stress this because I am convinced that these points which marked the failure of neo-scholasticism in the past form the central problems of present-day apologetical theology.

Resistance to the privatization of Christianity by the middle-class subject is clearly reflected in the Church's social teaching generally and the papal encyclicals dealing with social teaching since the time of Leo XIII and Pius XI. What is regrettable is not so much that forces have emerged in opposition to the middle-class movement and liberalism or that the absorption of the social praxis of Christian faith by the purely private moral praxis of the middle-class Christian has been opposed, but rather that this resistance has been too little the result of radical Christian faith itself. It was therefore possible for the resistance offered by those practising the Church's social teaching to be so misinterpreted that it came to be seen in the end, at least in the German-speaking world, simply as a defeatist defence of the middle-class attitudes of late capitalism.[13]

The militant nineteenth-century apologists were both clearsighted and blind to the truth at the same time. This is particularly true of the French traditionalists who, as lay theologians, developed the most carefully reflected and most suitable form of theology as far as social questions were concerned that was available at the time. We would be seriously underestimating the theological and

29

political importance of this movement if we were to maintain that it was no more than a cynical and arrogant rejection of the ideas of the Enlightenment. The traditionalists were, after all, aware of the great danger inherent in the cult of abstract reason and in handing down a rationality that was independent of subjects. They were also conscious of the perversion of political power that occurred when politics became subject to a similarly abstract concept of freedom and reason. Traditionalism also draws attention to another consequence of the abstract nature of middle-class reason and its dissociation from history and the human subject. It is that the rejection or destruction of tradition and memory does not simply lead to increased freedom and autonomy. On the contrary, it usually results in a new form of stultification, in which man is easily manipulated or corrupted.

The traditionalists were mistaken not so much in their attack against middle-class religion as in their conviction that it could be replaced by a movement back into an earlier, supposedly utopian form of Christianity. The level of the traditionalists' criticism of the Enlightenment and the middle-class subject should not be lowered, nor is it possible for theology to return to a period before the middle-class revolution.

Only if the Enlightenment is scrupulously questioned and re-examined (partly in the light of the resistance offered by what we have called the apologetical front in the ninteenth century), theology will finally be able to respond to the challenge presented a long time ago by Marxism in its struggle for a new subject. This challenge is accepted in particular by practical fundamental theology as a political theology of the subject, in an attempt which will go beyond its debate with the post-idealist thinkers in their criticism of religion and ideology, since this debate has too often been disassociated from the human subject and therefore conducted at too abstract a level.

Notes

1. See J. B. Metz, 'Apologetics', *Sacramentum Mundi*. For the history of fundamental theology as a theological discipline, see B. Welte, *Auf der Spur des Ewigen* (Freiburg, 1965); see also, for the development of fundamental theology in Protestantism, G. Ebeling, 'Erwägungen zu einer evangelischen Fundamentaltheologie', *op. cit.*

2. What was discussed in these theological polemics was neither the foundation of Christian faith, the Trinity nor Christology, but rather the Church. It was therefore no coincidence that the first manual of fundamental theology dealt not with systematic theology, but with canon law and the nature of the Church. It was written by Robert Bellarmine.

3. J. R. Geiselmann's studies are particularly relevant here. See also H. Fries and G. Schwaiger, eds., *Katholische Theologen Deutschlands im 19. Jahrhundert*, I (Munich, 1975).

4. The Tübingen school (and Drey in particular) was ultimately dependent on Schleiermacher and consciously sought to enter into dialogue with his philosophical theology, which ought to have been simply a 'theological fundamental knowledge'. See R. Stalder, *Grundlinien der Theologie Schleiermachers*, I (Wiesbaden, 1969).

5. For this question, see especially R. Mate, *El ateísmo, un problema político* (Salamanca, 1973).

6. I shall deal with the whole question of the content of Christian faith in connection with this theme in a book that will appear shortly: *The Faith of Christians*.

7. H. Fries' theological studies point in this ecumenical direction. It is not just by chance that various attempts have been made in recent years to formulate a fundamental theology in the Protestant tradition. See G. Ebeling, 'Erwägungen zu einer evangelischen Fundamentaltheologie', *op. cit.*, and W. Joest's fundamental theology (Stuttgart, 1974).

8. See Metz, Moltmann and Oelmüller, *Kirche im Prozess der Aufklärung* (Mainz and Munich, 1970). E.T.: *Religion and Political Society* (New York, 1974).

9. I have developed this idea already in an essay, 'Weltverständnis im Glauben. Christliche Orientierung in der Weltlichkeit der Welt heute', *Geist und Leben* 35 (1962), pp. 165–184. See also my *Theology of the World* (London, 1969), pp. 13–55. Similar views will also be found in the religious and philosophical works of K. Rahner, H. Fries and H. R. Schlette.

10. Friedrich Gogarten has already developed this idea of secularization in his book, *Verhängnis und Hoffnung der Neuzeit. Die Säkularisation als theologisches Problem* (Stuttgart, 1958), on the basis of the Protestant distinction between law and gospel, introducing in this way the much quoted distinction between secularization and secularism. See also Harvey Cox's theory of secularization which this author developed in succession to Gogarten and Bonhoeffer: *The Secular City* (London, 1966).

11. It ought to be clear that a theology of the world is more acceptable for our understanding of the Church than the critical form of political theology. In connection with the former, there is always the possibility of the Church's flight from society (which is often a secret desire on the part of many members of the Church) and the establishment of faith in a ghetto that is easy to defend. Such a situation would not be disputed by the objections of a world that has become secular. 'Purity', however, in relationships and competence is not a Christian or biblical category. In the Bible, it is a 'Pilate' category, that is, a category of appeasement.

12. T. Rendtorff's theory of Christianity is, from the theological point of view, the argument in favour of this kind of secularization that makes the greatest claims.

13. See the work, published by F. Hengsbach, of the field of studies known as 'Kirche und Befreiung.'

3. Political theology of the subject as a theological criticism of middle-class religion

Far from being diametrically opposed to present-day theology, Enlightenment or contemporary thinking certainly has a right to be domiciled in theology, even though that right may perhaps be vague and difficult to distinguish. The right to domicile does not mean that its criticism of the Church and theology will always be understood or even heard or that it will have, in modern theology, an equal partner in debate. Much that was called into question in the Enlightenment is still waiting for an answer in theology. What, however, is firmly established in modern theology—and, what is more, in the theological thinking and the different theological positions of all the various Christian confessions—is the formal Enlightenment or contemporary principle of the subject. The deepest level of theology has in fact been reached in this principle of the subject and attempts have been made to reconstruct it as a specifically religious subject, going back beyond the Enlightenment, in Protestant circles to the Reformation and in Catholic circles to mediaeval theology. It is, however, worth pointing out here that the supremacy of the subject in theology in the abstract sense has not become more easily distinguishable in the process. By this I mean that it is difficult to distinguish, in the Enlightenment itself, the validity of speaking about man as such and his reason, autonomy, freedom and other abstract attributes. No real, critical clarity existed here with regard to the concrete subjects intended and defended in the idea of man or the subject, in other words, with regard to the social reality expressed in this concept.

A most important achievement made in the debate with religion and the criticism of ideology is that problems should not be discussed without reference to the human subject or independently of their social and political background. This is an important aspect of the so-called enlightenment of the Enlightenment,[1] which is constantly required and without which neither contemporary thought itself nor those who receive it can remain rational and subjects can remain subjects.

In this perspective, it is necessary to question what is really meant, in the sense of actual social subjects, by such theological abstractions as man, existence, person or subject in modern theology, which is obviously able to include and deal with the Enlightenment and contemporary thought as a purely theoretical intellectual process dissociated from the human subject. Does modern theology know, in other words, what is taking place when it defends, as a specifically religious subject, the subject of the modern era, whose problematical social situation it does not always necessarily take into account?

This is perhaps the time to summarize briefly what has to be discussed in this chapter, as opposed to the preceding chapter. Although the Copernican revolution did give rise to a crisis in theology and the Church, which was recognized and eventually overcome so that it is no longer a crisis, this was not the cause of the extreme crisis that has continued to be felt in Christianity. This crisis in theology and the Church, which has not yet been grasped in its real proportions, let alone overcome, is due to the breakthrough at all levels of the new man or middle-class citizen with reservations towards, and what one might call a 'division of labor' relationship to, the Church. This new man emerged in the Enlightenment. He is the subject in the subject. He is concealed behind the rational, autonomous man who has come of age in the modern era.[2] He is finally also the creator of that form of religion which is used, as it were, to decorate and set the scene, freely and in private, for middle-class festivals and which has for a long time been current even in normal Christianity. Theology, which believes that it is bound to defend the contemporary human subject uncritically as a religious subject, is, in this perspective, simply a late reflection of this middle-class religion (*'bürgerliche Religion'*). It is not my aim to make this religion an object of scorn by examining it so intensely. The aim is rather to elucidate what is meant by the fact that religion no longer belongs to the social constitution of the identity of the subject, but is rather added to it.

I shall therefore attempt in the following sections to throw a little more theological light on the Enlightenment and its consequences. In this, I shall try to avoid the common practice of German scholars in the past, who believed that it was possible to overcome the effects of the Enlightenment by means of political restoration and a return to periods of human consciousness which preceded the modern era and had been superseded.[3] My attempt will take the form of a theological enlightenment of the Enlightenment and its subject, the middle-class citizen. The latter does not present us with a theological problem in his origin. This theological criticism is only necessary in the citizen's self-assertion and absolute value. We know, after all, from the dialectics of the Enlightenment that the process of liberation ceases at the point where it becomes an unconscious and mechanical self-defence.

We have therefore to go back to the Enlightenment, not in order to define the reaction of theologians or the Church more precisely or critically, but rather in order to acquire a better understanding of the crisis itself that has come about as a result of the Enlightenment and the middle class or perhaps as a result of the gradual disappearance of the Enlightenment into the middle class. This improved understanding of the crisis will inevitably be directed above all towards theology and the Church.

In the following six divisions of this chapter, then, the central elements of the crisis caused by the Enlightenment will be examined and subjected to theological analysis. These include the phenomenon of privatization, the loss of tradition and the crisis of authority, the reduction of reason to rationality and of religion to the sphere of private religion. The concluding section contains a number of indications pointing to the need for a political theology of the subject.

1. Privatization

Privatization, the most important phenomenon in the crisis caused by the Enlightenment and therefore the first to be discussed here, had its origin in the conflict between the Church and the State that began in the late Middle Ages and became more acute during the period of the religious wars and divisions. The two confessions which were in conflict with each other at that time were in no sense private religions. They were both above all sovereign expressions of the social life of their period. This conflict made it increasingly impossible for the political unity of the state to be based on religion in those parts of Europe where it was no longer possible to enforce religious and confessional uniformity. If the state, then, was to have a chance of survival and was to carry out its tasks of creating unity and guaranteeing freedom, it had to be emancipated from religion. Even before the widespread process of privatization took place in the Enlightenment, then, this home-made form of privatization already existed in the Christian religion.[4]

A distinction was always made in the Enlightenment between the private and public spheres as one of the fundamental conditions for a humane society and I do not intend to question this good aspect of the Enlightenment phenomenon of privatization. I am only concerned here with what is in my opinion the continuing problem of the subjects of that process of privatization.

The way of life of the middle-class citizen is ultimately contained within the concept of 'private'. The middle class is no longer sustained by any all-embracing traditions, let alone religious traditions. It owes its existence and survival largely to an economic and political struggle against social systems and economic structures, such as feudalism and absolutism, that were sanctioned by religion. It is supported by a new principle which regulates and underpins all social relationships—the principle of exchange. Production, trade and consumption are all determined by this middle-class principle of exchange. All other values, which may have had a decisive effect on society in the past, but which no longer directly contribute to the functioning of the modern middle-class society of exhange, have receded into the sphere of private, individual freedom.

From the economic point of view, the property of the middle-class citizen forms the basis of and safeguards his freedom to dispose of materials, services, technical processes and so on. From the political point of view, this results in his claim to self-determination and self-government on the one hand and a precarious separation between private and public interests on the other. Religion has become a private matter. It is possible to make use of it to satisfy cultural needs, but it is no longer necessary to have it in order to be a subject.

Religion is no longer the expression of a primary need. Pascal was aware of the rise of this new man and was passionately opposed to it. It was not the fact that men would have found different answers to the ultimate questions from those provided by Christianity, but rather that they could live without having or even seeking any certainty with regard to those questions that made them so difficult for Pascal to understand. Indeed it was this life without ultimate certainty that made him call the phenomenon of the middle-class subject, which had hardly made its appearance and which he did not really know himself, 'monstrous'.[5]

I have in this context to correct an error that is frequently made in theology: namely, that the Reformation was the period when the new middle class and the principle of privatization emerged. Luther was not the middle-class citizen who sustained the processes of the Enlightenment and impressed them with his personality. His question about the certainty of salvation was quite different from the questions asked by the new man of the Enlightenment. It is possible that a pre-middle-class subject appeared at the time of the Reformation, but what certainly did not appear then was the phenomenon of middle-class, privatistic subjectivity which led to the crisis in Christianity and the Church and which can therefore not so easily be given theological honours.

2. The crisis of tradition

I have already alluded to the crisis of tradition caused by the Enlightenment. I must now discuss the extremely important and legitimate aspects of that crisis. The Enlightenment was not, after all, a process in which man ultimately became practical in his freedom in the face of the direct constraints of tradition.

In the Enlightenment, tradition undoubtedly lost its power to determine human activity and to direct man's life. It also became an object of historical knowledge or a storehouse of information to satisfy the needs of reason in the Enlightenment. This technical association between history and tradition was given scientific expression in historicism. Obligation and normativity can no longer be based on historical reason as a medium of tradition—historical knowledge is a medium by which history is made relative and less important. As a result, what Lessing called a 'horribly wide ditch' has appeared between the origin of religion, and especially the Christian religion, and its present, historically mediated claims.[6]

Theology could certainly be usefully occupied with a study of tradition and its loss of power to determine human action and to direct a consensus, a loss that was observed by Lessing, and it is true to say that it has indeed been concerned with this question from the time of Kierkegaard onwards. Karl Barth and the representatives of existential or transcendental hermeneutics have studied it. There is, however, a more profound reason for the need to make even greater efforts to understand this question theologically (it has become again and again clear that theology is impotent in the sphere of hermeneutics). The reason is that Lessing's difficulty remains because it cannot be understood and overcome purely as a theological problem. Its existence compels theology and the Church to enter into dialogue with the subject of historical reason—middle-class society.

The Enlightenment criticism of tradition can only be properly understood in the light of the phenomenon of the rise of the new man, the middle-class citizen, and the society of exchange that was fashioned by him. It can be understood above all as endangering what has no exchange value.[7] One of the greatest dangers of middle-class life is that everything that does not conform to calculating reason and the laws of profit and success is left to individual and private choice.[8] By making religion a purely service religion to which he turns as a private individual, the middle-class citizen has also made tradition a value of which he makes use as a private individual. The 'culture industry' (Horkheimer's and Adorno's term) is a recent expression of a process that began in the Enlightenment.

The citizen is, however, generally regarded as favourably disposed towards history, traditional and, in that sense, conservative. If my analysis is correct, on the other hand, and what I have said about the growth of the middle-class consciousness is true, then this common view of the middle-class subject must clearly be corrected and he must be seen as conservative only in a very limited, partial and privatistic sense. He will, in other words, subordinate everything, including his own love of the past and of tradition, to the rules of the exchange game.

This ought to make the Church, which apparently regards the citizen as reliable in this respect, think. This loss of tradition can, moreover, perhaps be seen most clearly in our attitude towards the dead. There can, of course, be no relationship of exchange with the dead. According to Kierkegaard, our love and mourning for the dead is the only form of love that cannot be included within the framework of a society based on exchange and the satisfaction of needs. For this reason—and that is why Kierkegaard made this criticism of the middle-class Christianity of his own period—community with the dead has been thrust further and further into the background. It has lost its importance and has become privatized. There is in modern society a rapidly increasing loss of power and value in traditional values such as friendliness, thankfulness, attention to the dead, mourning and so on for which there is no corresponding counter-value and for which one gets nothing in return. In the firmly established Socialist societies, there is really no human solidarity of a totally new kind, simply the perpetuation of earlier middle-class society with all its inner tensions. One symptom of this situation is the fact that in those Socialist societies people are still, as in the West, forbidden to show any sign of mourning. No prohibition has even been publicly issued, but the socially accepted ban on mourning has for this reason continued all the more obstinately.

In view of this fact, the frequently expressed opinion that our contemporary concept of tradition originated in the Reformation and that the Enlightenment criticism of tradition was already present in and anticipated by Luther's criticism is, in my opinion, naive and even wrong. It is true, of course, that the practice of going back to Scripture is in certain respects a criticism of ecclesial and theological traditions, but it should always be subject to the condition that this tradition has a normative effect on Christian life and action. An appeal to Scripture is ultimately in itself an appeal to a particular tradition.

Since the Enlightenment and the rise of middle-class society, tradition has clearly become less important. Yet it forms a constitutive element in religion. For this reason, theology is bound to have an interest in overcoming this loss of historicity in the case of the middle-class subject and therefore in this sense in overcoming the Enlightenment itself.

What, then, at first appears to be a process of liberation from the anonymous oppression of unknown traditions in which the new longing for freedom is not expressed conceals a radical danger, not only for the existence and identity of traditional religion, but also for the identity of man and his state as a subject.

However well-founded, legitimate and necessary the Enlightenment criticism of traditions may have been, we are bound, if we follow its development into the present time, to recognize that memory is not only the object (which is gradually losing its objectivity), but the inner element of the critical consciousness that is trying to gain clarity about its interests and the direction of its own criticism. This topic will be discussed in greater detail later in this book (Chapters 5 and 11). In the meanwhile, I must consider the problem of the loss of authority which has accompanied the loss of tradition.

3. The crisis of authority

Together with tradition, authority, which cannot derive anything from reason, is also in a state of crisis. In his well-known attempt to define Enlightenment (*Die Beantwortung der Frage: Was ist Aufklärung?*, 1784), Kant said: 'Enlightenment occurs when man leaves the state in which he has not yet come of age and which he has brought about himself. This state is marked by a lack of ability to make use of his intellect without the guidance of another person. Man brings it about himself if the cause is not a lack of intellect, but rather a lack of decision and courage to make use of oneself without the guidance of another'. This definition of Enlightenment is obviously critically aimed at the state in which man is prevented from coming of age by an authority which cannot be tested or questioned with regard to its legal status. This kind of authority was diametrically opposed to the Enlightenment principle of equality. There is also an inevitable tendency that it will go on producing or reproducing new inequalities and new forms of tutelage.

The authority of the Church is particularly endangered by this spontaneously critical aspect of the Enlightenment. A continuous insistence on an authority which is no longer universally convincing and has ceased to be socially plausible can easily assume the character of coercion and authoritarianism. When this occurs, criticism inevitably intensifies.[9]

There is always a temptation in the Church and theology to reject criticism of religious authority on purely theoretical grounds, while at the same time preserving what is often authoritarian in the Church and decisionistic in theology. What is generally overlooked, however, is that the middle-class subject or middle-class society has been concealed behind the Enlightenment criticism of authority. Its characteristics must be investigated critically if the Enlightenment criticism of authority is to be rejected successfully by theology.

The equality of the partners is, at least in principle, assumed in the middle-class concept of exchange. This equality is assumed so that society, which is based on exchange, will function smoothly. For this reason, authority, as a principle of inequality and subordination, almost automatically loses social plausibility. It has come to be regarded as a relic of feudal society and its patriarchal and hierarchical structure that have been successfully overcome by the middle class. The aspect of authority that is retained and can still command the respect of middle-class reason is competence, which can be described as authority in the form of knowledge.[10]

As authority increasingly becomes part of (calculating) reason, both the feudal survivals of authority and what is authoritarian in authority on the one hand and the saving aspect of authority on the other disappear, as in the case of tradition. Authority cannot be separated from tradition. It is the force of tradition, its persistence and urgency, with which it remembers and must be sued. Insofar, however, as tradition is a constitutive part of critical reason, the latter must always have elements of authority. Without them, it has no power to liberate.

In middle-class society, authority is threatened as a precondition and inner aspect of critical and liberating reason. What is threatened, in other words, is that authority to which men give their consent when they affirm their own state as subjects or the possibility of others being subjects. This authority is the authority of freedom and justice on the one hand and suffering on the other. This kind of authority can never have much exchange value. This is why it can hardly ever be regarded as competent by the forum of calculating reason.

This authority, which can and should be defended by theology and which cannot be interpreted by the criticism of ideology as an alienated form of knowledge, enters the state of crisis that is synonymous with that of the religious subject whenever the latter is unquestioningly absorbed by the contemporary subject. In other words, this crisis occurs when the religious subject ceases to be proof against the middle-class imagination.

At this point, I make a brief aside, which is nonetheless closely connected with what I have said so far about the Enlightenment criticism of authority. The problem confronting authority in religion and the Church is above all that, when that authority has not assumed authoritarian aspects, it tends to reveal aspects of that form of authority which are both permitted and produced by middle-class society and which also constitute a great danger to religion. These aspects include routine, bureaucratic forms of authority, the worst forms of hierarchical authority, overgrown with administration and unapproachable, and authority as a management of truth without any social basis.

It is not possible for authority in the Church to avoid this danger altogether, but it should certainly not be completely absorbed by these forms of authority. A form of authority which was legitimately required by the Enlightenment should therefore develop within the Church's praxis. This is an authority based on competence. This competence is not an administrative or a legal competence of the kind that is prominent in middle-class society. It is also not a purely cognitive competence which presupposes the silent absorption of authority by knowledge (this would be the kind of competence required by a liberal theology, based on a false understanding of the Enlightenment). The type of authority needed is one that is based mainly on religious competence. In so far as this kind of authority is really competent, it would be able to learn from the Enlightenment and, in so far as it is not purely functional, but really religious, it would be able, at least to begin with, to overcome the effects of the crisis in which authority found itself placed by the Enlightenment and middle-class society.[11]

This authority based on religious competence could be a critical and liberating authority in middle-class society today. A new kind of authority based on being authority rather than having authority would gain in importance as political and social life approached the model of a complex administration more and more closely. It would become more and more significant as all functions in society became increasingly structuralistic, anonymous and divorced from the human subject and as the relationships between responsibilities

41

became less and less distinct. It might also be one of the central places where the unconditional demands of the authority of freedom, justice and suffering could always be expressed on behalf of the majority. It could be a means of saving Enlightenment reason from banality and collective obscurity.

4. The crisis of (metaphysical) reason

The Enlightenment led to the creation of a new community of mutual consent that was not based on the metaphysical reason that formed the silent and unquestioned basis of mutual consent on which feudal societies were founded. The Enlightenment was, after all, a consistent criticism of classical metaphysics.

The Reformation was, of course, also a criticism of metaphysics, that is, the metaphysics of scholasticism, but this criticism took place on the basis of a completely Christian community of mutual consent. The process of the social differentiation of reason, which was at the heart of the Enlightenment criticism of metaphysics, had not begun at that time.

The appeal made for the first time during the Enlightenment to reason, the subject and praxis points to a totally new process. This is that reason was, also for the first time, no longer thought of as independent of the subject and its practical aspects. Whereas the metaphysical use of reason concealed the question raised by its social and political context, the Enlightenment threw light on the background to this abstract use of reason. In other words, the usurpation of metaphysical reason for a definite power that remains in the background and functions as a social subject is revealed. What has taken place is the acceptance of universal reason by a control that is on the one hand ecclesiastical and on the other political.

According to Kant's definition of Enlightenment, the màn who has the freedom 'to make public use of his reason in all things' has come of age. I shall examine this idea later on, but in the meantime I would point out that it has primarily the value of a moral appeal. It is not in the first place a call to create new social conditions of freedom. On the contrary, it is directed to what already exists and to those who already have—perhaps latently and perhaps partly openly—the social power to come of age and who only need to be set free. As Kant himself said in the same essay of 1784: 'Laziness and cowardice are the reasons why so many men, even after nature has set them free from alien guidance, still do not come of age throughout the rest of their lives and why others find it so easy to become their tutors and guardians. It is so comfortable not to come of age'. To whom is Kant referring in this passage? He is not really saying that mankind as a whole, which has not yet come of age, should achieve freedom from tutelage. He is rather referring to a particular subject who is in danger of being 'lazy', 'cowardly' and 'comfortable'. This subject is the propertied citizen who lacks the moral strength to make use of his own intellect and to become politically what he has already been both socially and economically for a long time.

It is, of course, true that the pathos of the Enlightenment was certainly directed towards making all men come of age as subjects of the use of their intellect. Without distinction, knowledge and knowing more, education and being more educated were proclaimed, encyclopaedias were published and indeed what Lessing called the 'education of the human race' could be regarded as the basic programme of the Enlightenment. At the same time, however, the language used in the Enlightenment should not deceive us into thinking that the Enlightenment aim was to make the propertied citizen the bearer of political reason. Nor was the coming of age of the Enlightenment a coming of age for those without property, the population living on the land or the peasant classes, who were almost all illiterate at the time when the great encyclopaedias were written. What asserted itself, then, in the criticism of metaphysical reason and the emphatic affirmation of coming of age and the subject was ultimately a new élite or a new aristocracy. In other words, what was given prominence in the Enlightenment was in a reversed image in the mirror, so to speak, precisely the same phenomenon against which the Enlightenment was fighting.

The characteristics of this middle-class élite, however, also entered into Enlightenment reason itself and its concept of praxis and the subject. In the logic of this reason, praxis developed not as a praxis of liberation, but as a praxis of control, which was not control in the earlier, direct sense of the word, but a control of nature in the interest of the market.

That is why the reason that supports the subject in his control of nature is a universal theme in the middle-class society which was first reflected and first became conscious of itself in the Enlightenment. This is, then, a technical reason which at once reduces everything to the level of an object and makes it marketable and profitable. If this is forgotten and reason, praxis and the subject are used in the abstract sense in theology, without also taking into consideration the middle-class society of exchange that is expressed in these three concepts, the consequence might be that the middle class may imperceptibly be given those theological, religious and ecclesiastical honours which were denied to it in the beginning because a better instinct prevailed and which will now help it at this late stage to justify itself.

5. Religion in a state of crisis

The criticism of metaphysical reason which was initiated in the Enlightenment must become a criticism of religion when religion and metaphysics condition each other. If metaphysical reason, which is divorced from the subject, loses its (political) innocence in the light of the Enlightenment, then religion, which also makes use of this abstract metaphysical reason to justify its universal claim to validity, at once becomes suspect. The criticism of religion that was undertaken in the Enlightenment at first on the basis of a completely different title (the criticism of tradition or the criticism of authority) is deeply rooted in this phenomenon.

Initially, then, the criticism of religion in the Enlightenment was a criticism of ideology. This was more clearly the case in France than in the German Enlightenment. It was in France that religion was traced back by the 'atheists' of the Enlightenment to self-seeking deceit on the part of priests and it was Voltaire who on the one hand rejected religion in itself, but on the other recommended it because of its socially useful function in stabilizing the *status quo* in society and preserving private property.[12]

The Enlightenment did not simply criticize religion in the sense of providing a criticism of ideology. It above all affirmed religion, although this affirmation was not the same as that of positive religion in Christianity. It was also in no sense indebted to the Reformation criticism of religion. The religion of the Enlightenment, in critically rejecting the idea of revelation, was *religio naturalis*—a natural religion or a religion of reason.

This natural religion of the Enlightenment was at first thought of as the rational religion which was in accordance with all men's needs and which could be justified on the basis of the history of mankind. This understanding of natural religion was accepted into many liberal theologies, in which religion was—and sometimes still is—generally described as a feeling of simple dependence (Schleiermacher) or as the expression of the numinous depth of existence (Tillich).

This general summary of the religion of the Enlightenment is, however, misleading, because the so-called natural religion of reason which apparently applies to all men is as élitist as the enlightened reason itself. It is in fact only applicable to the new man of the Enlightenment, the citizen, as the subject of reason. The natural religion, then, is an extremely privatized religion that has been, as it were, specially prepared for the domestic use of the propertied middle-class citizen. It is above all a religion of inner feeling. It does not protest against or oppose in any way the definitions of reality, meaning or truth, for example, that are accepted by the middle-class society of exchange and success. It gives greater height and depth to what already applies even without it.

The concept of a natural religion is therefore in no way neutral or historically innocent. It is no more neutral than the middle-class citizen himself. It is therefore impervious to experiences and testimonies both of the biblical and of the non-biblical religions. It could hardly be used as a leading concept for an encounter and a dialogue between religions.

It is here that the element of truth that is present in the criticism of religion made by 'dialectical' theologians (Barth especially and, even more radically, Bonhoeffer) is revealed. The distinction made by these theologians between faith and religion is, in my opinion, problematical for several reasons. They have, however, possibly in opposition to their basic intentions, managed to save the very concept of religion that they rejected in their terminology. They have above all recognized what is deeply middle-class in religion and have drawn attention to the danger in which Christianity would be placed if it were to be absorbed by the weakest level of liberal religion as left behind by the enlightenment and the middle class.[13] There is a great deal of contemporary theology in which only the natural and rational elements in Christianity are accepted as valid and a great deal in the Church of today, which, at least in Germany, is too closely identified with middle-class religion, that points to the fact that this process of absorption has already begun to take place.

6. The need for a political theology of the subject

This assessment of the process which took place in the Enlightenment and which can be summed up as a process in which religion became a private affair of the middle class can certainly be said to have a bearing on the concept of a practical fundamental theology of the subject. According to the latter, the Enlightenment cannot be received or inherited in a purely abstract form and the subject, the person and existence should not be taken over uncritically by theology as a result of the modern era and its process of privatization.

The private middle-class reality which resulted from the Enlightenment and characterizes the modern era cannot be completely identified with the subject, the person or existence in a way that is strictly relevant to religion or theology. What we have here, then, is the process of atrophy that takes place in the state of all men as subjects in the presence of God, a state which is the concern of any political theology and which is only possible if religion is not simply added subsequently to the social constitution of the subject.

It would certainly be wrong to use such direct contrasts as private and public, inward and outward realities, theory and praxis or mystical and political as a means of illustrating the significance of a political theology of the subject. It would be equally wrong to apply in a rather condescending way the categories of public, outward, practical and political to it. This distinction is in itself the result of the very process of Enlightenment of which a political theology inevitably tries to be critically conscious. Whenever this critical consciousness is lacking, theology is bound to continue to exist without reference to the subject. Alternatively—and this amounts to the same thing—it will try to conceal, by speaking very generally about the subject—or the contemporary subject—all the contradictions which go to the very heart of the Christian identity and which are the result of the socially differentiated history of the subject in the modern era. Theology will in that case hardly be able to develop any critical means for the defence of the middle-class subject (the source of the various crises of identity in Christianity that were revealed in the Enlightenment) as the really religious subject.

I am bound to stress here, and I shall later discuss systematically, the fact that this theological criticism of middle-class religion will certainly not result in an abstract negation of the individual, including the middle-class individual. All that the theologian can do here is to question whether the middle-class principle of individuation is the only valid one and whether it is strong enough to carry out the task given to it by religion. The religious task here is to stand up for all men as subjects in the face of violent oppression and of a caricature of solidarity in a violent absorption by the mass or an institutionalized hatred. This theological criticism of middle-class religion does not in any sense amount to an abstract devaluation of middle-class values.[14] All that it does is to question whether these values can be saved and defended simply and solely by means of the middle-class principle of individuation.[15]

Notes

1. See, for example, Kleist's statement on Enlightenment (in his *Marionettentheater*): 'eating of the tree of knowledge for the second time'.

2. For this interpretation of the Enlightenment, see L. Goldmann, *Der christliche Bürger und die Aufklärung* (Neuwied, 1968).

3. For the special difficulties that German philosophers have experienced with the Englightenment (as opposed to the way in which it has been assimilated in Anglo-Saxon pragmatism, French positivism and socialism), see the important works of G. Picht and K. Scholder.

4. See E. W. Böckenförde, *Kirchlicher Auftrag und politische Entscheidung* (Freiburg, 1973).

5. See Groothuysen in Schellong, *Bürgertum und christliche Religion* (Munich, 1975), p. 17.

6. The fundamental problem of theology to which this 'horribly wide ditch' refers was given its classical expression in G. E. Lessing's essay of 1777: *Über den Beweis des Geistes und der Kraft*. Another much quoted statement is also to be found in this essay: 'Chance historical truths can never become proofs of necessary rational truths'.

7. See M. Horkheimer and T. W. Adorno, *Dialectics of Englightenment* (New York, 1971; London, 1973), *passim*.

8. Adorno called tradition 'essentially feudal' and Sombart similarly insisted that the feudal economy was 'traditionalistic'. R. Koselleck has shown in his writings how tradition and history lost their plausibility and ceased to be examples for the present as middle-class and industrial society developed after the feudal period.

9. Acceptance of this kind of bare claim to authority is characterized by blind decision and therefore has decisionist aspects. It is therefore not surprising that theologies of faith have tended more and more since the Enlightenment to become theologies of decision, that is, theologies that interpret faith as a 'leap'. Paradoxical, existential and personal theologies are similar in this respect.

10. It would be wrong in this context to regard the criticism of authority expressed in the Reformation as the model for the Englightenment criticism. Luther's conflict at that time was not a conflict between authority and knowledge, but one between authority and authority. The 'freedom of a Christian', about which Luther spoke, was developed on the basis of an appeal to the indisputable authority of Scripture.

11. Authority should not be confused here with charisma. Any attempt to separate office and charisma, however, should also be resisted. To do this would indicate that there was no such thing as a charisma of authority. It is, however, not sufficient for the Church authorities to appear in a private sense as religious or 'pious'—the authority of those holding office ought rather to be charismatic. For the idea of the authority of witness, see J. B. Metz, in *Kirche im Prozess der Aufklärung* (Mainz and Munich, 1970), p. 79.

12. In the article on religion in his *Dictionnaire philosophique,* Voltaire said that faith in God and belief in the punishments of hell could not in any way be regarded as without value from the political and functional point of view. They were, in his opinion, indispensable for the preservation of private property and the exercise of what was at the time legitimate power. It is only one small, consistent step from this position adopted by Voltaire to the critical change of this position in Marxism.

13. To this extent, there is a hint in Bonhoeffer's 'religionless Christianity' of the possible rise of a post-middle-class Christian 'religion'. See T. R. Peters, *Die Präsenz des Politischen in der Theologie D. Bonhoeffers* (Mainz and Munich, 1976), pp. 79 ff, 195 ff.

14. This seems to me to be the case of the dialectics of the Enlightenment as outlined by members of the Frankfurt school such as Horkheimer and Adorno.

15. The present discussion in the Federal Republic about fundamental values can only be conducted on the theological side, distinctions can only be made and the argument can only be properly orientated if the problem outlined here (and in the following chapter) is constantly borne in mind.

4. The concept of a political theology as a practical fundamental theology

Like every other new theology, the new political theology had problems in establishing its legitimacy and authenticity and still has them.[1] We may apply what Walter Benjamin has said in another context to these problems and say that the political tendency of a political theology can only be accepted as valid if its theological tendency is valid. The reverse is not true. A political theology must be consistently orientated in this direction and must recommend this criterion to all theologies, because none can, without practising self-deception, regard itself as being entirely without a political tendency or as politically innocent. A political theology of this kind is therefore able to expose and combat every prejudice that is active in theology and the praxis of the Church, according to which a theological tendency is valid if its tendency in politics is more or less right wing and conservative in the usual sense of the word.

In this chapter, I shall attempt to extend further the beginning that has already been made with political theology as a practical fundamental theology that seeks to work out the basic problems of Christianity. In Chapter 1, these problems were elucidated as a point of departure for a contemporary theology. In Chapter 2, they were worked out in a process of systematic historical reflection. In Chapter 3, this practical fundamental theology was already seen to be effective as a theological criticism of middle-class religion or of the silent but repeated identification of the middle-class and the religious subject.

The present chapter plays a central part in my argument and in it I am concerned with the task of working out the theological structure of this approach and of correcting earlier attempts at political theology and introducing considerable differentiations.[2] In this practical fundamental theology, the main concepts are *praxis* and the *subject*. In the first section, I shall attempt to throw light on the meaning of the primacy of praxis or the practical foundation of all Christian theology. This practical fundamental theology will then, in the second section, be presented as a political theology of the subject and its claim to authenticity will be justified in the strictly theological controversy about direct theologies of the subject and in the wider dispute concerning man's ability to be a subject. As a direct consequence of this, the importance of the religious subject in the historical struggle for man will be discussed in Section 3. Finally, in the last section (4), I shall suggest a theological definition of faith. This section is, like the book itself, entitled 'the faith of the Christian in history and society'. My definition of this faith will, I hope, arise out of the approach made in the earlier sections. In it, faith will also be defined, in a nutshell, in such a way that its theological validity need not be gained by obscuring the contrasting social experiences and positions by means of which it can be cancelled out or made to disappear nowadays.

1. The practical foundation of Christian theology or the meaning of the primacy of praxis

The term 'practical fundamental theology' is in itself unusual and may surprise many readers. I use it, however, to draw attention to the fact that theory and praxis are not dealt with here in the usual order of priority, in which praxis is regarded as the continuation, implementation or concrete application of a previously defined theory. Practical fundamental theology is, on the contrary, directly opposed to a non-dialectical subordination of praxis to theory or the idea. In it, great emphasis is placed on the intelligible force of praxis itself, in the sense of a dialectical tension between theory and praxis. To that extent, it is a theology that operates subject to the primacy of praxis.[3]

What, then, is the situation here? Is it something more than simply an emphatic, overlegitimized and therefore extremely abstract use of praxis? Or will a theology that is made subject to the primacy of praxis not inevitably be thought to be uncritical and divorced from theory? We are, however, bound to ask in the context of this question what 'critical' and 'theoretical' really mean here. The starting point for a practical fundamental theology is that all attempts made to base theology on pure theory or absolute reflection must be regarded as uncritical or only apparently theoretical. Practical fundamental theology does not appeal primarily to an understanding of theory and criticism which is valid outside the sphere of theology and according to which all pure theories are seen within a wider context of communication and action, with the result that they cannot be critical without reference to praxis. On the contrary, practical fundamental theology is based on the practical structure underlying the logos of Christian theo-logy.

a. The practical structure of the logos of Christian theo-logy

In itself, the Christian idea of God is a practical idea. God cannot be thought of at all unless this idea irritates and encroaches on the immediate interests of the person who is trying to think of it. Thinking about God is a review of interests and needs that are directly related to ourselves. Conversion, metanoia and even exodus are not simply moral or educative categories—they are also and above all noetic categories. Stories of conversion and exodus are therefore not simply dramatic embellishments of a previously conceived 'pure' theology. On the contrary, they form part of the basic structure of this theology. This practical structure of the idea of God is the reason why the concept of God is basically narrative and memorative. (Narrative and memory are not added as an ornament to a 'pure' idea of God.)

This practical structure applies with particular clarity to our Christological knowledge.[4] The praxis of imitation forms a constitutive part of Christo-logy, if the logos of this Christology, like that of Christianity itself, cannot ultimately be united with the logos of Greek philosophy which has to be regarded as pure and for which Christ was always 'folly'. It is true of any Christology that Christ has always to be thought of in such a way that he is not simply thought of. All Christology is nourished, for the sake of its own truth, by praxis and particularly the praxis of the imitation of Christ. It is, in other words, expressed in a practical knowledge. In this sense, then, all Christology is subject to the primacy of praxis. This might be called Christological dialectics or the dialectics of imitation. These dialectics are not in any sense idealistic conceptual dialectics expressing a tension between two ideas (divorced from the subject). They are rather dialectics of theory and praxis or

51

dialectics of subject and object. It is only when they imitate Christ that Christians know who it is to whom they have given their consent and who saves them. This Christo-logical dialectical tension can be clearly recognized in the accounts concerning the imitation of Christ in the New Testament. There is, in those accounts, no adequate distinction between narrative and commandment, with the result that the listener is able first to hear the stories of Jesus and then reflect about the consequences that he may or may not draw from them and apply to himself. These New Testament stories of the imitation of Christ are in themselves appellative and imperative. They attempt to change the listening subject in the telling of the story and to make him ready to imitate Christ. Christological knowledge, then, is not handed down primarily as a concept, but in such stories of the imitation of Christ. It therefore has, as the theological idea of Christ itself also has, a narrative and practical character.[5] I shall try to show in the following pages the extent to which this Christological knowledge in its practical aspect is and must be, in accordance with theological thinking as such, political.

In the meantime, however, it is important to indicate the constitutive part played by such practical concepts as imitation, conversion and exodus in the structure of theology as such. This also automatically raises the question of the status of praxis or the specific relationship between theory and praxis in fundamental theology.

In my earlier considerations concerning an approach to a political theology, my point of departure was the primacy of praxis, to such an extent indeed that this primacy of praxis or the relationship between theory and praxis that was expressed in this primacy became the key concept in my approach. In the perspective of the debate about the foundations of theology as such, we may say that the so-called hermeneutical problem of theology was not really a problem of the relationship between systematic and historical theology or between dogma and history, but rather a problem of the relationship between theory and praxis or between the understanding of faith and social praxis.[6] The concept 'praxis', however, had too great a content and this led to misunderstandings and equivocation, with the result that it was necessary to introduce differentiation into the concept. Karl Rahner's theology was influenced by Kant's transcendental teaching and his question about what conditioned the possibility of knowledge generally. Unlike Rahner's theology, political theology was, to begin with, more emphatically orientated towards the traditions of the practical philosophy of history and society, in other words, towards Kant's teaching about the primacy of practical reason and the dialectics of theory and praxis in Marxism.[7] The constant point of departure for political theology was that the change to the primacy of praxis in philosophy (Kant, the Enlightenment—Marx) should be regarded as the real Copernican revolution in philosophy and that it was therefore very important not only to solve the basic problem of theological reason as it were this side of idealism, but also to try to do theology on the other side of idealism.

The praxis that was central in Kant's teaching and on the basis of the intelligible force of which practical reason was built up is moral praxis (this has already been explained in some detail in the preceding sections). Kant's practical philosophy of history and society was therefore developed above all as ethical teaching.[8] From then onwards, there could be no critical logos which was not practical in its intention as ethics. No differentiation had, however, as yet been made between moral and social praxis or, to express this in another way, social praxis was (as we have already seen above in Chapters 2 and 3) the same as the moral praxis of the subjects who had already achieved power in the social sense. Social praxis was, in other words, identical with the moral praxis of the citizens. Individual moral imperatives in Kant's teaching replace the question of social action and conceal the fact that coming of age is a question not only of the moral exertion of the individual, but of social structures and relationships. It was Marx who first made it clear that individual moral praxis was not in any sense socially neutral and politically innocent and that the so-called purely ethical interpretation of social praxis always worked with substitutions. Reference is made to 'man', but what is meant in each case is the socially established subject. Although this cannot be discussed in detail here, the same obviously also applies to Kant's categorical imperative.

I did not make a clear enough distinction in my early attempt to formulate a political theology within the concept of praxis between moral and social praxis. In so doing, I placed the teachings of Kant and those of Marx too much at the same level.[9] The political statements made in this theology were therefore often purely moral, in the nature of an appeal or an exhortation. They were therefore able to be used in widely different contexts.

It is theologically important that moral praxis not be socially neutral and politically innocent. If the primacy of praxis in theology is taken seriously, this has a bearing not only on moral praxis in the narrower sense, but also on social praxis. This can be illustrated by reference to Kant's postulate regarding coming of age. Kant was able to describe coming of age as a moral task, because he had in mind only people who had been of age for a long time in the social and economic sense, that is, people who already existed as socially powerful subjects. There is, however, clearly a situation in which man has not yet come of age and is impotent and oppressed which is not simply due to the moral weakness of those who have not yet come of age or are impotent and oppressed. And who can doubt that this socially conditioned failure to come of age, this impotence and this oppression—in a word, this poverty—forms an important object of Christian praxis? Who would deny that Christian praxis must inevitably be concerned not only with man's state as a subject in the presence of God, but also with the fact that men can become subjects and can live as subjects rising from misery and oppression?

I may conclude this section by saying that the practical structure of theology, as outlined here, includes not only moral, but social praxis. In other words, the forms of behaviour such as metanoia, exodus and the imitation of Christ which are constitutive in my idea of God and Christological and eschatological knowledge in general have a social and political structure. This understanding points clearly to the very deep meaning and significance of my idea of a political theology.[10]

b. The practical hermeneutics of Christianity

It is clear that Christian praxis as social praxis ought to be more precisely defined. It should therefore be discussed within the framework of practical hermeneutics of Christianity of a kind that could be described cautiously as practical and dialectical hermeneutics, since it does not simply have its object, Christian praxis, outside itself.

We must first define these practical hermeneutics more precisely with regard to other theological attempts to define practical Christianity, in other words, with regard to univerally historical, eschatological and transcendental hermeneutics.

We must, for example, ask, in the light of the approach that has been elaborated here, whether, in his extremely valuable attempt to develop universally historical hermeneutics, Wolfhart Pannenberg's anticipation of a total meaning in history is not too little interrupted or irritated by what is described in the apocalyptic tradition as a universal catastrophe, in other words, as the reign of the Antichrist. According to Pannenberg, praxis is of secondary importance and subordinate or else it is in danger of becoming a praxis that is orientated towards a previously conceived totality of meaning. But does history really follow its logical course in this sense? And, if it is really uninterrupted in its course, does it then (as Max Horkheimer, for example, correctly asked) fulfil its human destiny?

Jürgen Moltmann's concept of an eschatological hermeneutics of Christian praxis is very close to my own ideas about a political theology and for this reason I am bound to point to a clear difference. His book, *The Crucified God,* was in many respects quite splendid, but since its publication Moltmann has used the concept of praxis increasingly to describe a theology in which the history of the suffering of the Son and the world is rooted within the Trinity. Praxis, which can only prevent the danger of speculative gnosis in such an approach, is no longer an intelligible principle in Moltmann's theology. On the other hand, this intelligibility is required in the attempts made to find a narrative and practical approach to Christology and soteriology and indeed in the idea of a practical fundamental theology as such.

I will have more to say about Karl Rahner's transcendental hermeneutics of Christian praxis in the following main section (2) of this chapter and later in Chapter 9, when I shall be attempting to answer the question 'A transcendental and idealistic or a narrative and practical Christianity?' Even when one has to go emphatically against his teaching, one can still learn from Rahner.

These hermeneutics of Christian praxis have, however, to be clarified with regard to theories of action that are outside the sphere of theology. It is clear that both theories of action which work analytically and scientific and linguistic theories are ultimately social theories which owe their alleged autonomy to a social division of labor that is not reflected in the analytical approach to knowledge.[11] They have therefore to be examined within the framework of a theological theory of history and society. What is more, these theories are, in my opinion, characterized by a non-dialectical logic of development and I shall consequently have to question them and narrow down their theoretical status again and again in the course of my reflections and especially in my chapter on 'noncontemporaneous theses on the apocalyptic view' (Chapter 10 below).

Here I shall confine myself to a brief outline of the most important aspects of this practical and dialectical form of hermeneutics which will then remain normative for the two following sections (2 and 3), where this praxis will be characterized as having solidarity and liberating in the interest of the process by which all men become subjects.

1. Christian praxis as social praxis—also in view of what I have just said about Kant's teaching—remains ethically determined. This is because the demand for the social conditions and constellations of moral action to be considered does not have as its aim a process by which moral praxis is simply interpreted as social praxis and the moral subject is also made simply relative. A consideration of the social dependences of moral action can be regarded as a necessary condition, but not a sufficient one, in determining Christian praxis.[12] The consequence of this ethical determination of the Christian's social praxis is that this praxis cannot lead to an abstract or a violent negation of the individual. This moral determination of social praxis also makes possible and guarantees the fact that it will become really practical as a criticism of violence or of the recording of violence continuously by means of a logic of hatred, so that it becomes possible to overcome violence only by further violence.

2. Christian praxis as social praxis continues to be determined by an excess of historical determinations that are the noninferred function of the prevailing social totality. This is where the hermeneutics of memory as a dangerous phenomenon or as subversion and rebellion plays an indispensable part. Every utopian concept of liberation which questions and breaks through what is currently held to be plausible is ultimately rooted in this kind of memory, which is in turn not simply a reflection or reproduction of the contemporary factors determining society and economics. Otherwise, from what source could interests and norms be gained that could be

applied to the practical task of criticizing existing relationships? A materialism based on the conviction that society is determined strictly by economic factors could never be revolutionary unless it unreasonably demanded of matter itself a kind of teleology of freedom.[13]

It is here, however, that the idea of narrative plays a part in heremeneutics, insofar as it determines praxis on the basis of dangerous stories which call the social conditioning of human activity into question and which are directed against a kind of history in which, under certain structures and systems, the subject, who can never be accurately calculated by anyone, is made to disappear. It is precisely this excess of historical determinations that are communicated by memory and narrative which can prevent new forms of praxis from being purely sporadic, from standing simply symbolically for a new reality and not raising this up and therefore from being re-absorbed too easily by the existing system. Innovatory praxis must therefore be accompanied by a making present of a collective historical memory.

3. Christian praxis as social praxis is guided by an understanding of praxis that also takes what may be called the pathic structure of this praxis into consideration. In other words, praxis is seen not simply as action—which means that it is regarded as the subjection and control of nature—but also as suffering. Sorrow, as a category of opposition to the prevention of sorrow and melancholy by a society of achievement and triumph, and joy, as a category of opposition to man's increasing inability to celebrate the meaning of life, are both examples of the pathic or suffering structures of human praxis that can be regarded as forms of opposition to the prevalent apathy of society. Another example of a pathic structure is solidarity as openness to past suffering, in other words, as solidarity with the dead and those who have been overcome. Almost all the themes discussed in this book are characterized by an attitude of resistance to the interiorization and privatization of these pathic forms of expression of social praxis. The claims made by this pathic or suffering structure of social praxis are outlined in 'The future in the memory of suffering' (Chapter 6 below), in which I also make clear that an emphasis placed on this pathic structure of human praxis does not in any sense lead to a paralysis or a calming down in the sphere of political action. On the contrary, it can only liberate

praxis from its exclusive orientation towards an anthropological model, according to which man is viewed one-sidedly as a subject exerting control over nature and human history, the latter being regarded as a non-dialectical history of progress and triumph or conquest. At the end of this process, man is bred back to nature and his status as a subject ceases, because his control of nature is ultimately exercised with the help of a model of knowledge and action which is itself orientated towards natural processes that lie outside the sphere of history.[14]

It is obvious that the category of memory—in the form of a memory of suffering—and the category of narrative—as a linguistic identification of the stories of human suffering, which escape the system of the history of progress and triumph—is given greater importance here. Similarly, the category of solidarity in its extended sense of anamnesis or the memory of the sacrifices of history also gains in importance. In the same way too, these categories are, in the various arguments used in the course of this book, directed against any attempt to interpret the history of suffering in terms either of evolution or of dialectics and indeed against all attempts to define the subject only on the basis of his actions, not on the basis of his suffering.

This, then, concludes my introductory clarification and differentiation in the concept of praxis in the idea of the primacy of praxis. In Section 2 of this chapter I shall try to define it more precisely. In the meantime, however, it is important to deal at once with two questions that arise in connection with the idea of the practical foundation of Christian theology.

c. The question of the subjects and the functions of theology

In addition to the question of the relationship between the subject and praxis, which is of fundamental importance and will have to be discussed in greater detail, there is also the question of suitable and competent subjects of theology, in other words, who is competent to do theology? In a truly practical fundamental theology, we should above all be conscious of the fact that theology should not simply elaborate and pass on themes without reference to the subject, but that it must again and again be interrupted by praxis and experience. The important questions to be asked by theology, then, are: Who should do theology and where, in whose interest and for whom? Is it sufficient in this context simply to point to the usual division of labor within the Church? Is it, in other words, enough, to have recourse to the standardized subjects of theology (professors, teachers and specialists in theological studies), places (universities, seminaries, colleges), the normal forms of communication (books, lectures, discussions) and interests (the Church's teaching mission)? It is important that theology itself poses these questions and that they are not imposed on theology from outside, in the spirit of a criticism of ideology.

In this context, we are bound to consider very briefly an objection to the new political theology. Overemphasising the word 'political', the objection is made that there is a rather dubious attempt in political theology to place lay people in a position of tutelage in the Church by means of a professional, official theology. What is often overlooked when this criticism is made is that this political theology in fact looks forward to the emergence of a new subject of theology. It is in no way assumed that the only adequate exponent of this political theology is the professional theologian or the one who, as it were, specializes in God because of his office. On the basis of the intentions of this theology, the distinction between official and lay theology ceases to exist. Indeed, it is possible to say that the abolition of this distinction is to some degree a presupposition of this whole approach, on the basis of the theory of knowledge. In other words, political theology transcends, in its intentions, the narrow sphere of professional theology, whether this is practised by official representatives of the Church or laypeople.

d. The question of truth within the primacy of praxis

We must now briefly consider the very important question of the meaning of truth within the primacy of practical reason. What, in other words, is the position of truth in a practical fundamental theology? Is truth in this context not simply made subordinate to praxis? Is truth not re-interpreted as relevance? And does this re-interpretation not simply conceal (because it is in fact a semantic deception) what really happens, namely the liquidation of the concept of truth, insofar as a truth that is orientated towards praxis is no longer truth?

In a practical fundamental theology, the difference between truth and relevance is in no sense simply a matter of personal discretion.

In such a theology, the idea of truth without reference to subjects is irrelevant and even dangerous, with the result that truth and relevance are bound to converge to the extent that truth becomes the type of relevance that applies to all subjects. In other words, in a practical fundamental theology, truth is what is relevant to all subjects, including the dead and those who have been overcome or conquered. I shall attempt to show in the following section how this understanding of truth is in accordance with the understanding of the subject in political theology.

It is only if truth is previously conceived as correlative with pure reason or theory or as the result of absolute reflection that this objection to practical fundamental theology and its supposed attitude towards truth can be sustained. The same objection could also be made to the biblical traditions. Towards the end of this book, when I deal with the categories of memory and narrative (in Chapters 11 and 12), I shall attempt to throw some light on the narrative and practical structure of knowledge and truth. This is analogous to the practical structure of the idea of God.[15]

2. The struggle for the subject or practical fundamental theology as a political theology of the subject

If political theology, as a practical fundamental theology, is to avoid the danger of divorcing its praxis from the subject, it must be elaborated as a theology of the subject. I must therefore elucidate this essential aspect of political theology and define it more precisely, on the one hand because it is often suspected of obscuring the subject too much in the interests of history and society and, on the other, because the theologies that are often criticized by political theology are also regarded as theologies of the subject (of a transcendental, existential, personalistic or paradoxical and dialectical kind). What, then, has to be done is to define in greater detail what I have already said in Chapter 3 above about the political theology of the subject.

a. The idea of God—constituting the subject and forming identity

The history of the biblical religion is a history of the way in which a people and the individuals belonging to that people became

subjects in the presence of their God. In this sense, the word subject does not refer to the isolated individual, the monad who only
afterwards made sure of his co-existence with other subjects. Experiences of solidarity with, antagonism towards, liberation from and
anxiety about other subjects form an essential part of the constitution of the religious subject, not afterwards, but from the very
beginning. The question about the relationship between the individual subject and other subjects is unreasonably expected and is the
product of later abstraction. The universal solidarity that existed
among biblical subjects, then, is a fundamental category in the political theology of the subject. It does not point to a subsumption of
individual religious subjects at a later stage. On the contrary, it is
the form in which those subjects existed in God's presence and
through him.

The Old Testament and New Testament histories of faith cannot
be added as a kind of superstructure or accompanying phenomenon
to mankind that has already been constituted in its subject state.
They are rather histories of the dramatic way in which men were
constituted as subjects through their relationship with God. Those
men were called out of the anxieties and compulsions of archaic
societies in order to become subjects of a new historical process.
The terms of their state as subjects were dynamic—being called in
danger, being called out of fear, the exodus, conversion, the raising
up of their head, the imitation of their leader and so on. Religion
was not an additional phenomenon. It was an active part of the process by which Israel became a subject. In the Old Testament, it was
in the exodus that the people most clearly became subjects.

Their relationship with God was not an expression of slavish submission and weak subjection. It did not humiliate them as subjects,
but compelled them again and again to be subjects in view of the
extreme dangers of that state. Prayer therefore impelled the one
who prayed to remain a subject and not to avoid his responsibility
in view of his own guilt. It made him become a subject in the presence of his enemies and in the midst of fear to lose his name, his
own face and himself.[16]

This shows us, then, how essentially practical the biblical and
Christian idea of God was and is. As such it is not an expression of
a subsequent overcoming of the subject and his previously conceived identity by strange, alienating powers that are not under-

stood. As such it is not the result of a projection of the endangered subject, who is impelled by archaic fears, into a state beyond danger and destruction. It is in no sense a superstructure onto an already formed identity of the subject. It is above all an idea that forms identity and enters deeply into the basis of existence. It is opposed to the formation of an identity of the subject that is orientated towards possessions and on the contrary constitutes the subject as solidly united.

In this idea of God, man's state as a historical and social subject is in no way suppressed or disregarded. On the contrary, it impels it into situations where it is seriously threatened. Just as this idea of God has, for example, to make itself responsible for guilt if it is to remain a subject, so too it has to oppose suppression and contempt of men if it is to become a subject. This can be expressed in a more dramatic way: the struggle for God and the struggle to enable all men to be free subjects does not operate in the opposite direction, but proportionally in the same direction.[17] It is clear that this concept of a political theology has to be further elaborated, both theologically, in contrast to the so-called direct—and in my view abstract—theologies of the subject, and in the secular perspective, that is, in view of the historical struggle for the subject and indeed in the form of a practical criticism of a culture of hatred and a culture of apathy.

b. Against the theologies of the subject that are divorced from the subject

In my earlier attempts to formulate a political theology, I directed my arguments against the various theologies of the subject that dominate the theological scene today. The thesis of deprivatization that was elaborated in it did not intend, in its use of the direct and in this sense abstract contrast between public and social on the one hand and private and subjective on the other, to move away from the subject and towards society (which is, if possible, regarded as independent of the subject). It was from the beginning determined by the impression that theology is in danger, because of the tendency to privatization, of failing to perceive the existence of the individual to whom it appeals. As I pointed out in my earlier work,[18] any existential and personal theology that claims to understand human existence, but not as a political problem in the widest sense, is an abstract theology with regard to the existential situation of the individual. The thesis of deprivatization therefore attempted to criticize prevalent theologies (such as the existential theology of demythologization, the personal theology and the transcendental theology) in an effort to get away from privatistic categories and the long established abstract contrast between the subject on the one hand and history and society on the other and to move closer to a new theology of the subject, even if this proved inadequate. The problems, however, remained.

In so far as they are relevant in this type of theology of the subject, history and society only appear as anthropological reductions. They can be regarded only as variables of a subject or an anthropology which tries to keep the subject out of its historical and social struggles for identity, as it were almost *a priori,* by means of a late and diminished form of metaphysics and which compensates for its suspected dissociation from history by a weakened idea of the historicity of the subject. The thesis that is critically presented and renewed here, however, is that this theological understanding of man must inevitably become more and more atrophied in view of the role that is attributed to him, namely that of being the subject of his own historical and social processes.

It would not be difficult to demonstrate how the eschatology of the universe that is directed towards history and society has receded more and more and has become almost completely overshadowed by the eschatology of the individual and how this process has gone hand-in-hand with the anthropological reduction of history and society in theology. The same applies to apocalyptic studies, in which attention has for a long time been exclusively concentrated on individual situations of catastrophe in the death of the individual.[19] The questions that are so deeply involved with the apocalyptic literature—to whom does the world belong? to whom do its suffering and its time belong? who is its Lord?—have been more successfully suppressed, it would seem, in theology than in any other sphere. They arise every day in a secularized form in the historical and social struggles for power which take place in our world and in which, it should be noted, the fate of man as a subject and particularly as a religious subject is at stake. The anthropological reduction of history and society that I have criticized above also takes place not where a beginning is made with the transcendental experience of the subject, man's openness, the true nature of his existence or the paradox of meaning and suffering, but where the intersubjective I-Thou experience is approached. In this approach, the mystery of suffering in historical life is reduced to the problem of the obscure Thou in the encounter between men. The list of questions could, of course, be enlarged. The aspect that has to be stressed, however, is that these questions point to the consequences of an abstract theology of the subject which is divorced from history and to which almost all modern theological approaches seem to be committed.

This reduction of history and society in the determination of man's state as a subject in the presence of God is resisted in the political theology of the subject. This does not mean that it makes the subject into a sliding function, a variable in historical and social processes. On the contrary, it tries rather to keep to a twofold structure that is constantly entire and to a mutual priority of subject and history-society. It can, however, only do this if it develops the theology of the subject as a theory of history and society, in opposition to the usual division of labour between systematic theology and theological teaching about society, and if it deals with and elaborates this theory as a practical one. What is above all problematical for the political theology of the subject in this context is the identification which takes place in the systematic theology that is divorced from the subject, in other words, that is generally unconscious of its social subject and which I have already considered above in my historical survey in Chapters 2 and 3. This identification is, of course, that between the middle-class and the religious subject.

The most enduring of these theologies, because it has been elaborated wih the most powerful arguments, and one which has an effect in all the Christian confessions, is the transcendental theology of the subject developed by my teacher, Karl Rahner. The questions of a political theology of the subject have partially been evoked by Rahner's theology, but they have remained captive in contradiction in it. Rahner's basic thesis of theology as anthropology[20] cannot be simply repeated in a political theology of the subject, but it can be made more historically and socially evident in it.

I do not want to repeat what I have already said elsewhere about Rahner's transcendental theology of the subject, nor do I want to anticipate my remarks in Chapter 9 below about the choice between a 'transcendental and idealistic or a narrative and practical Christianity'. I would like, however, to deal briefly here with the fundamental anthropological definition that is present in the transcendental theology. This can be expressed concisely in the following way: man exists as an anticipation of God and this anticipation conditions the possibility of his knowledge and his behaviour. I am overlooking the fact that it is difficult for a political theology of the subject not to recognize, in such a definition of man, the anthropology of a society which is basically still determined by religious aims and which is therefore only capable of consent when such social conditions prevail. The only question that I would like to ask in this context[21] is whether this anticipation itself has anything to do with history, in other words, whether the anticipation has temporal structures. This question can be expressed differently in the following way: does this transcendental anthropology take into account the fact that man's anticipatory existence is a historical existence?[2]

The concept of experience that has been elaborated in the transcendental theology of the subject does not have the structure of historical experience. The social contradictions and mutually antagonistic aspects which form the basis of suffering in historical experience and in which the historical subject is constituted in fact disappear, in this transcendental theology, in the absence of objectivity of a previously known transcendental experience in which these contradictions are already reconciled in a non-dialectical way.[23] The transcendental theology of the subject has the effect, then, of overlegitimizing the identity of the religious subject in view of the historical suffering of man.

If this safeguard of transcendental identity is abandoned, several questions are at once raised, for example, how can norms be obtained for the historical struggles for man's state as a subject? How can we be orientated and inspired to save his identity? How can we find a foothold in the turmoil of historical and social processes that are becoming more and more divorced from the subject if this can no longer be found by means of metaphysics or even by the late metaphysics of anticipation?

c. Memory and narrative as categories of salvation

The categories that can be applied in order to ascertain religious identity and to safeguard norms are those of man's historical consciousness—memory and narrative. These categories have a different part to play in a political theology of the subject from the one that they may play in a transcendental theology of the subject. In other words, they do not have a deduced or inferred significance as pure categories. They have, on the contrary, a fundamental importance. They do not, for example, act as a decoration, filling in the details of a previously conceived idea. They are rather fundamental categories used in ascertaining and saving identity in the historical struggles and dangers in which men experience themselves and are constituted as subjects. Memory (and narrative) are not to be understood in this context as categories of defeatism and resignation—they are dangerous categories (this aspect of the question will be discussed again and again in Parts II and III of this work).

Here, however, I will confine myself to an indication of the universal meaning of memory as the category of the salvation of threatened identity. If this question is approached from the negative point of view, we see that the destruction of man's memory systematically prevents him from becoming or remaining a subject in the context of history and society. It is, in other words, an obstacle to identity. For example, the uprooting of slaves and their deportation helped to destroy their memories and at the same time helped to establish them successfully as slaves. The destruction of memory therefore led to the confirmation of their existence as slaves and their systematic deprivation of power in the interest of complete submission. The reverse is also true—identity is formed when memories are aroused.

The historical process by which a nation, race or class become subjects almost always begins with their breaking through the power of the official idea of history by exposing it as propaganda on the part of those who rule them. This idea of history is called, in various contexts in this book, the history of triumph or conquest. In this history of conquest, those who are conquered and oppressed are not remembered. Peasants, for example, have revealed their memory of suffering in their chronicles and citizens have made that memory visible in their art. In this way they have derived the power to resist the threat to their identity. Workers have similarly begun to discover that the current works of history are silent about their suffering and have become dissatisfied with this state of affairs. In this, then, memory operates above all as a category by which historical identity is found and as a category of liberation.[24]

d. The state of all men as subjects

A political theology of the subject, for which memory, as a definite memory, is fundamental (this definite memory being that of men's process of becoming subjects in the presence of God), is bound to criticize the usual theological idea of man and the subject, especially when it becomes increasingly clear that this idea only acts as a camouflage for one definite subject (the central European) or when the idea of the modern subject in theology has the obvious aim of avoiding all the problems that have arisen in the last two hundred years.

The political theology of the subject will also keep to the idea of man and the subject with the help of the categories of historical identity and conscious of the concrete origin of these abstract concepts, since it cannot be concerned simply with an identification with some historical class subject or other.

A political theology of the subject which cannot, in the name of the memories that it tries to express, simply let the middle-class subject be a middle-class subject, will also not be able to let the comrade be a comrade. In other words, it will not be able to identify the socialist personality with the subject that it is seeking to express. With the help of its memory, which is neither absorbed by the existing structure of social relationships nor produced by that structure, the political theology evokes a subject that cannot be defined simply on the basis of antagonistic models of a class society, by the negation of whatever opponent appears at the time. When there is opposition (based on memory) to the refusal to allow man to be a subject, this opposition is not only to feudalism or capitalism, it is also to any form of suppression or institutionalized hatred. In this process, the God of this dangerous memory does not secretly become a political utopia of universal liberation. The name of God stands rather for the fact that the utopia of the liberation of all human subjects is not a pure projection, which is what that utopia would be if there were only a utopia and no God.

In this sense at least, the idea of God is indisputably political. It is moreover political in itself and not simply political in the sense of acting as a criticism of ideology, with the result that it is—as it would be in the latter case—not in continuous need of being set free from an association with particular power structures. It represents an option in favor of the state of all men as subjects—all men can be and must become subjects. The freedom of the Christian memory with regard to existing relationships and structures therefore does not consist of its imagining, rather as art does, a fictitious counter-world. In this freedom of memory, the history of men as subjects in the presence of God is evoked and Christians are compelled to respond to the practical challenge of this history. In its praxis what will emerge, at least partially, is that all men are called to be subjects in the presence of God.

Will Christians succeed in this important task of making man's religious state as a subject socially and visibly incarnate in the struggle for man and his history? Those who are not aware of any problems in this task because they believe that they know what the proper subjects of Christian praxis are ought to ask themselves whether they can deal with the crisis of religion that has been brought about by the middle-class subject in any way that is not defeatist. This way of dealing with crises of this kind has so far at least achieved very little. Church life in the developed world is tending to develop more and more into two patterns—on the one hand there is the Church with the liberal touch serving the middle class in its need for celebration and, on the other, there is the anxious, traditional Church as a sect. There is an increasing loss of deep inner conviction regarding faith in the official Church today, resulting in a corresponding loss of nerve and decisiveness. The life of the Church is characterized by a fear of powers and processes that are not understood. This anxiety has sapped the courage of Christians to take new steps, encourage the development of new, alternative forms of Christian praxis and to make new religious and political experiments.[25] This anxiety has led to a quest for stabilization in past forms.

In my previous arguments, I assumed that religion and man's becoming a subject were inseparably connected. I could not appeal to a transcendental theology of the subject which presented man *a priori* as absolutely transcendent. I can, however, go beyond the developed ideas and refer to a historical anthropology based on the history of religion. This historical anthropology is certainly able to support the idea that man did not transfer his state as a subject to God in human history seen as a history of religion, but that he only acquired identity as a subject and became the subject of his own history through religion, that is, in his relationship with God.[26]

This connection has been made even more plausible today by the simultaneous occurrence of a fundamental crisis in religion on the one hand and a social crisis of the subject on the other.[27] Is it purely by chance that the idea of the end of history should arise at a time when the universal history of man ceases to be understood as a history of religion? Is it a pure coincidence that suspicion about the death and collapse of language should occur at the moment when religious language is becoming increasingly atrophied? Is it fortuitous that the announcement of the death of man should follow that of the death of God? Theodor Adorno proclaimed the 'end of the individual'—or at least that of the citizen—many years ago and noted: 'The horror, however, is that the citizen has not found a successor'.[28] Is the subject dying out altogether, then? For determined structuralists, the death of the subject is already a fact. They regard man as an anthropomorphism and a 'remarkable invention of the eighteenth century'.[29]

In its struggle for the 'new man' and the state of the oppressed classes as subjects, Marxist socialism is firmly opposed to this paralysis of historical subjects (even though it is, at least in its western forms, irritated by adaptation to structuralism[30]). Where, however, has this struggle succeeded to such an extent that we can see, in this 'new man', the identity and solidarity of all men in their free state as subjects? I should like to be able to say that Herbert Marcuse is right, when he, who is reminded of Fascist praxis by the pure negation of the individual, including the middle-class individual, says that solidarity and community do not imply an abandonment of the individual, but are the result of autonomous individual decision and that this solidarity is a solidarity of individuals, not of masses.[31]

From where, then, do the forces producing a new individualization that is not the outcome of repression of others come? How does the strength to resist a systematically distorted form of solidarity based on hatred or the massing together of people come about? How can we at the same time avoid abandoning true solidarity which offers us the opportunity to perpetuate individual identity and a human status as subjects not in opposition to other weaker and socially deprived groups and classes, but together with them?

3. Religion in the historical struggle for man

Is it the religious subject who is particularly required here? It is, if that subject understands the practical interest in the process by which others become subjects, that is, those who live in a state of oppression and collective obscurity, as a necessary, although perhaps not sufficient condition of his own state as a subject in the presence of God. It is also, if the subject realizes that the Christian Gospel is only political and politically committed by proclaiming the state of all men as subjects in God's presence and by paying no less a price for this state as subjects in God's presence than for the struggle against oppression and hatred of the kind that make it impossible for the mass of the populations in many parts of the world to become subjects.

An example of this is the contrast, to which I have already referred, between the rich industrial countries of the North and the poor countries of the South. Because the population of these southern regions is to a great extent traditionally Catholic, this contrast between North and South cuts right through the one-world Church and, for example, affects the relationship between the central European and North American churches on the one hand and the Church in the Latin-American subcontinent on the other. Just as the Gospel to which the Church bears witness acts again and again as a challenge to political and social life, so too must the contrast between North and South become an irritation to the Church and make demands on it. How, then, can the one Church deal with the class contrasts that exist between the northern and the southern regions of the world, both of which are included in the same Church? How can these contrasts be reconciled with the living unity of the Church? How can they be brought into harmony with the Church as a eucharistic community of those who are called out and should raise their heads in order to be subjects of a new history? How can we deal with the fact that entire populations in the one Church live in collective obscurity? Can the rich churches of the North only redress the balance between them and the poor churches of the South that has been destroyed by what has been recognized as the mechanics of exploitation and structural injustice by means of almsgiving? As long as the attempt made by theologians (especially in this case those responsible for the theology of liberation) to make sure of their point of departure by means of an analysis of the world situation is criticized as too general and suspected of being a concealed manoeuvre on behalf of foreign interests, there can be no real awareness in the Church of the extent of these problems.

These considerations should not be understood as an attempt to raise the kingdom of God to the level of politics and economics. They do, however, point to the fact that religion has been made guilty by its attempt to purchase its political innocence by not participating in the historical struggles for all men and their status as subjects. In the earlier considerations of political theology, which took the form of a criticism of ideology, this presumed innocence and neutrality of the Church and its members were criticized almost exclusively. Now, however, political theology is also expressed as an option in favour of the state of all men in solidarity as subjects.

There is certainly religion in an authentic form even when there is oppression. The God of the Christian Gospel is, after all, not a God of conquerors, but a God of slaves. This would be the case even if middle-class theologians were not allowed to justify a strict division between 'person' and 'work' and thus to infer a completely interiorized state of man as a subject in the presence of God—a state that they patronizingly offer to all men and especially to slaves.[32]

Whenever Christians bear this fact firmly in mind, they are able to express the principle of the religious individualization of man with conviction in the face of all opposition and conduct the struggle for God as a struggle for the process by which all men are able to become subjects in the face of any collective misunderstanding of man's new solidarity and of the creeping death of the individual in an evolving world.

The question of men's ability to become subjects in solidarity with each other and that of the religious subject are convergent. Here the reserves of religion to save identity are required more than ever. These reserves, which can resist apathy and a distorted collective life that is divorced from the subject, are, however, clearly not unlimited. They are dependent on the historical ability of living religion to resist and on faith in the state of all men as subjects in God's presence. This state as subjects in the presence of God is one of solidarity in a universal sense—not only with regard to those who are oppressed, deprived and needy, but also with regard to those who have been overcome or conquered and those who have died in the world's history of suffering.

One of the indispensable ways in which this solidarity is expressed—and this has to be stressed—is prayer. In this, religion is fundamentally different from that pure utopia to which no one prays and which is clearly only a promise for those who are still to come—a paradise for the victorious—but not for those who suffer unjustly and die. A society which has lost its interest in the continuing state of its people as subjects and which has abandoned its community of interest with the dead will inevitably become weaker and weaker in the historical struggle for the state of the living as subjects and fall victim to evolutionary apathy.[33] The God of the living and the dead is a God of universal justice who destroys the norms of our society based on exchange and the satisfaction of needs, saves those who suffer unjustly and die and therefore calls on us to become subjects, to help others to become subjects in the face of hostile oppression and to remain subjects in the face of guilt and in opposition to apathy and the massing together of people.

Surely the identity of modern man is extremely fragile. Fitted into the complex structures of contemporary society which function almost without reference to the subjects of that society, he is in constant danger of losing his face and his name (in the biblical sense) more and more. His dreams and imaginings are less and less frequently creative, but are, on the contrary, levelled down more and more. In the name of evolution and technological progress, he is increasingly subject to a process of back-breeding to the state of a very adaptable animal or a quietly functioning machine. From time to time he tries to raise up his state as a subject on the basis of those artificial 'great' subjects that are the most pitiful imitations of the state of being a subject in the face of the most radical danger that threatens it.

Responsibility, which is not sustained by structures, is a disappearing value. The state of being a subject in solidarity with others is weakening. The art of suppressing or banishing guilt and obligation to others is widely practised. Politics tend to be less and less successful and to give way to administration and power structures. Is it perhaps true that we are living in an age of apathy? It is certainly true to say that human apathy is as bad as hatred and as disastrous in its effects on the process by which men become subjects in solidarity.

4. The faith of Christians in history and society

I would like to conclude this part of my book, in which I have dealt with concepts, by attempting to define the faith of Christians in the light of a political theology conceived as a practical fundamental theology. I therefore propose the following definition: The faith of Christians is a praxis in history and society that is to be understood as hope in solidarity in the God of Jesus as a God of the living and the dead who calls all men to be subjects in his presence. Christians justify themselves in this essentially apocalyptical praxis (of imitation[34]) in their historical struggle for their fellow men. They stand up for all men in their attempt to become subjects in solidarity with each other. In this praxis, they resist the danger both of a creeping evolutionary disintegration of the history of men as subjects and of an increasing negation of the individual in view of a new, post-middle-class image of man.

I shall now explain this attempt at a definition rather briefly, on the one hand bringing together the various considerations that have preoccupied me in this part of the book under theological headings and, on the other, providing a number of emphases and perspectives that point forward to the considerations that concern me in Part II.[35]

a. With an apocalyptical sting

This theological approach is strongly characterized by the primacy of eschatology and faith is primarily expressed in it as hope in solidarity. I have already justified and given meaning to an eschatologically-orientated theology in earlier reflections about a political theology and do not wish to repeat this discussion here.[36] One new aspect of this eschatological orientation of political theology, however, can be mentioned in this context and that is its apocalyptical character. The theological primacy of an apocalyptically-directed eschatology has important consequences both for theology and for practical Christianity. In particular it affects both the practical and the temporal structure of Christian hope, which is here seen as imminent expectation. This hope could only be deprived of its temporal character by an (objective) semantic deception in respect of the biblical traditions and re-interpreted as the timeless existential aspect of being a Christian, in other words, as constant expectation.[37] I shall deal in greater detail with the full scope of this attempt to express once more this apocalyptical aspect of Christian eschatology that has for so long not been considered in view of the present challenges facing Christianity in Chapter 10 below. In the same chapter, I shall also try to show the extent to which Christian hope, understood as imminent expectation, can provide the practical basis for a criticism of an evolutionary understanding of time, in which God himself becomes more and more vague and eventually unthinkable and in which the way is prepared for the end of history and the death of man's state as a subject.

b. God of the living and the dead

On the basis of this theological primacy of an apocalyptical eschatology, there is one fundamental theological statement that includes all other statements made about God and his existence as creator. It is that God is a God of the living and the dead and a God of universal justice and the resurrection of the dead.[38] This faith in the God of the living and the dead shares the Marxist socialist interest in the process by which man becomes a subject and in particular deprived and oppressed man's state as a subject and is opposed to a technological and scientific culture which produces apathy and in which the death of the subject, the destruction of language and the end of history are anticipated, at least in theory. This faith, however, also examines critically the teaching of historical and dialectical materialism, in which the reasons for the historical struggle for universal justice and the existence of all men in solidarity as subjects are to be found. It also questions whether the dialectics of freedom that are attributed to nature or matter are not in fact weaker than those of religion. An understanding of history as a dialectical process of liberation cannot, if it is divorced from or opposed to religion, remain uninfluenced by evolutionary thinking. This is, in my opinion, clear, in theory at least, in the remarkable hybrid form of structural Marxism.[39] Is it not true to say that there is evidence here of the beginning of a victory of an (ultimately undirected) evolution over history as a history of freedom and of the disclosure of dialectical materialism as an evolutionary idea, the paralysis of man's consciousness of solidarity by a growing sense of apathy and the disappearance of historical subjects in administrative structures?

This same faith in the God of the living and the dead also questions post-theological theories of history and society, asking especially whether they do not simply bisect history and thus cause it to end. The dialectical version of these theories remains firmly tied to the historical unity of mankind, but gives a relative value to the idea of universal justice that qualifies this unity. It does so by applying this universal justice exclusively to future generations and not to the dead and the sacrifices of history. The dead, after all, also belong equally to the universal community of all men in solidarity with each other.

'It is deeply inhuman to forget or suppress this question of the life of the dead, because it implies a forgetfulness and a suppression of past suffering and an acceptance of the meaninglessness of that suffering. Finally, the happiness of the descendants cannot compensate for the suffering of the ancestors and social progress cannot make up for the injustice done to the dead. If we accept for too long that death is meaningless and are indifferent towards the dead, we shall in the end only be able to offer trivial promises to the living. We are often told nowadays that there is a limit to the growth of our economic potential. This is, however, not all—our potential in meaning seems to have limits. It would seem as though our reserves of meaning are running low and as though there is a danger that the great words that we use to guide the course of our own history—freedom, emancipation, justice, happiness—will be leached and dried out until little meaning remains in them'.[40]

As soon as this faith of Christians in the God of the living and the dead, the God of universal justice, is critically introduced into the historical struggle for the state of all men as subjects in solidarity with each other, however, it is confronted with critical counterquestions. Where, for example, is the historical and social basis of the claim made by Christians to be the advocates of this universal and undivided justice? Where can concrete examples of the history of liberation be found in Christianity? Is the Christian promise of universal justice in the resurrection of the dead no more than an impotent idea without reference to human subjects? Is it not, in this sense, simply opium of the people? Does it not merely provide a soothing element in the historical struggle by which all men can become subjects? It is quite clear from these questions that the crisis in Christianity today is not primarily a crisis of the content of faith and its promises, but a crisis of subjects and institutions which do not measure up to the demands made by faith.

c. Hope in solidarity

In my definition of the faith of Christians, I spoke of hope in solidarity. Solidarity here should be understood in a strictly universal sense as a solidarity that has to justify itself not only with regard to the living and future generations, but also with regard to the dead. In this hope, then, the Christian does not primarily hope for himself—he also has to hope for others and, in this hope, for himself. The hope of Christians in a God of the living and the dead and in the power of that God to raise men from the dead is a hope in a revolution for all men, including those who suffer and have suffered unjustly, those who have long been forgotten and even the dead. This hope does not in any sense paralyze historical initiatives or the struggle for the state of all men as subjects. On the contrary, it acts as a guarantee for the criteria which men use again and again to oppose, in the presence of the accumulated sufferings of those who have been unjustly treated, the prevailing unjust structures and relationships.

d. Praxis again

Religion is not absorbed by existing structures and relationships, just as art, for example, is not absorbed in this way. Indeed, we may say that religion is not absorbed by any structures or relationships. God is not just an early, mythological name for what Ernst Bloch has called transcendence or for a transgression of existing structures. The name of God means rather that transcendence is not simply a symbolic paraphrase at a higher level or an impotent reflection of what simply happens, in other words, what ordinary historical events would have been if only they had been really transcendent.

We have, however, to pay a price for a statement such as this. If it is not to remain at the level of a pure assertion that is suspected of ideology, theology must be able to define and call upon a praxis in which Christians can break through the complex social, historical and psychological conditions governing history and society. What is needed, then, is a praxis of faith in mystical and political imitation.[41]

Notes

1. This is, for example, clear in the tendency on the part of many well-meaning critics who would like to accommodate this theology within the familiar pattern of systematic theology or else apply it to a previously conceived systematic approach. See, for example, G. Bauer, *Christliche Hoffnung und menschlicher Fortschritt. Die politische Theologie von J. B. Metz als theologische Begründung gesellschaftlicher Verantwortung des Christen* (Mainz, 1976) and, more recently, V. Spülbeck *Neomarxismus und Theologie,* Freiburger theologische Studien 107 (Freiburg, 1977). In his *Sprechen von Gott in heutiger Gesellschaft. Weiterentwicklung der 'Politischen Theologie'* (Freiburg, 1974), A. Ganoczy tried to relate my approach to the correlative process that he himself prefers. I have myself posed a number of critical questions in the foreword to this book and the controversy has clearly not yet come to an end. The following footnote (2) contains a selection from the available bibliography of political theology.

2. The first stage in the development of a political theology came to an end, at least as far my particular responsibility for it was concerned, with the publication of the article on political theology in *Sacramentum Mundi* (and later in *Encyclopedia of Theology: A Concise Sacramentum Mundi*) and the volume entitled *Diskussion zur 'politischen Theologie'* (H. Peukert, ed., Mainz and Munich, 1969). The aspects of political theology that emerged during this first phase remained dominant throughout the debate that continued in the years that followed. That is why it seemed to me to be very important to extend, in the first part of the present volume, the rather disconnected approaches that have been made so far and bring them together in a critical survey. In this context, too, it is important to mention some of the very many contributions that have been made to a political theology in recent years. I would divide these contributions into five main groups: larger independent works, volumes on political theological themes, recent bibliographies, articles in dictionaries and finally surveys.

1. Larger independent works. G. Bauer, *Christliche Hoffnung, op. cit.;* A. Ganoczy, *Sprechen von Gott in heutiger Gesellschaft, op. cit.;* V. Spülbeck, *Neomarxismus und Theologie, op. cit.;* M. Xhaufflaire, *La 'théologie politique'. Introduction à la théologie politique de J. B. Metz* (Paris, 1972); C. Geffré, *Die neuen Wege der Theologie* (Freiburg, 1973; French original Paris, 1972); G. Ruggieri, *Christliche Gemeinde und 'politische Theologie'* (Munich, 1973; Italian original Milan, 1971), *Religion and Political Society* (New York, 1974); M. Xhaufflaire, ed., *La pratique de la théologie politique. Analyse cri-*

*tique des conditions pratiques de l'instauration d'un discours chrétien libéra-
teur* (Tournai, 1974); W. R. Schmidt, *Die Eschatologie in der neueren
römisch-katholischen Theologie von der Schuldogmatik bis zur 'politischen
Theologie'* (Berlin, 1974); F. Strazzari, *Il Pensiero di J. B. Metz* (Padua,
1974); H. Rolfes, ed., *Marxismus—Christentum* (Mainz, 1974); R. Gibellini,
ed., *Ancora sulla 'Teologia Politica': Il Dibattito continua* (Brescia, 1975); J.
M. Bonino, *Doing Theology in a Revolutionary Situation* (Philadelphia, 1975),
Dios y la ciudad. Nuevos planeamientos en la teologia política (Madrid, 1975);
R. D. Johns, *Man in the World: The Political Theology of J. B. Metz* (Duke
University, Diss., 1975); J. Cuda, *La croyance et l'incroyance à la lumière de
la Théologie de l'Espérance. Essai d'une synthèse thématique fondé sur la
théologie de J. B. Metz* (Paris, 1976); S. Wiedenhofer, *Politische Theologie*
(Stuttgart, Berlin, Cologne and Mainz, 1976); A. Fierro, *The Militant Gospel.
An Analysis of Contemporary Political Theologies* (London, 1977; Spanish
original, 1974).

2. Volumes on themes in political theology: H. Assig and W. Trutwin, eds.,
Politische Ethik. Theologisches Forum, 9 (Düsseldorf, 1972); *Tijdschrift voor
Theologie* 2 (1972); *Internationale Dialog-Zeitschrift* 4 (1972); *Il tetto* (Feb.
1973); M. Baumotte et al., *Kritik der politischen Theologie* (=*Theologische
Existenz heute* 175) (Munich, 1973).

3. Recent bibliographies: H. H. Schrey, 'Politische Theologie und Theologie
der Revolution', *Theologische Rundschau* 36 (1971), pp. 346–377 and 37
(1972), pp. 43–77; K. Rahner, *Encyclopedia of Theology* (London & New
York, 1975); *Ephemerides Theologicae Lovanienses* 49 (1973), pp. 594–604;
50 (1974), pp. 336–347; 51 (1975), pp. 353–365. G. Bauer, S. Wiedenhofer
and V. Spülbeck, *op. cit.*, also provide extensive bibliographies in their works
mentioned above. There are also several recent books not mentioned in these
bibliographies. These include, among others, A. Gonzales Montes, 'Reflexión
teológica y razón politica. Un analisis histórico-teológico de la hermeneutica
politica de la fe', *Dialogo Ecum.* 8 (1973), pp. 119–154; G. Gomez Arango,
'La "teologia política" según J. B. Metz', *Ecclesiastica Xaveriana* 1973, pp.
68–115; T. Saraneva, 'Johann Baptist Metzin "poliittinen teologia"', *Eripainos
Teologinen Aikakauskirja* 1, 1973; *ibid.*, 'Transsendentaaliteologiasta "poliit-
tiseen teologiaan" Johann B. Metzin ajattelun muuttuminen', *Eripainos Teologinen Aikakauskirja* 2, 1974, pp. 122–130; G. A. Butler, 'Karl Barth and Political Theology', *Scottish Journal of Theology* 27 (1974), pp. 441–458; J. de la
Torre, 'Nuevos supuestos metodológicos de la teología política', *Studia Moralia* 12 (1974), pp. 183–256; A. Gethmann-Siefert, 'Die Einheit von Philosophie
und Theologie im Konzept der "Politischen Theologie" ', *ibid.*, *Das Ver-
hältnis von Philosophie und Theologie im Denken Martin Heideggers* (Munich,
1974), pp. 282–290; L. Oeing-Hanhoff, 'Thomas von Aquin und die gegen-
wärtige katholische Theologie', W. P. Eckert, ed., *Thomas von Aquino* (Mainz,
1974), pp. 245–306; H. Schelsky, 'Theologen: Vom Seelenheil zum Sozial-
heil', *Die Arbeit tun die anderen. Klassenkampf und Priesterherrschaft der In-
tellektuellen* (Opladen, 1975), pp. 317–329; F. J. Jiménez, Urresti, 'Crítica
teológica a la teología crítico-política de Metz. Reflexiones para la teología del
Derecho público eclesiástico', A. Vargas-Machuca, ed., *Teología y mundo*

contemporaneo. Homenaje a K. Rahner en su 70 cumpleaños (Madrid, 1975), pp. 515–543; Gregory Baum, 'Political Theology in Canada', *The Ecumenist* 15 (1977), pp. 33–46.

4. Articles in dictionaries: see especially the article by K. Füssel, 'Politische Theologie' in the tenth edition of K. Rahner and H. Vorgrimler, *Kleines Theologisches Wörterbuch* (Freiburg, Basle and Vienna, 1976 [10]), pp. 337ff.

5. Comprehensive surveys of criticisms of political theology will be found in the works of S. Wiedenhofer, *op. cit.*, pp. 39ff, 49–52, 55–67, and G. Bauer, *op. cit.*, pp. 268–270, 280, 292.

3. Shortly after the first phase in the development of a political theology, I became aware, through the work of some of my pupils, of the practical limitations of a purely theoretical critical theology. For this question, see above all M. Xhaufflaire, *Feuerbach und die Theologie der Säkularisation* (Mainz and Munich, 1972; French original, 1971); see also other works by Xhaufflaire on the subject of political theology above, note 2; F. van den Oudenrijn, *Kritische Theologie als Kritik der Theologie* (Mainz and Munich, 1972); L. Dullaart, *Kirche und Ekklesiologie* (Mainz and Munich, 1975). The text of section 1 of this chapter is basically an attempt to respond to this criticism. Matthew L. Lamb's penetrating article, 'The Theory-Praxis Relationship in Contemporary Christian Theologies', *The CTSA Proceedings* 31 (1976), pp. 149–178, is very important in my discussion of the dialectical tension between theory and praxis.

4. See especially the Christological passages in my book, *Followers of Christ* (London & New York, 1978).

5. None of the important modern Christologies (in the German-speaking countries especially) take this practical structure of Christology as their point of departure. In this sense, they are all idealistic and characterized by a non-dialectic relationship between theory and praxis. See especially Karl Rahner's transcendental Christology, which is the most influential and about which we shall have more to say later in this book, and the recent Christological studies of W. Kasper, H. Küng and E. Schillebeeckx. Küng has taken over several of the concepts and categories of political theology in his *On Being Christian* (New York, 1976; London, 1977), but has reproduced them in a distorted form by discussing them in the light of his own active understanding of 'praxis' and 'application' and not in accordance with the objective status that praxis has in political theology itself.

6. See my *Theology of the World, op. cit.*, p. 112.

7. For an elucidation and a description of the present situation of systematic theology on the basis of various interpretations of Kant's ideas, see J. B. Metz, *Kirche im Prozess der Aufklärung* (Mainz and Munich, 1970), p. 63, note 23.

8. For the status, in the history of philosophy, of the change to the primacy of practical reason and for the distinction between an anthropological philosophy based on the theory of knowledge and a philosophy orientated towards history and ethics, see O. Marquard, *Schwierigkeiten mit der Geschichtsphilosophie* (Frankfurt, 1973).

9. See my *Theology of the World, op. cit.*, pp. 111–112.

10. I have already dealt in detail with this question on the basis of the twofold mystical and political structure of the imitation of Christ in *Followers of Christ*. In this work, I have clarified the specific aspect of this political Christology of the imitation of Christ as contrasted with the Christological approaches which stress the

praxis of the imitation of Christ as an element of Christology (see Kierkegaard or Bonhoeffer)—in contrast with pure Christologies based on the idea—but which only acknowledge that imitation in the form of individual moral praxis.

11. See the relevant passages in H. Peukert, *Wissenschaftstheorie-Handlungstheorie-Fundamentale Theologie, op. cit.,* and K. Füssel, *Die sprachanalystische und wissenschaftstheoretische Diskussion um den Begriff der Wahrheit in ihrer Relevanz für eine systematische Theologie* (Münster, 1975).

12. Responsibility cannot in this context simply be handed over to all the social subjects; the individual subject must remain in view of his guilt. See J. B. Metz, 'Vergebung der Sünden', *Stimmen der Zeit* (Feb. 1977).

13. For the status of memory, see K. Füssel, 'Erinnerung und Kritik. Über Intention und Problematik einer politischen Theologie', *IDZ* (1972), pp. 335–344.

14. See my foreword to H. Rolfes, *Der Sinn des Lebens im marxistischen Denken* (Düsseldorf, 1971). For the systematic scope and meaning of the category of suffering, especially that of the *memoria passionis,* see J. Hochstaffl, *Negative Theologie* (Munich, 1975).

15. For the ways in which the theory of science affects the present debate about the concept of truth, see K. Füssel, *Die sprachanalytische und wissenschaftstheoretische Diskussion, op. cit.*

16. For the subject of prayer as a struggle for man's state as a subject in the presence of God, see my contribution to J. B. Metz and K. Rahner, *The Courage to Pray* (New York, 1979).

17. It would be wrong to assume that the religious subject should be defined according to the standards of a middle European subject. The theological concept of the subject is obviously already present in the biblical accounts of the way in which man becomes a subject.

18. See my *Theology of the World, op. cit.,* pp. 110–111.

19. The abstract anthropology that is active here is the consequence of a constellation of ideas found in the history of philosophy that is hardly reflected within this theology itself. O. Marquard has drawn attention to the ways in which this primacy of anthropology has come about and to the price that has to be paid for its cessation. He has pointed out that 'not every philosophical theory of man can be called anthropology, but only that one which is made possible by its turning away from the traditional metaphysics of scholasticism and mathematical science, in other words, by turning towards the living world and made fundamental by turning towards nature, in other words, by the resignation of the philosophy of history'. See Marquard, *op. cit.,* p. 138.

20. See, for example, Rahner's summary of this thesis in his 'Theologie und Anthropologie', *Schriften zur Theologie* VIII (1967), p. 43ff. (E.T.: *Theological Investigations* 9). See also my own position in *Christliche Anthropozentrik* (Munich, 1962).

21.This question could also, for example, be compared with Wolfhart Pannenberg's anthropology of anticipation.

22. Karl Rahner's attempt has clearly been influenced by J. Maréchal and in it he has made use of Kant's question about the conditions governing the possibility of human knowledge and has given a theological foundation to this question by means of

the concept of anticipation. As in the case of any question of a transcendental nature (about the conditions governing the possibility of knowledge), Rahner's concept has to be applied to one question, namely, whether the transcendental process takes into account the fact that the conditions governing knowledge in a changing world also change themselves, in other words, that they cannot simply be determined in a purely reflective way (as factors that are given or present).

23. Over and against this concept of transcendental experience, it is important to bear in mind that historical experience is not determined by an attempt to make the painful dialectical tension between subject and object disappear; it rather has to reveal it. (See especially T. W. Adorno, *Negative Dialectics,* New York, 1973.) The logic of Utopian thinking of this kind will only be appreciated when it is fully understood that historical experience is characterizd by this dialectical tension between subject and object. This Utopian thinking should not, however, be conceived as though subjects thought something out for themselves, had a definite aim in mind and looked for the means by which they would be able to realize this Utopia (which is depicted in anticipation in the imagination). This is a misunderstanding of Utopian thinking which is as trivial as it is widespread today. The starting point for authentically Utopian thinking is that the subjects themselves change in their practical anticipation of a Utopia and that the Utopian imagination consequently also changes. This is why this Utopia cannot be depicted graphically and why it at the same time has to be conceived in an essentially practical way.

24. The obvious question that has to be asked here is whether certain groups and states (the lay state, for instance) have not been prevented from finding identity in the history of Christianity and the Church itself because they have been denied their own history. The question of narrative as a category of the salvation of identity ought to be discussed in greater detail in the consideration of this whole problem. Narrative is nowadays suspected of being the category of a purely conservative way of historical thinking intending a pure history of the subject. While our writing of history was dominated by this idea of history as a pure history of the subject, it was in fact a history of privileged subjects, a history of the powerful or a history of conquerors. The view of history that is based on structural analysis is rightly opposed to this kind of history as a history of great subjects or as a pure history of persons. My critical insistence here on the category of narrative does not mean that I think of it as a return of all structural history to a pure history of persons or a pure history of rulers. On the contrary, it is seen as opposition to the attempt to solve the problem of the history of subjects by means of historical structuralism. Our understanding of history as structural may well have liberated us from a pure history of persons or a pure history of conquerors or rulers. In this process of liberation, however, it is not a question of finally eliminating the historical subject, but rather a question of extending that subject, so that not only certain groups of persons, but all men can emerge as subjects of history. The category of narrative is indispensable if this is to be accomplished and in this universal sense it continues to be a category of the salvation of identity.

25. For this phenomenon, see the fate of the exciting theology of liberation in the semi-official judgment of the Church and the assessment of new politically active basic communities in various countries and the movement known as 'Christians for

socialism'. For models of alternative ways of life with religious and political intentions, see the recent dissertation published by J. Caldentey Barceló, *Estudio sobre comunidades cristianas de base de Barcelona y su significado para una renovación en la iglesia* (Münster, 1977).

26. This argument, based on the history of religion, has been developed by Wolfhart Pannenberg in several of his works.

27. For this connection, see, for example, J. Habermas, *Legitimationsprobleme im Spätkapitalismus* (Frankfurt, 1973).

28. The first of these quotations will be found in Adorno's *Minima Moralia* and the second in *Prismen* (Munich, 1963), p. 267. In Adorno's work, the struggle for the subject seems to be already lost. For him, the middle-class subject has ceased to exist, the socialist subject cannot be regarded as a successor and the religious subject cannot be seen as authentic. The idea of a dialectical tension of the Enlightenment was therefore essentially submissive in Adorno's case.

29. Statements of this kind will be found in the work of the influential French structuralist M. Foucault.

30. I cannot go into the question here of the extent to which Althusser has been influenced by structuralism in his work as a whole and in his anti-humanism and his polemics against the concept of the subject in particular. Any discussion of this question would inevitably be very controversial, as so often happens in Althusser's work. See, for example, L. Althusser, *Elemente der Selbstkritik* (West Berlin, 1975); *id.*, *Ideologie und ideologische Staatsapparate* (West Berlin, 1977). See also Althusser's contributions to H. Arenz, J. Bischoff and U. Jaeggi, eds., *Was ist revolutionärer Marxismus?* (West Berlin, 1973).

31. See H. Marcuse, *Die Permanenz der Kunst* (Munich, 1977), p. 46.

32. In my opinion, E. Jüngel should have included this in his polemics against D. Sölle in the question of 'Christianity and socialism'. See, for example, his *Müssen Christen Sozialisten sein?* (Hamburg, 1976), p. 111 ff.

33. For prayer as an expression of man's becoming a subject in the face of extreme danger and as resistance to apathy, see my contribution to J. B. Metz and K. Rahner, *The Courage to Pray, op. cit.*

34. For the development of Christian praxis as imitation, see my *Followers of Christ, op. cit.*, in which I have outlined the twofold structure (mystical and political) of imitation and at the same time shown how the practical political attitude of human friendliness can make this imitation unambiguous.

35. A detailed elucidation of this definition is really only possible if the content of the Christian creed is examined. This will be done in my book on Christian faith, *The Faith of Christians*.

36. See, for example, J. B. Metz, 'Gott vor uns', *Bloch-Festschrift* (1965); *id.*, 'An Eschatological View of the Church and the World' and, closely connected with this essay, 'The Church and the World in the Light of a "Political Theology" ', *Theology of the World* (London, 1969), pp. 81 ff, 107 ff. See also F. Kerstiens, *Die Hoffnungsstruktur des Glaubens* (Mainz, 1969), which is important for its arrangement and penetration.

37. Quite apart from the fact that a concept such as 'constant expectation' is self-contradictory and cannot be checked semantically.

38. It is possible that many readers will suspect that there is a Christological defi-

cit in this definition of faith. For this question and that of the connection between Christology and apocalyptical eschatology, see Chapter 10 below.

39. In my view, structuralistic Marxism is not a reconciliation of a dialectical Marxist approach and an Anglo-Saxon analytical approach, but the cessation of dialectics because of evolution.

40. From the text *Unsere Hoffnung* published by the synod of German bishops (I, 3).

41. This praxis is completely apocalyptical; see my *Followers of Christ, op. cit.*

PART II

THEMES

Bearing in mind the self-understanding of the practical fundamental theology that I have outlined in the first part of this book ('Concept'), it should be clear that I shall not develop a 'closed' system in this part. In this second part, I shall be dealing above all with themes that arise nowadays in the Church and society (whose Lord is not theology). There are, of course, far more of these themes than can be discussed here.

It is, as it were, possible to recognize a consistent inner structure in this complex of themes, which can be described as stages on the way to a developing consciousness and a testing out of a concept and its content. The spectrum extends from paradigmatic attempts in which the theological idea is not (subsequently) exemplified, but is first attained itself, through the insistent question about the subjects and practical foundations of these theological thought-processes to the question of the relationship between apocalyptical and eschatological time on the one hand and evolutionary time on the other. It should be clear from the first chapter of Part I ('Between evolution and dialectics') that the basic problem gains in perspective when this relationship is considered

The contributions based on earlier research into these themes are not quoted here simply as additional evidence. I make use of them because of their relevance to the concept of a political theology as a practical fundamental theology today. They can be regarded as an attempt to work out, in a contemporary form, an invitation to Christianity.

5. The dangerous memory of the freedom of Jesus Christ
The presence of the Church in society[1]

1. The status of the theme in theology and the Church

The question of the presence of the Church in society is ultimately the question of the situation today of theology and the Church as such. The view that this is no more than a question of application or of practical concretization which does not touch the substance of theological truth or the essential being of the Church at all is frequently encountered. This view is, however, in my opinion, a very serious misunderstanding of the situation, both with regard to the position and the task of theology and with regard to the Church itself.

a. The situation and task of theology

We live in a period when all ideas and concepts, including our concept of God, are determined and deciphered by the criticism of ideology and the sociology of knowledge that have been developed since Idealism in accordance with their social interest and historical context. Because of this, it is only possible to make the irreducibility and transcendence of the eschatological message visible and convincing if their critical and liberating power is itself freed from these socially determining factors. Any theology that aims to justify Christian faith and its tradition critically in this way is bound to take this social and practical aspect into account. No such theological theory can allow any abstraction from such problems as public life, justice and freedom, in othe words, political problems. It has to be and indeed can be 'political' theology and, what is more, it can be this irrespective of the way in which the political theme should be taken into consideration in determining a Christian's eschatological hope.

b. With regard to the Church

It is important to bear in mind here that, as a historical and social reality, the Church is always active as a political factor. In other words, it is political and acts politically before taking up any explicit political position and therefore also before there is any question of criteria governing its present political attitude. The usual supposition that the Church is a priori neutral or politically innocent in its attitudes is either uncritical or else it consciously draws a veil over existing political alliances. It is essential to evolve a critical and political form of hermeneutics of the Church if we are to prevent the Church from being uncritically identified with specific political ideologies and thus having it sink to the level of a purely political religion.

That is why a 'political' theology does not aim to be a regional task of contemporary theology as a whole, but a fundamental task. It does not seek to offer a new sphere of activity to frustrated Christians—that of politics. On the contrary, it tries to carry out the same task that Christian theology has always carried out—that of speaking about God by making the connection between the Christian message and the modern world visible and expressing the Christian tradition in this world as a dangerous memory. In this task, theology cannot simply uncritically ignore the historical distance between the present time and the unrepeatable situation of the biblical testimony, nor can it belittle the importance of that difference. It cannot, in other words, presume that the content and intentions of that testimony are known and simply apply them to the contemporary situation. It has rather to take account of the fact that this historical and social difference again and again raises the question as to what the content and intentions of the biblical testimony really are. In this sense, 'political' theology is not simply a theory of the subsequent application of the Christian message, but a theory of the truth of that message with a practical and critical intention for the modern world.

2. The theological basis

The following thesis may serve as a theological basis for our theme: the Church must understand and justify itself as the public witness and bearer of the tradition of a dangerous memory of freedom in the 'systems' of our emancipative society. This thesis is based on memory as the fundamental form of expression of Christian faith and on the central and special importance of freedom in that faith. In faith, Christians accomplish the *memoria passionis, mortis et resurrectionis Jesu Christi*. In faith, they remember the testament of Christ's love, in which the kingdom of God appeared among men by initially establishing that kingdom between men, by Jesus' confession of himself as the one who was on the side of the oppressed and rejected and by his proclamation of the coming kingdom of God as the liberating power of unconditional love. This *memoria Jesu Christi* is not a memory which deceptively dispenses Christians from the risks involved in the future. It is not a middle-class counter-figure to hope. On the contrary, it anticipates the future as a future of those who are oppressed, without hope and doomed to fail. It is therefore a dangerous and at the same time liberating memory that oppresses and questions the present because it reminds us not of some open future, but precisely this future and because it compels Christians constantly to change themselves so that they are able to take this future into account.

This definite memory breaks through the magic circle of the prevailing consciousness. It regards history as something more than a screen for contemporary interests. It mobilizes tradition as a dangerous tradition and therefore as a liberating force in respect of the one-dimensional character and certainty of the one whose 'hour is always there' (Jn 7. 6). It gives rise again and again to the suspicion that the plausible structures of a society may be relationships aimed to delude. It also refuses to measure the relevance of its criticism in accordance with what 'an elderly, rather sleepy business man' would regard unquestioningly as relevant 'after lunch' and what often functions as a secret criterion for rationality and a sense of reality. Christian faith can and must, in my opinion, be seen in this way as a subversive memory. The Church is, moreover, to some extent the form of its public character. In this sense, the Church's teachings and confessions of faith should be understood as formulae in which this challenging memory is publicly spelt out. The criterion of its authentic Christianity is the liberating and redeeming danger with which it introduces the remembered freedom of Jesus into modern society and the forms of consciousness and praxis in that society.

The Church acts as the public memory of the freedom of Jesus in the systems of our emancipative society. It reminds us of an indebted freedom, God's eschatological history of freedom which is gained in the cross and resurrection of Jesus and which cannot be absorbed into the ideal of man's coming of age that is contained in the middle-class history of the Enlightenment or into the apotheosis of the history of liberation by revolution. The Church does not dispense us from the responsibility to take care of the history of freedom, but rather initiates us into it: 'All things are yours, whether Paul or Apollos or Cephas or the world or life or death or the present or future, all are yours, and you are Christ's and Christ is God's' (1 Cor 3. 21-23). In this sense, then, the Church is an emancipative memory, liberating us from all attempts to idolize cosmic and political powers and make them absolute. In the light of the Church, all political orders appear, in principle, as orders of freedom and the political ethics of the previously established order are enlarged to include political ethics of radical changes in freedom. Every power of perfection, reconciliation and peace, which presupposes human freedom and the conflicts involved in it, is reserved in this memory of God.

It is from the memory of this 'eschatological reservation' that the Church can and must draw its strength to criticize all totalitarian systems of government and all ideologies of a linear and one-dimensional emancipation. Whenever the history of freedom takes place without reference to this memory of the eschatological reservation, it always seems to fall a victim to the compulsive need to substitute a worldly subject for the whole history of freedom and this always moves in the direction of a totalitarian control of men by men. In the end, a history of freedom which has lost this eschatological memory can only be interpreted as a non-dialectical and to some extent abstract history of emancipation in which the new conflicts and disasters of the freedom gained are ignored and the idea of coming of age without reserved reconciliation threatens to sink to the level of a commonplace idea of pure survival or cunning animal adaptation.

Where, then, is this eschatological memory of freedom that breaks open our cognitive and operative systems alive? Who brings about those forms of freedom that are so often forgotten or thrust into the background by our emancipative society? One of those forms is the freedom to suffer the suffering of others and to respect the prophecy of others' suffering, even though the negative aspect of suffering seems to be forbidden. Another is the freedom to become old although the public character of old age is denied and even regarded as secretly shameful. There is also the freedom to contemplate, despite the fact that so many people are now hypnotized, in the ultimate stages of their consciousness, by work, performance and planning. Finally, who will achieve the freedom to make present for us our own questionable and finite nature, even though our public life is open to the suggestion that it will be made even more whole and harmonious? Who will respond to the claim of past sufferings and hopes and the challenge made by those who have died? Who will make men's consciences more sensitive to their claim to justice? Who will cultivate solidarity with those to whom we shall belong in the near future? Who can share his understanding of freedom with those who do not die a heroic death in the front line of a revolutionary fight for freedom, but will rather die the terribly commonplace death of every day?

Any society that ignores or thrusts into the background these aspects of the history of freedom must pay for this neglect by gradually losing its own visible freedom. The eschaton of that society is boredom. Its myth is a faith in planning. The silent interest of the rationality of that society is to abolish the world as resistance, in order not to continue to experience that world. As Ernst Bloch has said, what we have now 'in the West is a patronizing, pluralistic boredom and in the East an imposed oppressed and monolithic boredom . . . It looks like a partial eclipse of the sun. Everything is remarkably grey and either the birds do not sing or they sing differently. Something is wrong in any case. The transcending being is weak'. Or else the dangerous memory has been extinguished and the eschatological memory has become exhausted.

Has Christianity failed here historically? Has the Church ceased to function historically as the institutional bearer of this Christianity and its memory? Can the future of human freedom be determined only with secular utopias and ideas? All 'external' opinions and many of the opinions expressed within the Church would seem to suggest this. In the modern theories of society, the classical criticism of religion has concentrated its attention on the Church. The Church is often described as an organization with a consciousness that is not contemporary. It is thought to impose an institutional tabu on knowledge and productive curiosity. It is regarded as a remnant that is opposed to emancipation. It is thought to have no more than a simulated interest in freedom and the upright progress of man. It has been called an opium in suffering and unjust relationships. According to most modern theories of society, the Church has lost or is rapidly losing its function in contemporary society. In this way, emphatic criticism gives way more and more clearly to indifference or benevolent courtesy, a caricature of the sympathy that is shown to a dying man. Even militant communists are more and more restrained in their struggle against a totally privatized Church. In the vigorous futurologies of the West, the Church has hardly any part to play.

Are the statements made about the Church today in the preceding paragraph simply clichés, expressing one-sided views conditioned by the prevailing systems? Or do they express the fact that the Church is constantly challenged in the world of today, in other words, the suffering situation of the Church of the crucified Lord, which every believer has to take into account?

I am of the opinion that we should not give this theological answer too quickly, because it fails to take into consideration a profound aspect of the prevailing attitude in criticism of the Church. This is man's historical experience with the Church, his collective memory of disappointments caused by the Church, the historical conscience of generations who are aware of the Church's dubious alliances with the power structures of society and the frequent impression of imbalance in the Church as representing a religion that is not believed, but is constantly replacing itself. This memory has to be taken into consideration. It is much more difficult to efface than is often assumed. It is indeed the most pressing historical and hermeneutical problem confronting contemporary ecclesiology and far more important than, for example, that of finding historical evidence for the foundation of the Church and the apostolic succession. This problem cannot, moreover, be solved by providing a better or more subtle interpretation of the Church's past history. It can only be solved by a painful process of change involving proof of the spirit and strength of a new praxis.

The roots of the ethics of the reform of the Church are to be found here.[2] These ethics are concerned not with modern attitudes that uncritically accept the prevailing illusions of contemporary society, but with the fundamental question of the historical identity and continuity of the Church and its mission. Church in this instance means above all: we Christians who try to live in the memory of Christ and for whom the idea of a tradition of this memory which is completely free of the Church as an institution and which entrusts this memory exclusively to the private individual is an illusion.

3. Options with a practical and critical intention

I would therefore like to make at least three suggestions here with a practical and critical intention.

a. An important question in this context is that of spirituality and the formation of spirituality in the Church as a spirituality of liberated freedom which bears witness to and justifies in the extension of a freedom that is critical of society. The witness borne by this freedom will have characteristics that differ according to the different spheres of society. The forms of freedom that will be required and practised in the systems of the prosperous societies of the West will be those forms which I have already mentioned: namely, those that have been largely forgotten or thrust into the background. In the systems of the southern regions, the witness borne by this freedom will take the form above all of a courageous struggle against social misery. In these regions too, there will inevitably be striking evidence of the interference of this testimony to freedom in the sphere of politics. In this situation, it would be objectively dishonest to appeal to the great variety of interpretations of political realities as a justification of the Church's failure to take up a position in politics. Bishops and theologians can easily become mandarins in a Church that continues to practise the same unchanging form of integralism and to establish political alliances under cover of its traditional neutrality and political innocence and without regard for the actual suffering and real oppression that exist in society.

The freedom which is critical of society and which bears witness to itself in the spirituality of liberated freedom is never purely intellectual in its attitude. Its criticism has none of the characteristics of 'total' criticism. It suffers from the pain of self-denial, persistence, impatience and patience—these are characteristics demanded by the Christian memory of freedom as an imitation of Christ. Because of this, it is not simply a copy of the prevailing criticism of society. It cannot moreover simply be thrust into the alternative of prayer and action. It tries to gain from prayer the freedom that it needs from the plausible structures of social mechanisms and prejudices and the strength to be independent enough to take liberating action in the interest of others, the 'least of the brethren'. In this action, moreover, prayer can set itself free from the suspicion that it is no more than an opium of the people and that God's name is invoked simply to soften the anonymous fate that again and again befalls every human hope of freedom. The spirituality of liberated freedom cannot therefore be limited to a pure experience of cult that is isolated and free from all the conflicts, repressions and challenges of everyday life. This way to a purely cultic spirituality is often recommended today and it would certainly seem to be an objective need in the middle class. All the same, it is a wrong way. At the end of it is the esoteric Church, the opium of the intellectuals.

The spirituality of liberated freedom that is required here increases in strength as our willingness to suffer the sufferings of others grows. It also increases as men have a conscience not only about what they do or do not do to others, but also about what they let happen to others and as they cease to regard, in accordance with the rules of the society of exchange, only those who are of a like mind as their brethren and to treat all others as an anonymous mass. Only those who are cynically dedicated to power will dismiss these aspects of socially critical freedom as romantic.

Is the question of this one indivisible freedom not always associated with those impotent people who lack the power that presupposes the power of love and whose only ally is the dangerous memory of the hope of freedom? The Church should support the institutionalized, authoritative interest of this freedom and indeed be that interest in season and out of season, because of the radical threats and catastrophes that have punctuated the history of freedom. In this attempt, the witness borne by the Church to liberated freedom can only acquire authority (from religious competence!) if it remains linked to the interest of love that looks for its own way through history in the track of strange suffering. It is only when the Church listens to the prophecy of this strange suffering, poverty and oppression that it will truly listen to the word of Christ and that it will be, as the visible Church, at the same time the invisible Church of the Spirit of Christ. To achieve this, it will have to conquer new fields of testimony and acquire new forms of charisma to express this liberated freedom.

b. It is important that the processes within the Church leading to a critical public life, a transition from an emphatic to a constitutional freedom and a real culture of freedom in the Church should be encouraged and promoted as courageously and constructively as possible. Critical freedom in the Church cannot be measured against purely psychological or sociological themes or allowed to solidify into a jargon of helpless protest. The radical question that confronts the Church today is whether it is prepared to live with the conflicts arising from critical freedom and whether it can understand those problems as an aspect of itself. This is not simply a claim made by a small élite group of intellectuals in the Church, but a fundamental question for the people of the Church as a whole. It is, after all, not the critical intellectuals who will be a problem in the Church, so much as the so-called simple faithful who even now seem to be profoundly irritated, not so much by a critical theology as by the institution of the Church itself. As we shall see later in Chapter 8, it is the factual change in the Church that has given rise to confusion and crises of identity.

The frequently mentioned confusion among the members of the Church has come about because they have been exposed to change in an unloving and authoritarian way by the Church and yet have not been provided with a critical understanding of the reformability of the Church itself. How is it possible for the 'simple faithful' to continue to grasp the identity of the one Church in all its changes and for them not to feel that they have been deceived if they lack the critical appreciation of their Church that would enable them to perceive the continuity in the changes and to know that a process of change is an essential part of the historical identity of this one *ecclesia semper reformanda?* One of the causes of the crisis in the Church today is not that there is too much criticism, but rather that there is a catastrophic absence of fundamental and practised critical freedom in the Church. This absence of critical freedom has, moreover, made the simple faithful the focal point of crisis in the Church of tomorrow. The silent majority in the Church forms a very problematical body. The crisis of religious identity among the simple faithful should therefore not be underestimated. Who will, in the end, save himself from a dangerous indifferentism or a sceptical form of resignation, through which increasingly firm and fatal lines are being drawn between the Church as an institution and Christian people?

However much it is stressed that the Church is the people of God and the universal priesthood of all believers and however much emphasis is placed on the importance of lay people in the Church, the number of those who really feel themselves to be Church is nevertheless becoming smaller and smaller. Where a collective identification is impossible, there is always a danger of panic. As we shall see later (Chapter 8), if we blame those who have difficulties of identification for this situation and appeal prematurely to the Church as a 'little flock', the only way ahead that we shall be able to point out to the Church is the way to sectarianism.

c. I would therefore like to suggest that the third task confronting us is to prevent Christians from developing an increasingly sectarian attitude. The situation in the Church is alarming. Its increasing cognitive isolation in a world which it has no more influence to define threatens to drive it into a closed sectarian attitude or else to make it adapt itself in a modernistic way. There is obviously a danger that the Christian message will be completely adapted and Church Christianity will sink to the level of an unnecessary religious paraphrase of modern processes in the world. Over and against this danger that the Church will lose itself by a process of active adaptation there is the danger of loss through passive adaptation. The latter danger is far less in the foreground of our attention today than it would be if we were really concerned with the way that the Church should follow in society now and in the future. This danger is that the Church will become a sect in the theological sense. In other words, it is the danger of a traditional sectarian orthodoxy and a sectarian attitude in a closed Church.

The symptoms of an increasingly sectarian attitude would seem to be a noncreative preservation of traditions, in other words, a pure traditionalism, a growing inability or unwillingness to have new experiences and to apply them critically to a self-understanding of the Church and its constitutions and documents. Many aspects of the continuing controversy between Christian confessions are, in my opinion, sectarian, as are the zealotic language and the new militant behaviour in controversy within the Church itself: in other words, the transformation of active Church life into a joyless and humourless zealotism.

The Church, as the Church of the Son, cannot, however, remain closed to the 'strangers' in the historical world that it does not understand and expect to preserve itself in that closed state. This 'conditioning by strangers' is not something that was subsequently added to the Church. On the contrary, it is an element of the Church's constitution and part of its *specificum christianum*. The Church cannot, in other words, know in advance and without historical experience and debate both what is human and what is Christian in the full sense of the word. If this is forgotten in the Church, then there is a danger that the Church will become a sect in the theological sense.

This warning of the danger of sectarianism is not made in ignorance of the fact that the Church is increasingly becoming a minority in society as a whole now and in the future. The Church could not be defined as a sect in the theological sense simply because it is a minority. It could only be called a sect because of its attitude. It need not fear being a minority, nor need it be ashamed of that status, unless it regarded itself as the institution that brought about the history of liberated freedom in the world and thus misunderstood itself so completely that it thought of itself as an ideology that replaced its own hope of freedom. The minority status of the Church may even be a positive opportunity, giving it greater mobility, bringing it closer to the oppressed and overlooked minorities in society and taking it out of its para-political structures. It may in this way become, in the strict sense of the word, a purgatory, with the result that the freedom of Jesus himself, the dangerous memory of which is indispensable to the future of freedom as such, may be represented in a renewed and more vigorous way in the Church's life.

Notes

1. This chapter is an adapted version, rewritten to fit into the whole concept, of a text first prepared in 1970. It was originally given as a paper at the International

Congress of theologians in Brussels in September 1970 and was published for the first time in the special number of *Concilium* (1970–1971), devoted to that congress, under the title 'Zur Präsenz der Kirche in der Gesellschaft'.

2. See J. B. Metz, *Reform und Gegenreformation heute* (Mainz, 1969); *id.*, *Followers of Christ*.

6. The future in the memory of suffering
The dialectics of progress[1]

1. The socio-political context

'The future is no longer what it was'. This statement, which is both trivial and wise, provides us with a meaningful insight into the changed situation in which we are living in the world today.

Confidence in the supposed gradual evolution of technological civilization has gone. If 'progress' exists at all, it is only in opposition to its naïve generalization (as in some crude futurologies). Increasingly, the warm stream of teleology that helped our way of thinking in the past is drying up. Teleological reliance on a growing reconciliation of man with nature has collapsed. With its disappearance we notice for the first time how profoundly and tenaciously it gripped us, conditioning even our philosophical and theological interpretations of the future. But now Sisyphus has suddenly reappeared next to Prometheus, Camus next to Teilhard, Monod next to Whitehead.

We are becoming ever more conscious of the dangers and antagonisms that arise when technological and economic processes are left to their own nature. Laws and our political and social control systems break down: dying cities, ruined environments, population explosions, chaotic information channels, an increasingly aggressive and vicious intensification of the North-South conflict, leading possibly to a new outcome of the East-West power struggle, and so on.[2]

In addition there is the threat posed to man's apparent identity and freedom by the growing possibilities of psychological and genetic manipulation. One also suspects that, left to itself, the technologico-economic planning of man's future will produce the wholly adapted human being whose dreams and imagination can no longer keep up and are suppressed by the functionalism of technical systems, whose freedom degenerates into an instinctive animal adaptability to the superior power and complexity of preformed behaviour patterns and who has been deprived of the world as something over against him, in order, in fact, to rob him of the need any longer to experience it personally. The purely technologically and economically planned production of man's future would seem to foreshadow the very disappearance of man as the being who has nourished himself on the historical substance of his freedom, that is, on the power to find an alternative despite all need to conform. Hence there is no lack today of voices to follow up Nietzsche's proclamation of the 'death of God' with that of the 'death of man': the paralysis of human spontaneity and the burial of man in the grave of an economico-technical structuralism; and the fear that human thinking is losing its dialectical tension with the *status quo* and is being integrated with an all-encroaching and anonymous production process.

It is a characteristic of man's situation today and his relationship with the future that there is a serious threat that he will cease to be the subject of the processes of technological civilization and become their product. What seems to be happening is that man, as the subject who plans and controls technology and science, is becoming controlled by them. In this situation, it would appear, it is no longer possible to speak about the future in categories that are dissociated from the subject, that is, in categories such as development, progress or even 'process'. Instead we have to ask: whose development, whose progress, and whose process? And: development, progress and process in what direction? The question of the future of our technological civilization is a question not primarily of technology, but of the control and application of technology and economico-technological processes; a problem not primarily of means but of ends, and of the establishment of priorities and preferences. This means, however, that it is primarily a political and fundamentally a social problem.

But how can politics become the primary *topos* in our technological society for investigation of the future? Is politics, as something self-sufficient, not set over against technology and economics in its death throes? Is there not a growing anonymous dictatorship of structures and processes compared with which the dictatorship of individuals and parties seems harmless? Kenneth Boulding has said that we can conceive of a world where an invisible dictatorship is still making use of democratic forms of government. Is the euthanasia of politics not coming closer in our technological society? Are we not witnessing an increasing self-paralysis of political reason and its consequent degeneration into instrumental reason in the service of technological and economic processes and their anonymous 'power-systems'? Where are we to find a politics capable of controlling these systems and extricating them from the contradictions and catastrophes apparent today?

Would something like a radical 'scientification' of politics help here? Certainly political life is becoming less and less capable of doing without the mediation and mobilization of scientific knowledge. Yet it is not science which constitutes and guarantees the authenticity of political consciousness as opposed to technological controls. Our modern sciences themselves are technological essentially and not merely incidentally; this is, in fact, a presupposition for their success and is grounded in the mode of cognition specific to them as sciences. Admittedly this raises a multitude of questions that cannot be pursued here. I would remark only that if politics is to be more than a successful accommodation to the control systems of technical and economic processes, it must be grounded in something more and something other than science (as we know and understand it today).

Obviously this kind of politics will exist only when there is a fundamental change in our political life. But not the conversion of politics into purely technological administration and a computer-politics which in its programming merely reproduces the above-mentioned dilemmas, not an old-style decision-politics, and not Machiavellianism, a kind of stone-age politics in the twentieth century. What we need in the long run is a new form of political life and new political structures. Only when that arrives will there be any humane cultures at all in the future. In this sense, 'politics' is actually the new name for culture and in this sense, too, any theology which tries to reflect on Christian traditions in the context of world problems and to bring about the process of transference between the kingdom of God and society is a 'political theology'.

The answer that this political theology gives to the question: 'how can we achieve that change of mind that is necessary if all men are to live in freedom?' is to make a plea for man's identity to be safeguarded within the tradition of practical reason. Political theology, in other words, opts for a historical anthropology and a practice of education based on the Enlightenment that do not too easily give way to the illusion that salvation in the future can be found by means of genetic manipulation and a computer ideology. I should now like to mention some aspects of this new orientation and structural pattern of political consciousness.

a. History has now reached a stage at which all the really decisive problems of human society have a world-wide or global significance. Politics have become something with which everyone is concerned in a new way, because everyone's future is involved in them. Global interventions have become the concrete theme of political action. This is why politics can no longer be conducted simply within the framework of national action and exclusively with the interests of national security, which are often ideologically motivated, in mind. On the contrary, politics have now to take place in the universal arena of responsibility for everyone's life and survival.[3]

b. Our present situation requires a new association between politics and morals which refuses to remain content with the middle-class and ultimately trivial morality of the affluent society which is still preserved for us in the liberal distinction between politics and morals. As Jürgen Habermas says: 'There are indications that developed social systems already accept, or are on the point of accepting, certain international imperatives of life—namely, the elimination of war as a legitimate means of settling conflicts, and the removal of mass poverty and disparities in economic development. Even where these systems do not at present offer adequate motives for the solution of such global problems, one thing is nevertheless already clear: a solution of these problems is hardly possible without the application throughout life of those universalist norms which were hitherto required only in the private sphere. Someone still tied to the old categories might call this the "moralization" of politics. But this kind of idea ought not to be dismissed—simply on those grounds—as naïve enthusiasm'.

c. This connection between politics and morals cannot be ordained from above, and can and should not be allowed to relapse into the political canonization of a particular moral system. It requires the mobilization of spiritual and moral forces by means of

103

a radical democratization of the social infrastructure, a nourishing from below of freedom and effective responsibility.

d. The form of political life that would allow a culture of freedom in our economico-technological processes cannot, in my opinion, afford to ignore the reserves of moral and political imagination that appear in the present subcultures and counter-cultures of our technological society. Far more than the conventional generation conflict is expressed in this 'youth culture'. It is, in a certain sense, our western form of the cultural revolution, the experimental quest for an alternative to the control systems of our technological society. Anyone who merely expects the escapists to return penitently like lost sheep to the established system has misunderstood both this culture and his own situation.

Is it not true to say that movements of this kind display clear symptoms of the crisis that exists in the way in which western affluent societies understand freedom, especially in view of the fact that a form of freedom that is increasingly formal and without content is being cultivated in those societies with the liberal pluralism? It is justifiable to ask whether these youth cultures are not trying, since the failure of their direct confrontation with our society, to renew that society as it were from its beginnings with new symbols of social identity and productive models which can be used to achieve a form of freedom with a specific content. We may therefore ask whether they are not really trying to anticipate a pattern of human life that is no longer dominated by production and performance alone.

Of course this new political life, whose aims are not confined to what is deemed plausible by our economico-technological controls, does not intend to bypass technology and economics altogether. There is neither an alternative to technology, nor (to date) an alternative technology. What is sought for and demanded is instead a new form of mediation, a new instrumental control of this technology and these technical and economic processes. One thing, above all, must be avoided: the dissolution of political imagination and political action into the pure business of planning. Only the independence of the political dimension can guarantee the possibility of a humane future.

You will perhaps remember the story of the fight between the two giants. One of them is weaker and is on the brink of defeat yet manages to keep going and finally free himself from the other's grasp. He is able to do this because a tiny hunchback sits in his ear, urging him on and continually whispering new defensive ploys. This might serve as a parable for the struggle between technology and politics, between purely economico-technological planning and a political draft for the future. Political imagination will prevent itself from ultimate absorption by the restrictive grasp of technology, so long as it keeps the moral imagination and power to resist that have grown out of the memory of the suffering accumulated in history. The dwarf stands for the memory of this suffering: in our advanced social systems, suffering is pictured as insignificant, ugly and better kept out of sight.

Political consciousness *ex memoria passionis,* political action in the memory of mankind's history of suffering: this could indicate an understanding of politics that would lead to new possibilities and new criteria for the mastering of technological and economic processes. It offers inspiration for a new form of solidarity, of responsibility towards those most distant from us, inasmuch as the history of suffering unites all men like a 'second nature'. It prevents a purely technical understanding of freedom and peace; it excludes any form of freedom and peace at the expense of the suppressed history of suffering of other nations and groups.

The history of human suffering provides us with criteria by which we can examine planning reason—enlightenment and education instead of encroaching on the inherited structure, a change of consciousness instead of enlarging the brain, a humanization of nature instead of producing man from a retort and letting people die instead of making them survive in despair.[4]

The memory of human suffering forces us to look at the public *theatrum mundi* not merely from the standpoint of the successful and the established, but from that of the conquered and the victims. This recalls the function of the court fool in the past: he represented an alternative (rejected, vanquished or oppressed) to his master's policy; his function was strictly political and in no way 'purely aesthetic'. His politics was, so to speak, a politics of the memory of suffering—as against the traditional political principle of 'woe to the conquered', and against the Machiavellian ruler. Today it is a question of sublating the 'division of labour' in political life between the powerful on the one hand, and the 'fool' with his powerless imagination of suffering on the other. Here I see the significance of a new association of politics and morals. From it there ultimately emerges a conception of political life and political responsibility for which the great moral and religious traditions of mankind could also, possibly, be mobilized, once they have been comprehended at their deepest level of meaning.

2. Nature and history

It is clear from what I have already said that political and social action can be orientated towards the future and provided with norms for this action not on the basis of a universal theory of nature, but rather on the basis of a historical system of justification. Would this not, however, once again place the future on an unreliable and shaky foundation? If political and social action determines the priorities of technological, scientific and economic development and if this action is itself nourished and determined by man's historical consciousness, is the future not exposed to the antagonisms of historical interests and parties? Ought we not, then, at long last, cease burrowing in the exploited and exhausted mysteries of history? Ought the future not be determined, at least experimentally, on the basis of a universal theory of nature?

As soon, however, as the problems of the preservation of the environment, the safeguarding of the sources of raw materials and an enlightened attitude towards the future are taken seriously, it becomes clear that history cannot be supported by a theory of nature, but that, on the contrary, nature must be safeguarded by a reflection about our historical responsibility for nature, so that it is not exploited without restraint. It also becomes apparent how far-reaching the effects are of an understanding that politics are the new name for civilization, since, if we regard it as an essential task to preserve nature as a pre-condition for a rational future, then civilization will justify both its original name and its claim to be able to overcome barbarianism. The category of responsibility for one's own actions, for others and for nature clearly demonstrates that civilization must justify itself in politics. In this way, the species becomes conscious of its own original process of life. This consciousness makes it possible for us to understand the unity of reason and reality as the reconciliation between nature and history.

Every attempt to reconcile nature and man has an essentially utopian character which is therefore also historical and dialectical. This is so because the human spirit, which rises above natural originality, is the same spirit that tries to objectivize its lasting dependence on nature in the form of dominating nature. If this spirit is, as history, different from nature in so far as it points to the state that liberates us from the compulsion of nature and even reconciles, then it is no longer the same in so far as it continues as a technique of natural compulsion of nature in increasing exploitation and control of nature. In this dynamic tension, the species is present as a natural element that can overcome itself and is therefore in conflict with itself and always harming itself. This is why the process of becoming man is characterized by suffering and there can be no teleological and final mediation between man and nature.

This argument would seem to be emphatically confirmed by modern science and especially by the anthropologically orientated branches of science such as human biology. One has only to read Monod against Teilhard and Whitehead! Monod has tried to invalidate a concept of evolution based on a combination of continuity and mutations by stressing the element of chance. In this attempt, he simultaneously tries to undermine the idea of man as the summit of evolution who has been driven to this point by necessity. Monod's man is the 'chance shot' of nature, the cosmic 'accident'. It is not possible to discuss Monod's theory in detail here, but I should like to stress that this element of chance in nature is not a spectre that can threaten a theology of history, which has learnt not to think of reality in terms of a closed cosmos that exists without surprises.

It is the idea of suffering that is so strongly opposed to an affirmation of the theory of reconciliation between man and nature. Any attempt to affirm this reconcilation eventually degenerates into a bad ontology of human passion. Suffering stresses the contrast between nature and history, teleology and eschatology. There can be no 'objective' reconciliation and no visible and manageable unity between them. Any attempt of this kind would be below the status of human suffering. This is particularly clear in the attempt to un-

107

derstand suffering as a universal interplay between *actio* and *passio* in nature. This attempt is, in the doubly negative sense of the word, no more than a scholasticism of suffering! The slightest trace of senseless suffering in the world of human experience gives the lie to all affirmative ontology and all teleology and is clearly revealed as a modern mythology.[5] Human suffering resists all attempts to interpret history and historical processes in the light of nature and nature as the subject of such historical processes. The pre-condition for this, of course, is always that there is, in suffering, a consciousness of identity in the negative sense which cannot be reduced to the trivial identity of natural persistence in time. Not only the anthropocentricity of power over and control of nature, but also the anthropocentricity of suffering, which asserts itself over all cosmocentricity, are both expressed in this consciousness of identity. It would therefore not be idealistic pride, but respect for the dignity of historically accumulated suffering if we were to try to understand nature in the light of history (if we were, in other words, to interpret the relationship between nature and history dialectically rather than teleologically) and to interpret the milliards of years of natural time as opposed to the time of human suffering as what Ernst Bloch has called 'inflation time'.

The substratum of history, then, is not nature as evolution or a process without reference to the subject. The natural history of man is to some extent the history of his suffering. In that history, the absence of reconciliation between nature and man is not suppressed, but preserved—against all teleological projection and all ontological generalization. The history of man's suffering has no goal, but it has a future. It is, moreover, not teleology, but the trace of suffering that provides us with an accessible continuity of this history. The essential dynamics of history consist of the memory of suffering as a negative consciousness of future freedom and as a stimulus to overcome suffering within the framework of that freedom. The history of freedom is therefore—subject to the assumed alienation of man and nature—only possible as a history of suffering. Every idea of a history of freedom that goes forward in a non-dialectical progression proves to be abstract and ideological. This, however, links political and social action firmly to man's historical consciousness and makes both a stoical withdrawal from the antagonisms of history and a teleological optimization of the contradictions of history impossible.

3. The future in the memory of suffering

Christianity does not introduce God subsequently as a kind of 'stop-gap' into this conflict about the future; instead, it tries to keep alive the memory of the crucified Lord, this specific *memoria passionis,* as a dangerous memory of freedom in the social systems of our technological civilization. This assertion, which is central to any practical fundamental theology and which is to some extent implicit in all that is said in this book, must be developed and explained in far greater detail.

a. 'Memory' would seem to be a middle-class counterpart to hope, leading us deceptively away from the risks of the future. In what sense can it be practical and critical and even dangerously liberating?

There are some very different kinds of memories. There are those in which we just do not take the past seriously enough: memories in which the past becomes a paradise without danger, a refuge from our present disappointments—the memory of the 'good old days'. There are memories which bathe everything from the past in a soft, conciliatory light. 'Memory transfigures', we say, and at times we experience this in a rather drastic form, for example when old soldiers exchange war yarns at a regimental dinner. War as an inferno is obliterated from such memories: what seems to remain is only the adventure experienced long ago. Here the past is filtered through a harmless cliché: everything dangerous, oppressive and demanding has vanished from it: it seems deprived of all future. In this way, memory can easily become a 'false consciousness' of our past and an opiate for our present.

But there is another form of memory: there are dangerous memories, memories which make demands on us. There are memories in which earlier experiences break through to the centre-point of our lives and reveal new and dangerous insights for the present. They illuminate for a few moments and with a harsh steady light the questionable nature of things we have apparently come to terms with, and show up the banality of our supposed 'realism'. They break through the canon of the prevailing structures of plausibility and have certain subversive features. Such memories are like dangerous and incalculable visitations from the past. They are memories that we have to take into account, memories, as it were, with a future content.[6]

It is not by chance that the destruction of memory is a typical measure of totalitarian rule. The enslavement of men begins when their memories of the past are taken away. All forms of colonialization are based on this principle. Every rebellion against suffering is fed by the subversive power of remembered suffering. The memory of suffering continues to resist the cynics of modern political power.

There is an obvious danger today that everything in our consciousness that is determined by memory, everything outside the calculations of our technico-pragmatic reason, will be equated with superstition and left to the private whim of the individual. But this does not necessarily mean that we are freer and more enlightened. We merely fall prey to the dominant illusions all the more easily and are deceived in another way. There are many examples. In this sense the remembrance of suffering contradicts the contemporary prophets of the disappearance of history. This memory prevents us from understanding history either as a mere background for an occasional festive interpretation of our existence, or merely as distanced material for historical criticism. As the remembered history of suffering, history retains the form of 'dangerous tradition'. This subversive tradition resists any attempt to do away with it by means of a purely affirmative attitude to the past (as, for example, in hermeneutical theories) and by means of a wholly critical attitude to the past (as, for instance, in ideology criticism). The 'mediation' of the memory of suffering is always practical. It is never purely argumentative, but always narrative in form, in other words, it takes the form of dangerous and liberating stories.

b. Bearing in mind what I have said so far, it should be clear that this memory is a memory of suffering. In our social life, there is a kind of prohibition, a structure aimed at deluding, which either disturbs or completely blocks our vision of the original cognitive and practical function of suffering.

Modern scientific knowledge is marked by the model of a dominative knowledge of nature, and in this view man understands himself anthropologically above all as the subject exercising control over nature. *Scientia et potentia in idem coincidunt:* Bacon's proposition characterizes the modern conception of science as knowledge of control. Accordingly, in a society universally determined by this kind of scientific knowledge, other forms of human behaviour and knowledge (such as suffering, pain, mourning, joy, play and so on) enjoy only a functional and derived validity and are largely underestimated in their cognitive and critical meaning. Hence it is significant that there should be a kind of anti-knowledge *ex memoria passionis* forming in our society, in which the existing identification of 'praxis' with 'control of nature' is banished.

Our idea of history is also unilaterally affected by a screening out of the importance of suffering. We tend, consciously or unconsciously, to define history as the history of what has prevailed, as the history of the successful and the established. There is hardly any reference in history as we know it to the conquered and defeated or to the forgotten or suppressed hopes of our historical existence. In history, a kind of Darwinism in the sense of the principle of selection (*Vae victis!*) tends to prevail. Again it is of decisive importance that a kind of anti-history should develop out of the memory of suffering—an understanding of history in which the vanquished and destroyed alternatives would also be taken into account: an understanding of history *ex memoria passionis* as a history of the vanquished. I shall discuss this question in greater detail in another context.

c. Christian faith declares itself as the *memoria passionis, mortis et resurrectionis Jesu Christi.* At the midpoint of this faith is a specific *memoria passionis,* on which is grounded the promise of future freedom for all. We remember the future of our freedom in the memory of his suffering—this is an eschatological statement that cannot be made more plausible through any subsequent accommodation, and cannot be generally verified. This statement remains controversial and controvertible: the power to scandalize is part of its communicable content. For the truth of the passion of Jesus and the history of human suffering as we remember it in the word 'God' is a truth whose recollection always painfully contradicts the expectations of the individual who tries to conceive it. The eschatological truth of the *memoria passionis* cannot be derived from our histori-

111

cal, social and psychological compulsions. This is what makes it a liberating truth in the first place. But that also is at the root of its nature and constitutionally alien to our cognitive systems.

What is required is theology as a form of hermeneutics of eschatological change that does justice to man, the object and time. This theology has the task of mediating an eschatological concept of change by means of a technologically rational form of change that will to a very great extent determine the pattern not only of technical developments, but also of social mutation. An eschatological criticism of the existing situation cannot make direct critical use of the category of change, because the existing situation has, in the rational sense, become a situation that is constantly changing. The new element in the eschatological kingdom of God has to be expressed with a justified and purposeful change in mind if it is not to shoot past the real target, which is a reduction in the difference between an existing lack of humanity and a humanity that is really possible. When it takes part in debate with the humanities, technology and political science, theology must look for categories that can be accepted as validly constituting a dialogue. Suffering on the one hand and an essentially human way of life on the other would be a suitable pair of categories. Their theological counterpart would, of course, be Good Friday and Easter or the *memoria passionis et resurrectionis*.

This memory of the suffering and resurrection of Jesus reveals its dynamic power in the question about the direction and aim of change. It is not a complete leap into the eschatological existence of the 'new man', but rather a reflection about concrete human suffering which is the point at which the proclamation of the new and essentially human way of life that is announced in the resurrection of Jesus can begin. What emerges from the memory of suffering is a knowledge of the future that does not point to an empty anticipation, but looks actively for more human ways of life in the light of our experience of the new creation of man in Christ.

In this sense, the Christian *memoria* insists that the history of human suffering is not merely part of the pre-history of freedom but remains an inner aspect of *the* history of freedom. The imagination of future freedom is nourished from the memory of suffering, and freedom degenerates wherever those who suffer are treated more or less as a cliché and degraded to a faceless mass. Hence the Christian *memoria* becomes a memory which shocks us out of ever becoming prematurely reconciled to the facts and trends of our technological society. It becomes a dangerous and liberating memory over against the controls and mechanisms of the dominant consciousness and its abstract ideal of emancipation.

A society which suppresses these and similar dimensions in the history of freedom, and in the understanding of freedom, pays the price of an increasing loss of all visible freedom. It is incapable of developing goals and priorities which prevent the creeping adaptation of our freedom to a society that is becoming increasingly anonymous and more and more completely divorced from the subject.

I should like to make two explanatory additions to the foregoing interpretation.

It might well be objected that in this approach Christian memory is unilaterally reduced to the status of remembrance of suffering, and that the memory of the resurrection of Jesus is put into the background, if not altogether obscured. Obviously it is impossible to make a simple distinction between the *memoria passionis* and *memoria resurrectionis*. There is no understanding of the resurrection that does not have to be developed by way of and beyond the memory of suffering. There is no understanding of the glory of resurrection that is free of the shadows and threats of the human history of suffering. *A memoria resurrectionis* that is not comprehensible as *memoria passionis* would be mythology pure and simple.

But what of a *memoria passionis* which understands itself in faith as *memoria resurrectionis?* What does it mean to make 'resurrection' accessible by way of the memory of suffering? Can such a resurrection faith also be expressed in socially communicable symbols which possess some critically liberating force for us? I believe that such a resurrection faith is expressed inasmuch as it acts 'contra-factually' in making us free to bear in mind the sufferings and hopes of the past and the challenge of the dead. It allows not only a revolution that will change the things of tomorrow for future generations, but a revolution that will decide anew the meaning of our dead and their hopes. Resurrection mediated by way of the memory of suffering means: The dead, those already vanquished and forgotten, have a meaning which is as yet unrealized. The po-

113

tential meaning of our history does not depend only on the survivors, the successful and those who make it. Meaning is not a category that is only reserved for the conquerors!

This must be taken into account by a church and a theology where the 'memory of suffering' occupies a central position. Only then will they be able to prevent themselves degenerating to the level of a church or a theology of the victors, and therefore of political religion (in something like the Constantinian sense). On the other hand, faith in the resurrection of the dead has a wholly social and social-critical significance. It enables us to insist firmly on the memory of the suffering that has accumulated in history, in order thereby to determine our behaviour and our hopes.

Such an understanding of the unity of the *memoria passionis* and *memoria resurrectionis* is also opposed to the attempt to make the conventional distinction between a wordly history of suffering and a history of glory transcending this world, in fact between secular history and salvation-history in the usual sense of the words. Secular history and salvation-history are not two factors that can be equated by means of theological speculation, nor can they (nor ought they to) be merely paradoxically contrasted. Salvation-history is, instead, secular history in which a meaning is conceded to obscured and suppressed hopes and sufferings. Salvation-history is that secular history in which the vanquished and forgotten possibilities of human existence that we call 'death' are allowed a meaning which is not recalled or cancelled by the future course of history.

We must also determine more precisely what is actually understood as 'suffering' in this context. Which 'suffering', then, is intended in the *memoria passionis?* Is it not very dangerous to talk about 'suffering in general'? Does the 'memory of suffering' not lose then all its critical, and above all its social-critical and political force? Does that not mean that suffering is wholly privatized and internalized? Does everyone not suffer, in a certain sense, in this view? Does a rich playboy in his luxury bungalow not suffer? Where are the requisite differentiations, the bases of a critical awareness in the interest precisely of those who suffer and are oppressed unjustly? Does this not lead to the entry of political commitment into the boring, non-specific vagueness which is for the most part the today of the social and political countenance of the world Church? Surely everything tends then towards that kind of consolation that ultimately consoles no one, since it intends exactly the same consolation for all. In the light of the Christian memory of suffering, it is clear that social power and political domination are not simply to be taken for granted but that they continually have to justify themselves in view of actual suffering. The social and political power of the rich and the rulers must be open to the question of the extent to which it causes suffering. It cannot escape this reckoning by invoking the specific suffering of the rich and powerful. And this critical interrogation of domination and riches is part precisely of that consolation which the Gospel would bestow upon the rich and the rulers.

The memory of suffering in the Christian sense does not, therefore, merge with the darkness of social and political arbitrariness, but creates a social and political conscience in the interest of others' suffering. It prevents the privatization and internalization of suffering, and the reduction of its social and political dimension. In this memory of suffering, the history of suffering and the history of social oppression are not identical, but they are also not separable.

4. God as the eschatological subject of history?[7]

As a kind of initial thesis, I suggested that the problem of the future was primarily political and fundamentally social. I now ask: How is the Christian *memoria passionis* to be connected at all with political life, and what justification is there for such an association? What have the two really to do with one another? Does bringing them together not mean their mutual decay? As I have stressed, it is not a question here of introducing the Christian memory of suffering into the existing forms of political life, but of making this *memoria passionis* effective in the transformation of our political life and its structures—a transformation already shown to be the decisive requirement for tackling the question of the future. Yet the fundamental question remains: Does political life not fall victim to the reactionary influence of universalist norms once it is associated with the Christian *memoria passionis*? For this Christian *memoria*, as an eschatological memory, entails a particular interpretation of the meaning and subject of universal history.

But how can the question of the meaning and subject of history as a whole have anything to do with political life? Does all talk of a universal meaning of history in its political application not lead to totalitarianism or at least to an uncritical, fanatical kind of utopianism? All positivist theories of social and political life insist on this danger. These theories are, of course, subject to the question of whether their rigorous rejection of the question of meaning does not eventually subject political life to a purely instrumental form of thinking, and in the long run abandon it to technocracy. And positivism is also subject to the question of whether by its rendering tabu or just ignoring, the question of meaning, it does not close its eyes to those ideologies which constantly seek to enthrone themselves as the subject and bearer of the meaning of history as a whole, and consequently endanger our social and political action.

In contrast, traditional Marxism and its theory of political life wholly maintain the question of the meaning and subject of history as a whole. The intention here is essentially practical: to determine the content and goal of revolutionary praxis. (Marxism does acknowledge a politically identifiable bearer of the meaning of history and recognizes it as the proletariat, which in its political praxis sets out to realize this meaning.) But in fact it is difficult to see how such a fusion of the meaning of history and political praxis does not eventually end in a political totalitarianism behind that transformation of political life that we seek for the sake of our future.

In its 'liberal' theory of the political life, traditional idealism also preserves the question of the meaning and subject of history. This position, however, differs from Marxism in acknowledging no socially apparent and politically identifiable subject of history as a whole, and, indeed, in rejecting any attempt at a political identification of this subject. Hegel, for instance, calls the subject of history as a whole the 'world spirit', whereas others speak of 'nature', and yet others of 'universal humanity'. These are all apolitical predicates. Here reference to the bearer and meaning of history remains essentially abstract. Nevertheless, it is clear that this abstract discourse about history as a whole can have an eminently practical political meaning. It makes possible and helps to bring about the liberation of political life from universal forces and universalist norms. Political life is set free to assume a wholly pragmatic orientation; politics as determined solely by the 'thing itself'—what is 'really at issue'. But are these 'factual structures' really anything other than the actual structures and tendencies of our economico-technological processes? Where are we to find a contra-factual consciousness offering a political alternative to these processes and their anonymity, if not in a pure decision-politics? Undoubtedly its anti-totalitarian effect is important in this liberal understanding of political life; nevertheless, in its positive version it seems to offer no impulsion for the transformation of political life that we are looking for.

Let us look again at the association between the Christian *memoria passionis* and political life. In the memory of this suffering, God appears in his eschatological freedom as the subject and meaning of history as a whole. This implies, first of all, that for this *memoria* there is also no politically identifiable subject of universal history. The meaning and goal of this history as a whole are instead—to put it very summarily—under the so-called 'eschatological proviso of God'. The Christian *memoria* recalls the God of Jesus' passion as the subject of the universal history of suffering, and in the same movement refuses to give political shape to this subject and enthrone it politically. Wherever a party, group, race, nation, or a Church that misinterprets itself in the sense of Dostoyevsky's Grand Inquisitor tries to define itself as this subject, the Christian *memoria* must oppose that, and unmask the attempt as political idolatry, as political ideology with a totalitarian or—in apocalyptic term—a 'bestial' tendency. In this way, in the light of the Christian *memoria passionis,* political life is liberated as protected from totalitarianism. But, as opposed to the liberal version of idealism, this liberation is now Utopian in orientation and not undefined. The Christian memory of suffering is in its theological implications an anticipatory memory: it intends the anticipation of a particular future of man as a future for the suffering, the hopeless, the oppressed, the injured and the useless of this earth. Hence this memory of suffering does not indifferently surrender the political life orientated by it to the play of social interests and forces, which for its own part turns upon the presupposition of conflict, so that it always favours the powerful but not the friendly, and always acknowledges only that measure of humanity which is the estimated prerequisite for the successful pursuit of one's own interests. The memory of suffering, on the other hand, brings a new moral imagination into political life, a new vision of others' suffering which should mature into a generous, uncalculating partisanship on behalf

117

of the weak and unrepresented. Hence the Christian memory of suffering can become, alongside many other often subversive innovative factors in our society, the ferment for that new political life we are seeking on behalf of our future.

Notes

1. This chapter is an adapted version, rewritten to fit into the whole concept, of a text that first appeared in 1971. It was originally given as a paper at an international symposium of theologians in New York in November 1971 and published for the first time in *Concilium* (1972), pp. 9–25, translated by John Griffiths and entitled 'The Future in the memory of suffering'. There are certain additions to this text in this chapter, including my contribution to *Evangelische Theologie* (1972), Heft 4, 'Erinnerung des Leidens als Kritik eines teleologisch-technologischen Zukunftsbegriffs' and the whole of section 2.

2. See the impressive investigation in D. Meadows, ed., *Limits to Growth: Report of the Club of Rome on the State of Mankind* (1972). This study is quoted as a historical symptom. Its factual (and intended ?) political assessment cannot be made here.

3. For this structure of universal responsibility and the related question of the scope of Christian competence in this sphere, see J. B. Metz, 'Vergebung der Sünden', *Stimmen der Zeit* 195 (1977), pp. 119–128.

4. We have already indicated that criticism of this kind is underestimated or even suppressed by enlightened reason.

5. See Theodor W. Adorno and his criticism of an ontologization of suffering and especially his *Negative Dialectics* (New York, 1972).

6. See H. Marcuse, *One-dimensional Man* (New York, 1966).

7. It will be clear from the first part of this book ('Concept') why it has proved necessary to modify the argument in this section about God as the subject of history. I have done this in order to give greater clarity and validity to the part played by man as a subject in history, a rôle that is nothing less than epoch-making. See my argument in 'Vergebung der Sünden', *op. cit.*

7. Redemption and emancipation[1]

1. Accentuation of the theme

Today theological pluralism too often expresses no more than a mindless capitulation to the sorry status of theology itself. Pluralism has become more encrusted and sterile than all the systems so eagerly combated under its banner. If pluralism is to become dialectically dynamic and the question of truth—whose currency has been devalued into a question of viewpoints—restored as a serious question, then any given theological position must strive to appropriate precisely those elements which other positions see as lacking or neglected in it, and vice versa. Applied to the theme 'redemption and emancipation' such an approach would mean, on the one hand, that a 'political theology' would not shrink from an exposition of the substance of the Christian doctrine of redemption; and on the other hand, that a theology concerned only to be 'specifically Christian' and interested in a 'pure' theology of redemption (if that is possible) honestly grapple with the notion of emancipation or liberation. For the import of Christianity demands that we dare not barter away in its name either the sacred or the world, with its history of suffering, for a mess of pottage.

Perhaps I have hereby formulated the emphasis of the theme to my own advantage. As a fundamental theologian I do not wish to lose sight of the approach advocated by distancing myself too much from the work of the dogmatic theologian. Indeed, in my opinion, both disciplines are closely related, even interwoven.

2. Universal and total emancipation

In this context I understand emancipation as a kind of epoch-constituting catchword for our contemporary experience of the world. It is a universal, almost historico-philosophical category for characterizing that modern world, with its processes of liberation and enlightenment, within whose relationships (and not just, under whose

119

conditions!) we must seek to articulate and assume responsibility for the Christian message of redemption. In fact, this suggested universal usage of emancipation is not so self-evident or unobjectionable. There is a real danger of ideologizing.[2] Hardly any other word seems so excessively used, so hyper-legitimate, and so emotionally charged in present discussions. Just page through the educational literature, especially the religious educational material, on the subject.[3]

Nevertheless, it does not appear to me very meaningful or helpful to restrict the notion of emancipation to its original legal context, where it signified the benevolently guaranteed release of slaves and persons in bondage or the release of sons from paternal care and responsibility.[4] For it is precisely the disappearance of any connotation of paternalistic condescension and the emergence of autonomy in the act of emancipation—that is, the understanding of emancipation as a self-liberation of human groups and classes in the modern history of revolution and enlightenment—that has introduced that tension and that contrast between redemption and emancipation which we must now reflect upon. In what follows, therefore, emancipation is used as a universal, quasi-historico-philosophical category of the modern history of freedom, which accordingly is discussed in the context of a contrasting historico-theology of the redemption.

This determination of the theme is consequential enough. It forces theology, first of all, realistically to take into account what I would like to call the total and uncompromising character of the so understood emancipatory history of freedom. This understanding found its first programmatic formulation in Marx, but in its generalized form, it is also present in emancipatory theorists of very different persuasions. Marx stated: 'All emancipation is the referal of human relationships constituting the world back to men themselves.'[5] Such a history of emancipation has, so to speak, not only a categorical but also a transcendental character. For it touches on, and revolutionizes, the very roots of the understanding of human freedom. In the self-liberation of individual groups and classes from subservience, from an underprivileged status, and from social repression the 'general human emancipation'[6] emerges. It is this self-emancipation which Marxism opposes to any form of an assured, liberated or redeemed freedom as an illusion distracting men from winning real freedom for themselves.

Now the course of recent history has increasingly shown inherent contradictions within the process of universal human self-liberation. It has become apparent that the history of revolution has degenerated into new histories of violence and repression, that within emancipative societies new histories of suffering emerge; that industralization and technology advance new planet-wide mechanisms of dehumanizing regimentation and subservience, etc.[7] Ernst Bloch has said, for example, that 'in the citizen of the French Revolution lurked the bourgeois—God save us from what lurks in our comrades!'[8] This has not led the emancipatory theories of history and freedom, however, to retract an overstated, too abstract conception of emancipation. Instead it has led them to what I would phrase the 'dialectics of emancipation'—especially within the circle of the Frankfurt School. These dialectics, far from minimizing the aspirations towards totality and inexorability in the notion of emancipation, actually make it more unassailable, less tractable, and immunize it against external criticism in as much as they attempt to reassimilate within the notion those very social contradictions emergent in the process of emancipation.

Judiciously, yet deliberately, I propose that everyone inclined to see in the dialectics of emancipation an opening for a Christian understanding of the history of redemption reflect on its implications—whether they interpret the history of redemption reductively as no more than a remedy for a delayed history of emancipation or non-reductively as an emphatic duplication of this history of emancipation. The distinctions developed in the dialectics of emancipation between work and interaction, between technique and praxis, between empirical fact and anticipation and so on are not theological distinctions. They are conceptual tools for a dialectical analysis of social contradictions in the interest of total emancipation. This applies as well to those very theological notions which occur in these dialectics, such as the notion of 'redemption' in Walter Benjamin and Theodor W. Adorno,[9] as a 'resurrection of fallen nature' in Ernst Bloch, Herbert Marcuse and Jürgen Habermas,[10] and perhaps also such as the later Bloch's call for a new demonology and satanology.[11]

121

There is no theological foothold in the crevices of these dialectics of the history of emancipation! At best it must be taken in its entirety and so discussed; it cannot be compromised by theological half measures. Hence one would radically distort these emancipation dialectics were one to maintain that their negative critical aspects should be 'complemented' by the affirmative of a Christian doctrine on redemption. Such a superimposed reconciliation underestimates both the critically negative mediation of totality in the dialectical history of emancipation as well as the irrevocability of the Christian history of redemption. Otherwise commendable efforts, in my opinion, founder at this point, for example, those aimed 'at introducing the question of Jesus into the emancipatory process',[12] and at interpreting historical redemption as the surpassing and the perfecting of emancipation history.[13] Emancipation is not simply the immanence of redemption, nor is redemption just the transcendence of emancipation—as a rather well known formula for reconciliation would have it.[14] This approach fails, if not elsewhere, on the totality of the dialectical history of emancipation which has appropriated the transcendental grounds of freedom. Such an approach fails, just as those other theological attempts at a neatly compromising distinction between redemptive history and emancipatory history fail—whether the latter are abstractly understood in the paradigm of a two-kingdom doctrine, or in a paradoxical soteriology of transcendentalist or existentialist vintage. All these efforts do not break the spell of emancipative totality which seems to haunt the modern history of freedom. Instead, they unintentionally strengthen that spell by their extreme lack of concrete history.

Concisely, I would assert that a theology of redemption does not become critical by assimilating the critical theory or by inserting itself into, or superimposing itself over that theory. Theology would thereby remain uncritically aware of the totality-aspiration at the origin of the modern history of emancipation. Only if theology takes the entirety of this history into account in its evolutionary version, can theology confront it in such a way that theology will neither regressively and undifferentiatedly fall short of the modern problem, nor from the very start, falsely seek to immunize its understanding of redemption from the criticisms of the history of emancipation through abstract and unhistorical distinctions, nor, finally, simply subordinate the logos of redemption to the logos of emancipative reason.[15] Attesting to the Christian legitimacy of the modern history of emancipation might be an important presupposition for avoiding those pitfalls.[16] However, it does not substitute for a theological determination of the relationship between redemption and emancipation, nor does it, of itself, dissipate the suspicion that the Christian message of redemption has, through its own historical realization, brought about a situation in which it has finally made itself superfluous, so that now emancipation successfully inherits the place of redemption.

3. History of redemption—history of freedom—history of suffering

For this reason, I suggest discussing a liberating redemption in and through Jesus Christ, an emancipatory, revolutionary and critical self-liberation of man, and a soteriological and emancipatory history of freedom, within the framework of what I term sweepingly and with some hesitation, 'the history of human suffering'. I realize how the latter history exists *plurale tantum* as the brittle and devastating histories of suffering narrated by those experiencing them, how they cannot be systematized in argument. More about this later. Now this history of suffering is rather boldly addressed as a medium for a redeeming and emancipating history of freedom. And this primarily accentuates the distinction and difference between liberation through redemption and self-liberation through emancipation. It does not drift into that orgy of equivocations, the superficiality of which blur the distinction between the notion of liberation and of deliverance, where so many contemporary facile compromises (as well as contrasts) are erected between redemption and emancipation—to the detriment of both in my view.

These histories of suffering are here understood as embracing all the actually experienced histories of suffering. They are not limited, then, to a social history of repression and a political history of violence, as these are thematized in the emancipatory history of liberation. Instead, they necessarily involve as well—especially in our discussion—a history of suffering as a history of guilt and as the fated destiny of finitude and of death. Only so understood in its entirety does the history of suffering provide a context for articulating

123

Christian redemption as deliverance. Redemption becomes an assured deliverance from the suffering of guilt and from the sinful self-degeneration of man, aspects elaborated in the so-called staurological (satisfactory) soteriology and as an assured deliverance from the suffering of finitude, of mortality, of that inner corroding nihilism of created being, as these are emphasized in the so-called incarnational soteriologies. I do not see how one could speak of Christian redemption as liberation and not discuss, or merely touch upon, the gifted deliverance from the history of suffering as a history of guilt and of deadly finitude.

This is not said with that type of low-bidding 'discernment of spirits' which pays no attention to the problem of how to communicate such redemption to men living in the age of emancipation. Quite the contrary. It is said in order to see clearly those very real historical and social processes—those very concrete and all-embracing histories of suffering—on which the dialectical and evolutionary notion of emancipative totality continually gets stranded, on which modern theories of emancipation with their historico-philosophical universality are shown to be abstract theories of an irrationally dichotomized history of freedom, and on which also, in my opinion, a purely argumentative soteriology gets caught in crisis.

a) The history of suffering as a history of guilt and the exonerating mechanism of an abstract-total emancipation

This concrete history of suffering was the acknowledged crux of a theodicy that had made God himself the subject of history. If I may say so, it became the decisive factor in expelling God from the center of history in the modern theories of history and of freedom. These theories replaced the *Deus Salvator* with *homo emancipator* as the universal subject of history.

However, once man had taken historical destiny in his own hands, the incriminating presence of the history of suffering did not disappear. Unhappiness and depravation, misery and evil, oppression and suffering have remained and have intensified and increased to planetary proportions. Who is to blame for this? Who is to bear the responsibility? Driven by such questions, the emancipative theories of history began to develop a type of 'anthropodicy' analogous to theodicy—with convoluted exculpating or exonerating mechanisms far outstripping the polemical hairsplitting of classical theodicy. Since God is no longer around to blame, it would seem that man as the maker of history must be blamed for the history of suffering.

Homo emancipator must 'justify' himself by taking the guilt and failure on himself as the responsible maker of history. *Homo emancipator* must live and recognize himself as *homo peccator*. Nevertheless, because he fears so much the possible heteronomy in the notion of guilt, he prefers to create new heteronomies. He tones down his historical responsibility. As a subject of history, he does not want to be taken so seriously. Faced with the history of suffering, he creeps away from the throne of the subject of history. With great subtlety, he develops 'the art of the alibi', as Odo Marquard said.[17] This exonerating mechanism can be illustrated in the predominant historico-philosophical theories of emancipation, whether they are of an idealist-liberal, a Marxist, or a positivist tradition.

Thus liberal and liberally minded Marxist theories of emancipation and enlightenment[18] imply historical processes that are divorced from the subject or, more precisely, they envisage a universal subject of history vaguely termed, in the tradition of Hegel, the 'world spirit', or, in the tradition of Schelling, 'nature'. The latter is an especially recurrent preference of the theorists of emancipation in the Frankfurt School.[19] These and similar entities function as transcendental subjects of history to which the dark side of emancipation, the history of guilt, can be attributed without repercussions, while the successes, victories and progressive strides on earth remain attributable to the emancipative acts of man as maker of history. A history of emancipation without a history of redemption is unmasked as an abstract history of success, triumph or victory. Hence a history of freedom dichotomized into a vague nature versus successful historical acts contains a perfect justification and exoneration mechanism for *homo emancipator* as the subject of history.

On the other hand, the classical Marxist version of the history of emancipation has conspicuously no qualms in designating a concrete, determinate subject of emancipative action: the proletariat. Here also, however, the history of emancipation is and remains, if reduced to essentials, a pure history of success, triumph or victory, in so far as it is attributed to this historical subject. It is in an unreal and inhuman fashion a history with no dirty laundry. For the failures, the guilt arising from the history of suffering, is exclusively

125

blamed on the others, on the opponents and enemies of this historical subject. Here the scapegoat or exonerating mechanism functions as usual. The alibi is the enemy with whatever power he still has over history. As an alibi-subject, the enemy will be passionately repudiated. A revolutionary theory of emancipation without a soteriology becomes enslaved to a compulsion for exoneration; a compulsion manifested in the need to cast human relationships within the context of enmity.[20] Within the neo-Marxist theories of history and society, the disquieting question of the failure of and the relationship between the struggle for freedom and guilt is always arising. At the same time, an awareness of the fact that misery and guilt are to be found not only in that relationship, but also possibly in ourselves is also present.

This view prevents us from interpreting the history of freedom simply as a history of success, triumph and victory. On the contrary, it forces us to draw attention to the constant paradox that exists between the history of freedom and the history of guilt. Something of the inner entanglement of struggle and guilt which does not simply exonerate the revolutionary fighter for freedom and stylize the revolutionary history of freedom itself as a pure history of success can be heard in the well known poem 'Emigration' by Bert Brecht. In this poem, addressed to those born posthumously, the author says: 'We, who wanted to prepare the ground for friendliness, cannot be friendly ourselves. But you, if it ever reaches the stage when one man really helps another, remember us with forbearance'. It is here that man's desire for emancipation, as a desire for innocence, would seem to be at least irritated.[21]

In the positivistic, technocratic conception of history and freedom—where the question of the meaning and subject of history is exposed as an ideology and dropped completely—this compulsion towards exoneration in the face of the history of suffering is not broken through, but finds its perhaps most sinister form. Processes of emancipation are here identified with processes of technological and economic progress. In the latter processes, however, the decisive agents become further divorced from the subject and increasingly anonymous. The history of freedom becomes in a new manner a 'history of nature'. It becomes a coercive mechanism of technological progress, a destiny of the second order, a post-historical, social structuralism with a teleology of emancipation that overlooks the subject of history. The mechanism of exoneration leads here to a total denigration of a responsible subject of historical action. Just as a certain theodicy of the Enlightenment, faced with the history of human suffering, sought to 'justify' the problem of God by simply denying his existence, so the mechanism of exoneration of an anthropodicy conceived as an abstract history of emancipation faced with the same history of suffering, attempts to justify and exonerate man by either insinuating or actually proclaiming his death as a subject.[22]

With these all too brief reflections I wish to indicate a central insight, namely that any emancipation cast as a universal historical totality is dangerously abstract and contradictory. A universal theory of emancipation without a soteriology remains caught under an irrational mechanism of exoneration or guilt-repression. A history of emancipation without a history of redemption, faced with the concrete history of suffering, subjugates the historical subject to new irrational constraints and either man is forced into a transcendental suspension of his own historical responsibility or he is forced into irreconcilable enmity or finally to negate himself as a subject. The refusal to accept guilt does not promote a definite, visible freedom but a painfully camouflaged heteronomy. The autonomy and coming of age of a total emancipation is loaded with inner contradictions. They are grounded on a partially or even totally cancelled identity of the acting subject. In the end, such an autonomy and coming of age, surviving because of repressed guilt which is projected onto alibi-subjects, and thereby denying any desire for redemption and reconciiiation, becomes exactly what Adorno so clearly feared—a banal expression of an abstractly dichotomized freedom. The history of freedom ends as the apotheosis of banality!

Christian soteriology, on the contrary, inexorably reveals the history of suffering as a history of guilt. It still entails, as Karl Rahner has said, 'a presentation whereby men are mystagogically initiated into a recognition of their guilt situation'.[23] Certainly this is not meant to inaugurate a new form of repression, by indoctrinating men with guilt-feelings, to establish or stabilize a cold-blooded interest in dominating them. It is not meant to endow the powerless with more guilt and the powerful with even more guiltless power or, by preaching guilt, more effectively to exonerate the privileged and those who give themselves privileges, so that the mystery of guilt is used as a calculated factor for subtly exploiting others. These are not imaginary dangers, they have happened often enough in the history of Christianity. Any soteriology must, with all honesty and determination and with an as yet undiscovered sensitivity, face up to the very pertinent criticism of religion as an ideology of guilt. It cannot speak of the history of suffering as a history of guilt without considering seriously the mechanisms of the history of repression and power. Therefore we can, in my opinion, speak of soteriology as a political theology of redemption. In this respect, nonetheless, it cannot evade that unpopular and, for many, long since mummified theme of 'guilt', sacrificing it on the altar of an abstract ideal of emancipation. Of what else does it speak when it discusses 'redemption'? How does redemption enter into the critical task of liberation which is to be accomplished within the contemporary history of emancipation? How is it able to contradict the defense mechanism of an abstract and total emancipation including the secret illusion of innocence which accompanies it; namely, the new opium of the totally emancipated in the presence of the concrete and all-encompassing history of suffering.[24]

b) The history of suffering as a history of the defeated and an ideology of emancipative progress

The real and all-inclusive history of suffering manifested in memory of Christian redemption includes the suffering of finiteness and of death as well as past suffering and the sufferings of the dead. In the presence of this situation, the liberating and meaningful message of redemption addresses itself to this concrete situation. For this dimension of the history of suffering is in no way merely added as an afterthought to the experienced histories of suffering. A Christian soteriology cannot be a casuistic cover-up for real suffering. The history of freedom remains much more and always a history of suffering.[25] Pain, sorrow and melancholy remain. Above all, the silent suffering of the inconsolable pain of the past, the suffering of the dead continues, for the greater freedom of future generations does not justify past sufferings nor does it render them free. No improvement of the condition of freedom in the world is able to do justice to the dead or effect a transformation of the injustice and the non-sense of past suffering.[26] Any emancipative history of freedom in which this whole history of suffering is suppressed or supposedly superseded is a truncated and abstract history of freedom whose progress is really a march into inhumanity.

Then again, this abstract history of freedom turns out to be a history of success, triumph or victory. The meaning of freedom in this history is one of triumph, the category reserved for those who come through *Vae victis!* However, *Vae victis* is no principle of interpretation for the history of freedom but rather the Darwinian definition of natural history. In both, what applies is the principle of natural selection, the survival of the fittest. Such freedom increases and marches forward over the prostrate backs of the dead as a *massa damnata*. The suffering of their fathers finds consolation in the happiness of the descendants, in past sufferings rendered worthwhile in a future harmony, as bitterly formulated by Ivan Karamazov.[27] A Darwinism of the second order, an objective cynicism against past suffering and the freedom of the dead and the conquered prevails. Finally, the history of freedom dissolves in this immense dichotomy of the theme of freedom.

On the contrary, Christianity in its message of redemption, does not offer definitive meaning for the unexpiated sufferings of the past. It narrates rather a distinct history of freedom: freedom on the basis of a redeeming liberation through God in the cross of Jesus. It is not by chance that this history of liberation narrates the descent into hell. This affirmation is by no means a mythological category which should be quickly deleted or relativized as a subsequent interpolation into the Christian memory of redemption under the pretext that it does not belong to the genuine concern of Jesus. In this way, the apocalyptical sting has been drawn from Christian soteriology and, in this way too, its decisive sense of freedom has been obscured. This descent, this being together with the dead on the part of the crucified Christ,[28] points to the original liberating movement of the history of redemption without which every history of freedom is reduced to the level of natural history and tendentiously aborts itself. The historical end of freedom as the apotheosis of nature!

All of this was not mentioned as appeasement nor as opium for present suffering. This history of redemption does not exempt us from the solidarity of historical existence. It encloses much more a superseded form of this solidarity. It wants to make us free, to enable us to be aware of the hopes and sufferings of the past. There is in the light of this history of redemption not only a 'forward solidarity' with the coming generations but also a 'backward solidarity' with the silent and forgotten dead. The latter is a practical solidarity of memory which looks from the standpoint of the conquered and the victims sacrificed in the world theatre of history. It does not only expose the non-sense of history against the probing optimism of the victor. The potential of meaning in our history of freedom does not only depend only on those who survive, who attain success and who come through. It narrates the counter-meaning of redemption.

This counter-meaning of redemption is obsolete only for a reason which, out of a pure anxiety of heteronomy, denies the respect for suffering that has accumulated in history, thereby even destroying the 'authority of the suffering' in the interest of abstract autonomy.

c. The history of suffering as the crisis of an argumentative soteriology

In view of the actual and comprehensive history of suffering of mankind, only purely argumentative soteriology is thrown into crisis. This is briefly specified in order to make certain that in all of our considerations up to this point, we do not understand the history of suffering as a third factor besides redemption and emancipation. The question therefore is: Can the theological idea of salvation and redemption hold its own against this history of suffering and the painful non-identity of historical life that is manifested in it? Does it not avoid from the outset, because of its idea of salvation in Jesus Christ and man's redemption and reconciliation with other men that have been brought about in that salvation, both the risk and the suffering of the non-identity of historical existence? Does it not set an ahistorical and ever suspiciously mythological being over the heads of a mankind plundered, humiliated and destroyed by the history of suffering? In the presence of historical suffering does soteriology finally reverse itself into an objective cynicism of history? Is there a theological mediation between redemption and history which as a history of suffering in general, is taken seriously in its historicality? Is there a theological mediation which does not fall into a stifling, high-sounding and finally self-deceiving speculative reconciliation with this history of suffering or is the existence of redemption itself rather suspended in view of this history of suffering? In my opinion, any purely argumentative theology fails in this problem of mediation which is formulated nowadays as the central problem of theology.

As I see it, there are three main attempts at a theological solution of this problem. The first depends on an existential and transcendental interpretation of the relationship between salvation and history. The question that is often asked in this context is whether a reconciliation cannot be sought by abbreviating 'history' to 'historicity', in other words, by withdrawing from the non-identity of historical life to a secret, unavailable and inexpressible point of identity in the subject or in existence itself.

The second attempt at a solution tends to a conditioning of redemption and salvation in the presence of the history of suffering. Salvation and redemption become extremely futuristic. They are at stake with regard to the non-identity of history as a history of suffering. But what is a redemption that is still at stake, if not a utopian redemption, which could only be used heuristically in the process of the human history of freedom? What is a conditioned redemption if not a cipher for a sought-after self-salvation and self-liberation of humanity which would again fall into the dilemmas we have already mentioned? This conditional soteriology dissolves itself into a practical philosophy of history which, as an inheritance of the Christian idea of redemption—since the Enlightenment—has incorporated utopian and political elements into itself. For example, Habermas has attested to the incapacity 'through consolation or trust so to outplay (or to overcome) the effective meaninglessness of contingent death, individual sufferings, private misfortune and in general the negativity of historically existential risks, as the expectation of religious salvation had achieved'.[29]

The third attempt at a solution, which is at present claiming a great deal of attention in the German-speaking countries will be discussed here in more detail and called by name. To begin with, it does not treat soteriology as purely precise nor does it see redemption as a definite (categorical) 'work' of God in Jesus Christ. It relates soteriology rightly not only to the theology of the Incarnation or to eschatology, but also to the specific definition of the Christian understanding of God in general, that is, to the theology of the Trinity. Suffering now becomes 'suffering between God and

131

God'.[30] The non-identity of the human history of suffering is, in the light of the *kenosis* of God in the cross of Jesus, taken up into the Trinitarian history of God.

One finds such an understanding in evangelical theology since Karl Barth, for instance in Eberhard Jüngel and above all in Jürgen Moltmann's latest book on the 'crucified God'. In Catholic circles, such considerations are found in Karl Rahner's suggestions on the unity of the immanent and the economic Trinity. Such considerations are also found within the context of Hans Küng's presentation of the historicity of God in his interpretation of Hegelian Christology.[31] (Right-wing Hegelians are always mentioned!). To my knowledge, however, the most impressive and forceful considerations are found in Hans Urs von Balthasar's interpretation of the paschal mystery within the framework of the Trinitarian understanding of God's history of self-emptying.[32]

There is a great deal that is praiseworthy in these and similar attempts.[33] I would, however, like to formulate a central consideration which is cast in an abridged and extremely formal manner. It is that the non-identity of human suffering cannot be cancelled out, in theological dialectics of Trinitarian soteriology, and still keep its historical character. For the painful experience of the non-identity of suffering cannot be identified with that negativity found in a dialectical understanding of the historical process, even that of a Trinitarian history of God. Whenever one tries to relate the history of redemption completed in Jesus Christ to the human history of suffering, not just by juxtaposing them in an ahistorical paradox (so that one is *sub contrario* asserted to be in the other), but to understand the alienation of the history of suffering itself as within the dialectics of the Trinitarian history of God, what occurs is a confusion between the negativity of suffering and the negativity of the dialectically mediated concept of suffering. A conceptual and argumentative mediation and reconciliation between real and effective redemption, on the one hand, and the human history of suffering on the other, would seem to me to be excluded. It leads either to a dualistic gnostic eternalization of suffering in God or to a condescending reduction of suffering to its concept. *Tertium non datur.* In my opinion, the dilemma cannot be solved by still more subtle and speculative argument, but only by another way of expressing a real and effective redemption in the non-identity of the age of suffering.

4. Towards a memorative and narrative theology of redemption:

My thesis is that a soteriology must neither condition nor suspend the event of redemption nor can it ignore or dialectically bypass the non-identity of the history of suffering. A purely argumentative soteriology cannot avoid these dangers. It must be made explicit in narrative. It is a fundamentally memorative and narrative soteriology.[34] It tries to keep the Christian memory of redemption alive in narrative form as a dangerous and liberating memory of redeemed freedom and to defend it by argument in the systems of our so-called emancipative world.

Later on, especially in Chapters 9, 11 and 12, I shall be dealing in detail with both the basic narrative structure of theology and the narrative structure of practical reason. I shall also discuss the inner connection between narrative and praxis. These are the important fundamental factors that form the basis of the position outlined here.

Notes

1. This chapter is an adapted version, rewritten to fit into the whole concept, of a text that first appeared in 1972. It was originally given as a paper at a conference of German-speaking dogmatic and fundamental theologians held at Munich in December 1972 and first published in its complete form a year later, entitled 'Erlösung und Emanzipation', in L. Scheffczyk, ed., *Erlösung und Emanzipation* (Freiburg, 1973), pp. 120–140. It first appeared in English as 'Redemption and emancipation' in *Cross Currents,* translated by Rev. Matthew L. Lamb and Sr. Jeannette Martin, C.S.C. This American translation has also been adapted to fit into the concept of the book as a whole.

2. R. Spaetmann, 'Autonomie, Mündigkeit, Emanzipation', *Kontexte* 7 (Stuttgart and Berlin, 1971), pp. 94–102.

3. See the overview of the relevant literature in religious education (*Katechetische Blätter*, Dec. 1971) with W. Offele ed., *Emanzipation und Religionspädagogik* (Einsiedeln, 1972).

4. On the history of the notion of emancipation, see M. Greiffenhagen, 'Eman-

zipation', in J. Ritter ed., *Historisches Wörterbuch der Philosophie,* II (Darmstadt, 1972), p. 448 f.

5. Karl Marx, 'On the Jewish Question', in Marx and Engels, *Collected Work,* III (New York, 1975), p. 146 ff.

6. Karl Marx, *op. cit.,* pp. 149–50.

7. See Theodor W. Adorno, *Erziehung zur Mündigkeit* (Frankfurt, 1972), 2nd edn., p. 146.

8. See *Spuren* (Frankfurt, 1959), p. 30. It is worth pointing out that, in the following passage especially, a rigoristic attitude is taken towards historical dialectical approaches and that this attitude cannot be reconciled with what I have said in part I of this book ('Concept'), at least not without some problems. It is taken in order to clarify the position and is preserved for heuristic reasons, even at the price of being too clear. In conformity with Part I, I continue to criticize the tendency that is inherent in these dialectics to totalize and to work without reference to the subject.

9. See T. Adorno, *Minima Moralia* (London 1973). In my opinion the usage of the notion of 'redemption' in Adorno, and especially in Walter Benjamin, deserves closer theological scrutiny. Cf. Benjamin, *Schriften* I (Frankfurt, 1961), p. 497 ff.

10. See Jürgen Habermas, *Toward a Rational Society* (Boston, 1970), p. 85 ff.

11. See E. Bloch, 'Aufklärung und Teufelsglaube', O. Schatz, ed. *Hat die Religion Zukunft?* (Graz, Vienna and Cologne, 1971), pp. 120–134.

12. See H. Kessler, *Erlösung als Befreiung* (Düsseldorf, 1972), p. 115.

13. Ibid., pp. 114 f., 122.

14. See Jürgen Moltmann, *Perspektiven der Theologie* (Munich and Mainz, 1968), p. 207. That Moltmann himself understands the relation between redemption and emancipation in a more differentiated manner than this formula would aver can be seen from his later work, *The Crucified God* (New York, 1974).

15. I have tried to show how one can expand on the relation between theology and specific modern problems precisely within this perspective; see my article, 'Grond en functie van de politieke theologie', *Tijdschrift voor Theologie,* 12, n. 2 (1972), pp. 159–170.

16. See W. Pannenberg, *Gottesgedanke und menschliche Freiheit* (Munich, 1972); J. B. Metz, *Christliche Anthropozentrik* (Munich, 1962) and my article, 'Prophetic Authority', in Metz, Moltmann, Oelmüller *et al., Religion in Political Society* (New York, 1974), pp. 177–209.

17. See his article, 'Wie irrational kann Geschichtsphilosophie sein?' in *Philosophisches Jahrbuch* 79, (1972), 246.

18. For the liberal version, see H. Lübbe, 'Geschichtsphilosophie und politische Praxis', *Theorie und Entscheidung* (Freiburg, 1971), pp. 111–133.

19. See M. Theunissen, *Gesellschaft und Geschichte* (Berlin, 1969).

20. See O. Marquard, *op. cit.,* p. 248.

21. I have taken this paragraph on neo-Marxism almost word for word from my article 'Vergebung der Sünden', *op. cit.,* p. 122.

22. M. Foucault, *Les mots et les choses* (Paris, 1966). Foucault regarded man himself, understood as a freely responsible subject, as an anthropomorphism or an 'eighteenth century invention'.

23. See Karl Rahner, 'Salvation', *Sacramentum Mundi* I (Freiburg & London, 1970), p. 405 ff.

24. Naturally there are many problems that could be pursued here, problems that are treated in such non-theological writings as E. Fromm, *Escape from Freedom* (New York, 1941), and A. Mitscherlich, *Die Unfähigkeit zu trauern* (Munich, 1967) among others.

25. This would hold true even if we were heading towards a social and economic order that would minimize contingency and fate, or a political order that would minimize the concrete differences among people. More than likely the history of suffering would be even more pronounced in such orders in so far as the latent despair, the 'jaws of death' (E. Bloch) that gnaw at our soul, could not be so successfully channelled, as they are now, into competition and social conflict.

26. See Theodor Adorno, *Negative Dialectics* (New York, 1973), p. 385.

27. See Fyodor Dostoyevsky, *The Brothers Karamazov*, trans. C. Garnett (New York, 1950), p. 292 ff.

28. See Hans Urs von Balthasar, 'Mysterium Paschale', *Mysterium Salutis* III, 2, p. 185 ff.

29. See Jürgen Habermas, *Philosophisch-politische Profile* (Frankfurt, 1971), p. 35.

30. See J. Moltmann, 'Die Verwandlung des Leidens', *Evangelische Kommentare* 5 (1972), pp. 713–717.

31. See Hans Küng, *Menschwerdung Gottes* (Freiburg, 1970).

32. See von Balthasar's article in *Mysterium Salutis,* III 2, pp. 133–326.

33. See, for example, H. Mühlen, *Die Veränderlichkeit Gottes als Horizont einer zukünftigen Christologie* (Münster, 1969).

34. It is not simply by chance that, for instance, some of the pertinent passages in von Balthasar and Moltmann (*op. cit.*) cut short the argumentative process and become an encoded form of narrative theology.

8. Church and People[1]
The forgotten subject of faith

The thoughts that follow could also be entitled simply 'The Forgotten People'. Forgotten people? Does not everybody speak about 'people'—even theologians and the Church? What, then, does it mean?

1. A short report on a 'schism'

In contrast to the Latin or Romance linguistic zones, the concept 'people' is not common in the German-speaking countries. In Germany especially, the word 'people' has for a long time been under a tabu. There is a good historical reason for this. Care has been exercised in the use of the word because of its misuse during the National Socialist period and there are also, I believe, sociological reasons for the continuing decline in its employment. In late technological societies, with a high degree of mobility, and an increasing loss of historical sense and interrelationship, it is becoming increasingly difficult to interpret and use the concept 'people' as an uncomplicated model of collective identity. (An attempt will be made in what follows to make a distinction here by alternating between 'people' and 'folk'.) All the same, the concept 'people' continues to be a central theological category with a thoroughly biblical content. It has also been given a much clearer emphasis in the thinking of theologians and members of the Church by the Constitution on the Church (*Lumen gentium*) of Vatican II, which defines and throws light on the Church explicitly as the 'people of God'. The question of the 'Church and people' can therefore be theologically justified and is in many respects a particularly contemporary one.[2]

In Germany at least, the religious situation seems to have been determined by a secret 'schism' between Church and people. The Church apparently is still a strong sphere of influence, but less and less of a people. It is increasingly concerned with the doubts of its

136

people—its 'simple folk'—and these doubts are much more severe than those of the Church's theologians and intellectuals. A silent exodus is taking place from the Church. The people are identifying themselves less and less with the Church.

Who is guilty? Modern theologians are accused publicly of confusing the people. 'The people do not know any more what to believe'. The problem would, however, be harmless enough if the only cause were a theology without a conscience. The recent Council did not produce this crisis; it simply exposed it. The cause is much deeper. The Church is paying the price of protecting its people too much. It is paying the price of letting the people become too little the subject of the Church, of allowing the voice of the history of the life and suffering of the people to become stifled and of letting the Church become the 'Church for the people' rather than the 'Church of the people'.

To look for the cause or causes of this crisis in 'others', in theologians or in the Church folk themselves will lead nowhere and only widen the gap between Church and people. One suggestion that is often made nowadays is that the Church should once again cut itself off from society in a new fundamentalism without humour or any sense of the interrelationship between Church and people. The phrase 'little flock' is enjoying a boom, but is functioning more as a defensive mechanism to protect the middle-class Church than as a dangerous and liberating memory of the 'Church of the little ones' of which Jesus himself spoke. The underground Church continues to expand hesitatingly and sub-cultures and counter-cultures are constantly imported. But they remain cut off from the people as the greater Church whose corrective they set out to be.

As for theology, almost its only subject is the professional theologian. But theologians find it difficult enough to develop a theology 'for the people', let alone a theology 'of the people'. They certainly find it almost impossible to write a biography of the ordinary folk. Theology—including progressive, socially and politically committed theology—is above all experienced in libraries and conferences, where the opinions and counter-opinions of one's colleagues plays a much more prominent part than the religious life and history of suffering of the Christian people. The mysticism of those people, which is usually hidden from the people themselves, features hardly at all. Theologians are afraid of lowering the scientific standard of their subject by popularizing theology and are therefore anxious to avoid being touched by the usually silent doubts of the ordinary Christian people. The ecclesiological key-phrase of the Second Vatican Council—the 'people of God'—has, in Germany at least, been diverted into very strange channels. It has led above all to a discussion of offices in the Church. The theme of 'people', which was placed on the agenda of the Council, has hardly been discussed at all. It is true that there has been a good deal of talk about the 'Church for the people', especially among pastoral theologians, but there has certainly been very little about the 'Church as people' or the 'Church of the people'. Yet the most important question of all is whether the 'Church for the people' can become a 'Church of the people'.

2. The Church and the history of suffering of a people—or the price of orthodoxy

A Church of the people—this is not something that can simply be accepted without question. This is most evident in the case of those churches that are still strikingly 'people's churches', in other words, in the churches where there is still a material identity between Church and people, as in the case of the churches in the Latin linguistic zones. For this reason, what follows is directed mainly at the situation in the Church in those countries, not in a spirit of condescension or criticism, but above all as an expression of hope, because what is involved there is possibly something that is already impossible or at least hardly possible any more in other situations in the Church. In the great body of the one Catholic Church in the world, the individual churches have special historical and social destinies, with the result that they have special tasks and missions in the history of the Church as a whole.

Many individual churches are today in a state of great upheaval and transition. Generally speaking, what is happening is that the 'people's churches' that have existed more or less up to the present are being transformed. In France, for example, and even in Germany, these transitional processes have tended to follow a very unpromising course. It is, however, possible that a transformation may take place in the Latin American countries by which a traditional people's Church may become a developed Church of the people, that is, not a Church that is without authority and has no offices, but a Church in which the people themselves can become in a more radical and vital way the subjects of the Church's community of hope.

The fate of 'church people' is often very similar to that of the people as a whole—those who speak most about them often know the least about them and are callous to their deepest injuries. Popular feeling is no guarantee of a friendly disposition towards the people. Is 'baptized people' something that can be accepted without question as the 'people of God' in the Church's understanding of itself? Is it in fact the Church as it defines itself in the name of Jesus Christ? The Church is not an original, natural people, but a people 'called out', a new people that has become the subject of a new and unsuspected history of God with men and has its identity in its narration of this history of salvation and its attempt to live by it. It is not possible to be the Church or the 'people of God' without bearing this new history. Being the Church is a movement. It is being 'called out', exodus, a 'lifting up of the head', a 'change of heart', 'imitation' and an acceptance of life and the history of suffering in the light of a great promise. There is no Church without this movement in which a people becomes the subject of a new history. That is why it began in history as a great movement of liberation—out of the compulsions of very early peoples. It is clear too from the early history of the Church how great a price it had to pay to liberate itself from the populism of the societies of the period and become a new people. The members of this new people were accused publicly of atheism and attacked on that account by the religions of the surrounding world.

Are the people of the Church really the subject of a new history of this kind and therefore the Church in this particular sense? Such terms as people's Church, people's religion and people's or popular Catholicism have at various times been current, but what have they really to do with the Church of Jesus Christ? We certainly have a much clearer idea now than we did in the past of the vast gulf between the existing faith of the people and the official faith of the Church, the religion of the people and the orthodoxy of the Church. The people often dismiss this orthodoxy as the expression of the religion of the Church's priests with which they have little to do because their own history seems not to be expressed in it or at the most hardly expressed at all. Who would wish to deny the existence of this alienation or 'schism'? There are many examples of it. Let us consider a few that occur in the popular Catholicism of Latin America.[3] They have parallels with the situation here.

According to a good deal of reliable evidence, faith in Jesus is not experienced in the popular Catholicism of Brazil as a faith that calls out, changes man's heart and mind and gives him hope and joy, but as a kind of mystical repetition of one's own painfully destroyed existence.[4] The following account of the experience of Holy Week in the Guatemalan Church is very characteristic: 'In Holy Week, there are frightening expressions of collective masochism in the processions of the heirs of the Mayas. Heavy crosses are carried. The participants share in the scourging of Jesus step by step in an endless climb to Golgotha. Amid cries of pain Jesus' death and burial become the participants' own death and burial, the worship of the destruction of the beautiful life in the distance. Holy Week of the Guatemalan Indians ends without the resurrection'.

I myself hesitated when I read this and felt that it was markedly Central European. I have quoted it, however, because it was written by a Latin American.[5] Other examples of Brazilian popular Catholicism show that the movement of conversion, the pathos of metanoia, openness to new life and the beginning of a new history in the presence of God are almost unknown in that country. There is strikingly magical and ritualistic association with the Church's signs and sacraments.[6] The Brazilian Catholic understanding of the Church is also problematical: 'In the eyes of the people, the Church is no more than the visible church building. It is a business belonging to the bishop and the priests in which certain needs can be satisfied. The idea that one can oneself be a member of such a Church is, of course, absolutely alien to this concept of the Church. The Church is seen as a "supermarket in which men buy divine goods" '. People buy these goods and pay the price that is asked without having anything further to do with the business itself. That is why the Brazilians pay without hesitation for the ceremonies that they have ordered, just as they pay the authorities for any service that is not necessarily religious. Even nowadays, despite the many reforms in liturgical matters, people still ask how much a baptism, a wedding or a mass will cost. What is almost completely absent, in other words, is a sense of responsible belonging to the Church.[7]

140

It should, incidentally, be noted in this context that these critical comments are not based on an ideal of a pure form of Christianity that can be separated from the 'pagan' traditions. There is, I believe, a form of paganism that is wanted by God even in the light of the Catholic traditions of Christianity. There is also a fear of contagion through contact with the pagans, which could be summarily described as 'typically Protestant'. Something else is clearly being criticised here—this Church for the people is obviously not a Church of the people and not even a Church in which this particular people sees itself as bearing the new history of God.

Who, then, is not happy about this schism between the official Church and the people? Who is alarmed about the prevalent heterodoxy of the people? A classical reaction on the part of theologians was to produce the doctrine of the implicit faith of the people and that of 'good faith', according to which everything that could not be justified as orthodox was attributed to good faith. These and similar interpretations did not, however, succeed in bridging the gulf between the Church and the people or in paying the price of orthodoxy. Such attempts are in the long run nothing other than symptoms of a new Christian populism that has taken the place of the earlier pagan populism. They try to make religion an instrument for the people. Christianity does not, however, present the people with any form of populism. On the contrary, it offers humanism. In other words, it fights with the aim of humanizing the people and makes it possible for the people to become subjects in the Church. It does not, however, do this on purely humanistic grounds. It does it in the knowledge of the price that must be paid for the orthodoxy of the people in the hope that the people will become the Church. It hopes, in other words, that the people will not simply be consumers of religion or an object of care and attention, but the subject of the Church and the new history of mankind with God that is made present in the Church. The aim of Christianity, then, is to enable the people to become the people of God.

With regard to the churches in those countries that we are primarily considering in this context, it is possible to say that the people there do not appear as the subject of the new history in the presence of God in the first place simply because they lack religious knowledge, theological education or information about the Church. The reason for this failure to become the subject of the new history

141

is because they are prevented from becoming that new people by the form of their history of suffering as a people. They are to some extent socially excommunicated by that history and excluded from the possibility of orthodox faith. The fact that it is impossible to be orthodox in certain inhuman circumstances is an argument in favour of the humanity of Christian faith, but it would be inhuman of Christianity to come to terms with the inhumanity of those circumstances. In such cases, consolation is insufficient. A cure has to be effected by transforming the conditions of life itself.

This does not in any way mean that Christianity is borne up by an illusion of a world that is completely free of suffering. The ideal of Christian freedom is not an abstract ideal of total emancipation and freedom from all suffering, an ideal which recognizes the history of human suffering simply as the absolute pre-history of human freedom. Christianity is not an ideology of apathy,[8] in which all suffering is objectivized and regarded as capable of being removed. It is therefore opposed to all political and social Utopias in which the history of suffering is unquestioningly identified with a history of oppression that can be abolished. In the Christian view, the vision of a world without social classes cannot be a vision of a world that is completely free of suffering if that vision is not to culminate in an apotheosis of pure banality. Christianity is therefore bound to be critical of such 'progressive' societies and to combat the anonymous prohibitions that they place on suffering and sorrow. The weapon used is not an abstract counter-cult of suffering. On the contrary, Christianity attempts to make men capable of experiencing the sufferings of others through their own capacity for suffering and in this way of being close to the mystery of Christ's suffering.[9]

The Church must, however, also resolutely accept the fundamental fact that there is a suffering that cannot be passed over in silence or transfigured by religion, but that has to be combated and transformed. This is not a commandment given by an alien political ideology, but the price of the people's orthodoxy, the price that has to be paid if the people themselves are to become the Church in the full sense of the word, the people of God and the subject of a new history with God. There is, in other words, a history of the people's suffering that again and again prevents that people from finding a new and living identity even in the Church, from learning how to write the language recording the memory of their own history of suffering in the *memoria passionis Jesu Christi* and from understanding the Bible as the mystical biography of his own history. I am referring here to the suffering that lets men become silent in the 'sorrow of this world' (as Paul called it, to distinguish it from the sorrow of Christians). This is the suffering that so destroys men and makes them so unrecognizable that they become as though they were 'no man's son'.[10] Who would venture to deny, with the southern countries in mind, that this kind of suffering exists, a suffering that cannot be accepted by Christianity because it has destroyed man's capacity to accept and to be a subject? Who would venture to dispute that this suffering is not simply confined to extreme individual cases or extreme examples of private unhappiness or misfortune, but can be recognized in a situation of suffering that has darkened the lives of entire groups and peoples—even inside the Church?

There is, then, this form of the history of suffering and this way in which the people suffer that cannot be made into an instrument, that only cynics can interpret as the privilege of the nobility, that leads to a rejection and even hatred of oneself and that forces entire peoples to lead lives lacking any form of self-assertion apart from a search for a simulated identity and expressions of frenzy. This form of suffering is certainly not a memory of God,[11] nor does it contain any memory at all or any hope.

How is it possible, then, for the Church to be here and for people to be here who are 'called out', people of the exodus, people of metanoia, people who 'lift up their heads'? There is, of course, authentic hope even in oppression. God must, of course, be remembered and praised even in misery. There is, of course, longing in the religious sense even when the people are socially injured and this longing is more than opium to deaden their own anonymous pain. It is, of course, also true that even here Christian hope expresses a longing that infinitely transcends all needs and their fulfilment. Otherwise only those men and women who had achieved full social humanity would be valid bearers of that hope and hope would then be the privilege of the later products of social and political development, those who had succeeded, the ultimate conquerors. It is worth repeating that the concrete social effort that is required here is not subject to the control of an alien political

143

ideology. It is the price of the people's orthodoxy that has to be paid if the people are to become the Church. This price has to be paid by everyone. As Charles Péguy said, 'We must pay the economic, social and industrial expenses—the temporal expenses. No one can avoid that—there is no escape, even for eternity, the spirit or the inner life'.[12]

The question of the price of orthodoxy is not simply a question of applied Christianity, a subsequent moral justification and confirmation of Christianity or the Church's practical expression of itself in love. On the contrary, it is part of the Church's constitution, a development of orthodoxy. It is here that we should look for the theological meaning of the overworked concept of orthopraxis. Understood in its correct sense, the term should not call a blind activism to mind, nor should it be seen as subjecting all Christian praxis to the compulsive interpretations of a society based purely on the satisfaction of its own needs, in which all public praxis is identified with that satisfaction. On the contrary, the term 'orthopraxis' draws attention above all to the need to pay the price of orthodoxy.

Has that price, however, possibly risen too high? Has what Chesterton called the adventure of orthodoxy become too dangerous? Is there really a desire to take orthodoxy seriously as applying to all men? Is it still known that to have right faith can make men free and happy? If that knowledge still exists, can any price be too high?

This question of the price of orthodoxy is one that is asked of the Church throughout the world. The Church should not simply reproduce the social contrasts that exist in the world in itself. If it did this, it would simply be helping the critics of religion and the Church to interpret religion as a superstructure and a function of certain social relationships. We should not as Christians accept the way in which the Church is becoming more and more a purely middle-class religion in the West, a religion of those who are fortunate, exempt from suffering or simply apathetic, while, in other parts of the world, it is becoming the religion of the unhappy or worse—the religion of slaves. What is so scandalizing in this process is not so much the fact that Christianity is a religion of the unhappy people of the world, a religion of slaves, as the fact that the Church brings together in itself both the unhappy and those who look at that unhappiness, both those who suffer and those who turn

144

away from suffering and calls itself as a whole a communion of the faithful.[13] Ought the members of this one Church not to insist upon the idea that they are all a people of God together with the Guatemalan Indians? If all were one, who could regard himself as innocent and unconcerned? Should not everyone pay the price, so that a new people will really emerge from all the many members? One people beyond all the natural communities? Was it not agreed a long time ago to reduce the price? This agreement was indeed reached in a fatal 'modernism of the heart', as Péguy called it, and it was decided to pay nothing at all and to opt for a 'solemn and glorious apparatus'.[14] This question of the price of orthodoxy is not simply incidental to the foundations of the Christian understanding of the Church.

3. Paradigms of a Church of the people?

We are bound, in this context, to look, at least indirectly, for historical models of this Church of the people to which we have referred again and again in the preceding sections. It would be unjust to attribute the constant appearance of the greater Church as a Church for the people rather than as a Church of the people simply and solely to an evil desire on the part of those holding office in the Church for power or to the continuing saturation of Church life and structures by an early form of populism. It may perhaps only be possible[15] to develop different forms of Church within the one Church in which all men can be called and accepted, in their own way and more fully than in the past, into and by the Church as a whole. With regard to the history of the Church, it is hardly possible to claim that there have already been forms or even preliminary forms of a Church of the people. What is particularly noticeable (and the reasons for this will have to be considered) is that this kind of people's Church has so far at least appeared mainly in minority movements and groups in the Church, many of which have later become sects.[16]

These movements, which, according to Francis and Dominic, brought the Gospel *non equester sed pedester* to the people,[17] in other words, at their own level, often had the effect of a salutary shock on the greater Church or a dangerous memory, reminding the Church that the process by which the people were to become subjects in the Church had not been forgotten. Characteristically, these movements were often lacking in theology. They did not see the Bible primarily as a book for exegetes, but mainly as a popular book or a mystical biography of the people, in which a divine interpretation of their sufferings and hopes could be found. The theme of imitation and especially the imitation of the cross was predominant in these movements. Jesus was not a fool or a rebel, but they knew that he was similar to both, since he was mocked by Herod as a fool and crucified by the Roman soldiers as a rebel. Imitation of Christ therefore meant for these movements a readiness to interchange these two roles. The theme of Jesus the poor man and the Church as the Church of the poor made a clearer impact in these movements than in the greater Church. They stressed the fact that the poor and little people were the privileged as far as Jesus was concerned and they wanted to make these poor and little people the privileged members of Jesus' Church. They sensed that the Church would survive the persecution of the powerful and the scorn of the clever men more easily than the doubts of the little and impotent people.

One may have the impression that to appeal to isolated movements of this sort, many of which were unable to survive in the greater Church, is useless and cannot be justified from the theological point of view. Is the fact that a movement does not last very long sufficient to prove that it is not authentic and is unsound from the point of view of theology and the Church? Is this proof of inauthenticity established because a movement is obscured or even crushed by other movements, dies and sinks into oblivion? Is it a false movement simply because all traces of it are obliterated by later, victorious movements? Ought our point of departure not to be the power of the Spirit of God and the fact that this Spirit blows where it will and also when it will and for as long as it will? And why should those who wait until the breath literally goes out of a new and perhaps troublesome movement or a new experience that is not understood wish to triumph? Is the longer breath of those movements that survive without being contested always incontestably the breath of the Holy Spirit? Does the Spirit always act in the history of the people of God according to the principle of *Vae Victis*? Is the Spirit, in other words, always effective in accordance with the principle by which we judge the meaning and progress of the history of the world and sometimes even the meaning and progress of the history of the Church? Is the history of the Spirit purely a history of triumph and conquest? This is very much open to doubt. Yet we may and indeed must, precisely for this reason, always remain open to such suppressed and forgotten movements in the history of the Church. Not, certainly, simply in order to canonize them, but in order to take up a new position with regard to their message and intention. In this sense, the memory of such new beginnings made from time to time is bound to remain a dangerous memory, a memory with a future. This memory can then become a liberating memory with regard to the Church's task to evolve within itself increasingly vital forms of a Church of the people.

4. Theology and people

In this context, I also have to say something about the relationship between theology and people. What is it that makes theology a theology of the Church? What does its orthodoxy consist of? What is the meaning of a theology for the Church, for the people's being and becoming Church and for the process by which the Church for the people becomes a Church of the people?

Who, too, is the adequate subject of a theology of the Church? The scholar? The professional theologian or specialist in God? The preacher? The pastor? The mystic gesticulating with his own existence? The individual Christian articulating his own history in the presence of God? The communion of the new people themselves, writing their collective religious biography, as did Israel and later the early Christian communities in important passages in the New Testament? Theology would then be the language of the people who had become conscious of their own history and had attained a new collective identity in God's presence as the Church. It would certainly seem as though it is not possible to give a simple answer to these questions if I am to avoid either abbreviating and archaically transfiguring the functions of theology or else exposing them to a purely esoteric professional theology.

In what sense, then, is theology a theology of the Church? Is it for the building up of the people of God? It clearly has this purpose in its educative function—it trains priests for the Church and the people of the Church. In this function it is possible to distinguish an

147

indirect contact with the people. At the same time, theology also interprets the statements made by the Church's teaching authority and makes them accessible to the people. It has to some extent the function of an official spokesman in clarifying the teaching and intentions of the Church's authority and situating them in a wider context. It is hardly possible to dispute the existence and legitimacy of these tasks, but we are bound to ask whether the strictly Church identity of theology comes to an end with these functions. Is the orthodoxy of theology defined in these tasks? Does theology not also have to speak directly in the interest of the Church for the people and indeed from the people? Does it not have to do this in its representative function and, as Thomas Aquinas intended, within the framework of a division of labour in the Church as the people of God? The theology of the Church is always trying to carry out this task. The history of theology bears witness to this representative function of theology. We must also ask whether a further step can be taken here in the theology of the Church. I believe that it must. Ought not the theologian always be ready to help the people themselves to speak? Ought he not have a maieutic function with regard to the people? Should he not commit himself to the task of enabling the people to take part and persist in their need to become the subject of the Church? Surely he should do all this, not simply as a pure task of enlightenment, education or information, but rather for the sake of the orthodoxy of theology? There can be, in my opinion, hardly anything that theology needs more than the religious experience that is expressed in the symbols and stories of the people. It needs this heritage very much if it is not to die of hunger because of its own concepts which are so seldom an expression of new religious experience and which so often simply reproduce the expressions of earlier experiences.

'Faith from hearing'—*fides ex auditu*—is always a question of listening to what the little and the poor people are saying, those 'to whom it is given'. In other words, it is not simply that the people need theology—theology also has an even greater need of the self-expression of the people. The symbols and stories of the people are irreplaceable. Nothing will take their place if the narrative tradition is interrupted or completely broken off and the people's memories are extinguished.

This point of view cannot be easily reconciled with a critical theology that has an unsympathetic attitude towards the myths, symbols, stories and mystical chronicles of the people. It cannot be easily reconciled with a theology that is concerned with pure argumentation and is theoretical in its approach to the contents of the people's stories. This kind of theology is nourished, either consciously or unconsciously, by two distinctions, both of which raise problems. The first is the distinction between faith and religion. This distinction is based on the assumption that man, as a believer, is living an abstract existence and is not a subject involved in experiences and stories or in his own history, a subject who is again and again identified in telling these stories and articulating these experiences in a symbolic manner. The second is the even more common distinction made between the people's Church and the Church of voluntary membership, between a traditional Christianity and an elective Christianity. This distinction is founded on the assumption that there could be a Church without a people and that people's collective memories and that a Church that was based simply on the free choice of individuals would not exist in a void because it lacked a normative tradition that communicated above all the contents of individual decisions.[18] These two distinctions can therefore be seen as theological attitudes taken by a religion that has its roots in the loss of historicity of middle-class society.

There is a false attempt to bridge the gap between theology and the people which characterizes modern theology regarded as the theoretical exponent of a middle-class religion: it is the attempt of bridging that gap by means of pure sociology. This mistake is made by all élitist views. Sociology is, after all, as far removed from the history of the life and suffering of the people as theology. And to transform theology into a form of sociology cannot make up for the loss of the people and society in theology. To change theology into sociology is to assume that the experiences of the people themselves and not simply data about attitude are expressed in sociology. It is therefore hardly surprising, if this is borne in mind, that more can be learnt about sociological theories (originally formulated by others) than about the history of the life and suffering of the people in many branches of modern progressive and critical theology.

As against this, there is also a simple, romantically regressive transfiguration of the 'people' which ultimately achieves nothing but a defamation of the achievement of critical theology. That, however, is certainly not the intention. Ultimately, what we have here is really critical theology. The critical interest of this theology, however, must always be governed by the conviction that the symbols, stories and collective memories of the people in the Church are absolutely necessary to any theology that wishes to avoid losing all foundation. Its critical attitude, in other words, should not lead to direct criticism of the symbolic world of the people. It ought, on the contrary, to lead to making the people more and more the subject of their own symbolic world. If it did this, these symbols would no longer be signs of alienation. They would rather be criticized by those who used them. In this case too, attention would once again be directed towards the need for the people to become, even vocally, the subject of the Church.

In order to achieve this, theology must assess the language of narrative differently. As I have already indicated several times in this book, a critical and political theology is bound to be concerned with narrative language. This concern is in no way an expression of a theological movement back to a pre-critical attitude.

Criticism of myth and ideology is also not rejected by this theology, but rather defined more precisely and given a more correct form and address. It is possible to say that the main task of critical theology is not to eliminate the religious symbolic world of the people, but to correct a wrong evaluation of it and to give it the right address. This task is based on the assumption that religious knowledge and a religious attitude are not simply innocent in the political and social sense. This theology's criticism of myth and ideology should therefore not be directed primarily against the people and their world of symbols, but rather against those who use those symbols wrongly, exploit them and apply them to the wrong ends. The first task, then, of the theologian who is engaged in the criticism of ideology is to be found here. It is not symbols, mysticism, the collective memory and its images that corrupt religion and deprive the people of their independence, but the way in which these are exploited for alien interests and can be used against the religious indentity of the people.

One of the great strengths of this critical theology in the sense in which I have defined it is that it is constantly examining itself and the situation in which it is placed at any given time. In other words, it is always able to question itself about the way in which it can, from its armchair position, criticize the experiences that are concentrated in these symbols and the extent to which it is justified, in the light of its purely theoretical construction of 'modern man', made at a desk, in defaming and demythologizing these symbols and calling them irrational.

There is a limit to the theological approach to the suffering of the people. This limit applies also to any attempt to do theology together with the people and to have a maieutic function with regard to their expression of suffering. It exists because of the sufferings that cannot be shared by theology. Theological argument has to be interrupted in view of these sufferings. Theology can only continue to narrate the history of salvation in a practical way, in other words, by being ready to act in a saving way.

5. A vision of a world-Church as the Church of the new people

I would like to conclude by outlining very briefly a vision of a world-Church that is to a great extent a Church of the people, a Church in which the people have emerged from their natural collective patterns of identity as a nation, race and class. This vision, then, is of a Church in which the people have become, historically, a new people and have found a new identity in the presence of God, a Church in which the claim that the Church is present for everyone does not seem like an empty acceptance of the weak and inarticulate because all men have become subjects in it.

The success of this Church is of the greatest importance for the future of the Church and for the future of religion as such. There are, after all, many dangers confronting the identity of the life of the Church, even in those social systems in which the Christian religion still has a place. This place is defined in strictly functional terms within the system. In other words, religion is tolerated as a means by which anxieties that are not understood are neutralized, painful disappointments in society are absorbed and dangerous memories and hopes that lead to rebellion within the life of society are made harmless. In brief, religion is there to bring stability to complex societies. Yet, whenever religion and the Church are re-

151

duced to a perfectly functional state, they die. The Church can only resist this danger in the long run when it is really living as a religious community in which all its members have become sub- jects, in other words, when an identity has developed in the Church, not imposed from above, but emerging from the religious experience of people themselves.

The success of this world-Church must also inevitably augur well for the future of life in society. The problems and the sufferings of the world have assumed enormous proportions. It is no longer pos- sible for social sufferings, in which entire peoples and nations are denied identity, to be overcome on a purely national scale. There is also another social threat to identity that exists on a world-wide scale—the silent disappearance of the subject and the death of the individual in the anonymous compulsions and structures of a world that is constructed of unfeeling rationality and consequently allows identity, memory and consciousness of the human soul to become extinct. If these dangers are to be overcome, identities must be fashioned that cannot be formed simply on the model of a pre- viously established collective identity. Confronted with these great needs and conflicts, does the Church simply present us with an im- potent promise? Or can it, as a world-Church—and can the world- Church as the Church of the new people—become a productive model of that identity? This is, of course, a vision. But is it only a vision?

Notes

1. This chapter is an adapted version, rewritten to fit into the whole concept of the book, of a text that first appeared in 1974. It was originally given as a paper at a conference in Madrid in April 1974 and first published as 'Kirche und Volk—oder der Preis der Orthodoxie' in *Stimmen der Zeit* (December 1974).

2. For an explanation of the various levels of meaning contained in the concept 'people', see, for example, *Evangelisches Staatslexikon* (Stuttgart, 1966), pp. 2442–2447. For the concept 'people of God', see the relevant theological lexicons and commentaries on the Second Vatican Council. For a discussion of the so-called 'people's Church' in the German-speaking countries, see *Herder-Korrespondenz* (February 1974). The word 'schism' is used here not in the dogmatic or legalistic sense, but sociologically.

3. In the arguments that follow, I have relied to a great extent on a dissertation,

hitherto unpublished, by the Brazilian theologian Luis Alberto De Boni, *Kirche auf neuen Wegen* (Münster, 1974).

4. See De Boni, *op. cit.*, p. 383.

5. E. Galeano, *Die offenen Adern Lateinamerikas* (Wuppertal, 1973), p. 63.

6. See De Boni, *op. cit.*, p. 384 ff.

7. See De Boni, *op. cit.*, p. 391.

8. See J. Moltmann, *The Crucified God* (New York, 1974); D. Sölle, *Leiden* (Stuttgart, 1973); J. B. Metz and J. Moltmann, *Leidensgeschichte* (Freiburg, ²1974).

9. See J. B. Metz and J. Moltmann, *Leidensgeschichte, op. cit.*

10. These words are based on a statement made by Brecht in his poem on the unkown soldier beneath the triumphal arch ("Gedicht vom unbekannten Soldaten unter dem Triumphbogen").

11. Following a statement by C. Pavese.

12. Charles Péguy, *Wir stehen alle an der Front. Deutsche Auswahl* (Einsiedeln, ²1952), p. 97.

13. See a study by Simone Weil, *Das Unglück und die Gottesliebe* (Munich, 1953), p. 47 ff.

14. See C. Péguy, *op. cit.*, p. 98.

15. Despite what is said below in section 5.

16. For the difference between the greater Church and a sect (a distinction that is not without its problems), see the classical studies of Ernst Troeltsch and Max Weber. Here, the distinction is used, not primarily in its normative sense, but rather in its descriptive sense. For what follows in this section, see a number of individual comments in D. Sölle and F. Steffensky, 'Christianity as Joy in Sects and Fringe Groups', *Concilium* 10 (May 1974), pp. 113–125.

17. In a polemical statement against the bishop-dominated Church of their own time.

18. 'Tradition' is, of course, not a history reconstructed by historical reason, at least for as long as our historical reason continues to conceal its narrative and memorative structures.

9. A transcendental and idealistic or a narrative and practical Christianity?
Theology in the face of the crisis of identity contemporary Christianity

1. A historical crisis of identity of Christianity? Theories, symptoms and reactions

There can surely be no religion or philosophy which is capable of such world-wide application as Christianity. Yet at the present time, when human beings are becoming more and more fully present as human beings, not simply intellectually, but in real historical processes, Christianity seems to have reached a state of extreme historical crisis—a crisis of identity. There is increasing reference to the 'post-Christian' or 'post-religious' world in which we are now living. There is a great deal of discussion about the disappearance or marginalization of Christianity and about its relegation to a position of powerlessness.

On the one hand, there is the neo-Marxist theory of the historical and dialectical heritage of Christianity, its critical potential, its liberating effect and essence. According to this theory, Christianity is effective and even indispensable in history in certain points of differentiation with regard to the accepted Marxist criticism of religion. It is not, however, effective in the strictly religious sense, but in its consistently secularized form as a Utopia that is successful in the traditions of revolutionary freedom.[1]

On the other hand, there is the evolutionary abolition of the Christian religion or the theoretical reconstruction of its cultural functions (in the widest sense) in the history of the evolution of mankind[2] on the basis of a logic of evolution that I have mentioned in various places in this book in an attempt to clarify both its theoretical status and its social implications.

154

There are, then, two different views of the historical fate of Christianity that have become important especially in the West. The first is the theory of the historical discontinuity between Christianity and the present age (this has been suggested principally to establish the legitimacy of the modern age [3]). The second is the view of the almost silent atrophy of the religious consciousness itself, the progressive disintegration of the assurance of religious identity in wide sections of society. [4]

With regard to the situation of religion as an institution and especially that of the Christian churches, an interesting theory of the churches as 'cognitive minorities' has been developed. Peter Berger, one of the leading protagonists of this theory, has claimed that, as far as Christianity is concerned, we may be fairly certain that there has been a considerable decline throughout the recent history of the West in the unquestioning acceptance that characterized the Christian religion in the past. The main consequence of this has, according to Berger, been a dilemma. As socially plausible structures of Christianity, the churches can either try to adapt themselves to the definitions of reality made by the surrounding world or strengthen their own position as cognitive minorities with regard to the world around them. There are, however, considerable difficulties involved in both these alternatives for the inner structure of Christianity. The first alternative threatens the spiritual content of Christianity. This, Berger insists, can only be adapted to a limited extent if it is not to lose its central character. The second alternative is in collision with the Christian churches' understanding of themselves that has existed since the time of Constantine as institutions that are involved in many different ways with society as a whole. [5]

These non-Christian or non-theological theories about Christianity in the modern age cannot be discussed in detail here and considered without regard to the situation or the subject, although it should be obvious that the question is dealt with, at least indirectly, again and again in the first two parts of this book. What we have to remember, however, is that they have certain analogies in the awareness of a state of crisis that exists in the minds of Christians and the life of the churches as a whole. Not only Christian intellectuals, but believers in general (and this is, of course, much more alarming) are beset by more and more doubts and anxieties. Is it not possible, at least in central Europe, to observe for the first time perhaps a widespread disappearance of inner and intense convictions about faith? Is there not, at all levels of society, an inability not only to be sorrowful, but also to be consoled? Is this inability not increasing? Is consolation not understood except as an impotent form of pacification? These symptoms and others that are related to them [6] in the heart of Christian life today would seem to point to the real existence of a crisis of identity in Christianity of the kind that has already been established in theory.

The Church is reacting, at least in the West, with increasing fear and anxiety. The process in which the Church is at present involved can, I believe, be described as one of stabilization through fear, a process that can be organized by a successful Church administration. The danger, however, is obvious. Stabilization through fear is in itself without any perspective and extremely subject to crisis. In it, the anonymous pressure exerted by unknown dangers is not overcome, but suppressed.

In this situation, no help can be gained either from the theological reaction by which this historical crisis of identity in Christianity is assessed and interpreted by drawing attention to the constant situation of contestation and suffering in which Christianity has always been placed and which every Christian has always had to take into account. This datum is abstract in the light of the concrete historical situation of crisis which is, in the last resort, not simply a situation of crisis in Christianity alone. It can easily become an excuse mechanism which only looks for the causes of this crisis outside Christianity itself and therefore cannot lead to any new praxis among Christians. We cannot unfortunately go into the other direct and therefore typical apologetical reactions to this crisis as it is known or felt to exist. (These include, for example, the neo-fundamentalist tendencies and references not to a radical but to a 'pure' form of Christianity fostering a sectarian attitude and semantic.) We are, on the contrary, bound to direct our attention to theologically developed theories about the present situation of Christianity.

2. Theological theories about the present situation of Christianity: a spectrum of positions

There are different forms of theological theories of secularization. The history of what is known as secularization in the modern era (in the widest sense) is interpreted either as a history of falling away from Christianity (this is the traditional interpretation in Catholic theology) or else as the history of either the effect or else the fulfilment of Christianity. I shall not, however, discuss these theological theories or theses[7] here, as I have already done so earlier in this volume (in Chapter 2 above) and as they moreover are not directly linked with the theological approaches that are to be deliberated in this section (the traditional Catholic version forms an exception here).

I give the theories about the present situation of Christianity that have been elaborated in argument and are therefore effective from the theological point of view the rather cursory description of transcendental and idealistic theories. This title therefore includes such different approaches as the universally historical and the transcendental approaches. If I am lacking in consideration in my generalized description of these approaches, it is because I want to clarify in as few words as possible the intention underlying the post-idealistic narrative and practical-political approach.

Among the universally historical approaches that are described (critically) in this chapter as 'idealistic' are not only Wolfhart Pannenberg's influential ontology of history and meaning that is strongly orientated towards Hegel and in which the idea of a meaning of history is not a category of practical reason, but (following idealistic traditions) a category of reflection. A universally historical and idealistic conception—in the sense of a stage in the history of human freedom that can be eschatologically and messianically integrated into Christianity—has, I believe, been provided by Jürgen Moltmann, in his impressive attempt to interpret the present situation of Christianity in the light of the revolutionary history of freedom.[8] T. Rendtorff's theory of Christianity, which is based on liberal traditions, can also be regarded, for different reasons, as belonging to this approach. According to Rendtorff, the present position of Christianity is a form of expression guaranteeing the middle-class history of freedom. (This is, of course, an extremely

157

truncated version of Rendtorff's interpretation.) Despite all their individual differences, however, these theories have one thing in common—they all work with great precision on history as the place where the crisis of identity has occurred in Christianity and they are all developed in accordance with a universally historical and idealistic concept.

As opposed to this first group of theories, there is one consistently elaborated theological theory of the present situation of Christianity in the Catholic world (which has an influence far beyond Catholicism). This is the transcendental theory of anonymous Christianity as developed by Karl Rahner.[9] In describing this theory as a transcendental and idealistic concept, I take as my point of departure the practical fundamental theology that I have outlined above (in Chapter 4) as a criticism of the transcendental theology of the subject. I do this in the hope that the critical questions that I ask about this theory will direct our attention to a post-idealistic narrative and practical understanding of Christianity and the Christian identity. I have already had something to say about the position occupied by memory and narrative as categories of practical reason that have the function of saving identity in an earlier chapter (Chapter 4) and shall have more to say later in the last part of this book (Categories).

The theory of anonymous Christianity sees the historical crisis of identity in the form of the dilemma that arises on the one hand from the increasingly obvious social particularity of the Church and on the other from the universal nature of the Church's mission and of God's saving will as represented in the Church. This theory seems to me to be dominated both by the central theological idea of God's free and universal will to save and by human respect for the hidden depths of man's existence, which is not open to absolute reflection and within which man is always to some extent anonymous even to himself. In his theory of anonymous Christianity, Rahner has only extrapolated his transcendental view of man as the being who has withdrawn from himself into God or as the being who is 'condemned to transcendence', who is 'always already with God', even in every act of denial of God, and whose freedom consists (only) in accepting this being (in faith) or in suppressing it (in lack of faith). In his reflective articulation of this freedom, man has to take into account dissonances and even contradictions between what is explicitly said and what is done in fact, between acts of freedom and reflective self-assurance and so on. It would, of course, be impossible to examine here Rahner's profound and highly developed theory of transcendental faith, which is obviously based on an idealistic theory of knowledge and on the traditional doctrine of *fides implicita* and *bona fides*. All that I can do here is to point to the result of this approach when it is applied to a theological theory about the present situation of Christianity.

A distinction has to be made between a Christianity that understands itself in reflection and is institutionalized in Church orthodoxy on the one hand and that anonymous Christianity on the other hand in which man can freely and fundamentally decide in favour of God without this having or even being able perhaps to understand itself as such in reflection. (It is even possible for this decision to express itself—under the anonymous pressure of a pre-individual and socially structured 'atheism'—'atheistically'). Nowadays, the Church is no longer able to reach a great number of people and is bound to take seriously into account that it will not be able, in the future, to make many people and groups of people explicitly Christian. This means that, according to Rahner's theory, the salvation of these people can be seen by the Church as possible in an anonymous form of Christianity.

3. The theory of anonymous Christianity—a few questions

Without repeating what I have already said, I should like in this section to consider the theory of anonymous Christianity by asking a few questions. I do this rather than criticize the theory, because I cannot be sure that the level of what has to be criticized can as yet be reached by criticism (and also because no viable alternative has as yet been provided to the theory in questions).

1. Does the doctrine of transcendental faith that is at the basis of this theory of anonymous Christianity not bear too strongly the marks of an élitist idealistic gnoseology? The great mass of people are saved by viture of their *fides implicita* and their attitude of *bona fides*. The real relationships are known to the few who possess the 'high gift of the wise'.[10] Rahner, whose entire theological disposition makes him turn away from an élitist attitude perhaps more than

any other theologian, has himself raised this objection. His reference, however, to the marks of élitism in 'sublime aesthetic, logical, ethical and other forms of knowledge' which he believes apply to all men, but are only known to a few[11] does not convince me at least. Full and explicit (!) knowledge of faith is after all a practical knowledge. In its distinctive character, it is incommensurable with purely scientific or idealistic forms of knowledge.[12] It is possible to speak of an arcane knowledge in the case of a full knowledge of faith, but this arcanum cannot be the arcanum of a philosophical gnosis—an élitist idealism—but must be the arcanum of a practical knowledge. It cannot be the arcanum of a Socrates, but must be the arcanum of Jesus, in other words, the practical arcane knowledge of the imitation of Christ.[13]

2. Do we not have, in this form of transcendental Christianity, a form of over-justification and over-identification of Christianity in the face of the growing historical threat to its identity? Is the historical identity of Christian faith not fixed, in this theory, to a basic anthropological structure, according to which man is 'always already', whether he wants to be or not, 'with God'? It would certainly be a fundamental misunderstanding of Rahner's transcendental theology if we were to assume that its aim was simply to introduce Christian faith subsequently into a previously existing anthropological structure. The transcendental process works in the opposite direction, according to Rahner's explicit description of it. The actual historical experience of man in Christian faith is generalized and becomes the 'categorial' pre-condition for our understanding of man as an absolutely transcendent being. The question remains, however, as to whether it is possible to generalize by means of speculative thought a historical experience (such as that of Christian faith), which is always threatened because of its historical character and whose identity is always endangered for the same reason. It may in fact only be possible to generalize this experience by means of a praxis for which no theological compensation can be found by transcendental reflection, but which must be remembered and narrated.

If we are to elaborate the idea of a narrative and practical Christianity further, we have first to extend our criticism, both that of Rahner's transcendental and idealistic theory and also (at least in outline) that of the universally historical and idealistic conceptions. My criticism, then, is principally directed against the attempt to explain the historical identity of Christianity by means of speculative thought (idealism), without regard to the constitutive function of Christian praxis, the cognitive equivalent of which is narrative and memory.

4. A fairy-story—to be read 'against the grain'

To clarify what I mean by this criticism, I should like to recall one of the best-known German fairy-stories, that of the hare and the hedgehog. One Sunday morning, the hedgehog is going for a walk in a ploughed field and a hare teases him about his bandy legs. He challenges the hare to a race in the furrows of the field. First, however, he goes home to breakfast because, as he tells the hare, he cannot run on an empty stomach. He then returns with his wife, who is exactly the same in appearance as her husband, and gets her to stand at the far end of the furrow. He himself stands at the other end beside the hare in another furrow. The hare falls for this trick. He runs and runs in his furrow, but the hedgehog is (in both positions) 'always already' there. In the end, the hare falls dead from exhaustion on the field.

The 'little ones' of this world, who are always slow and therefore deprived in life and for whose encouragement this fairy-story was presumably written, may let me perhaps tell this story 'against the grain', in other words, against their own fully-justified intention and for a moment take the side of the hare, who runs and runs and in the end falls dead in the race, while the hedgehog wins by a cunning trick and does not even have to run. If we opt for the hare, we opt to enter the field of history, a field that can be measured in running the course or the race, in competition or in flight (one is reminded here of the images used in the Pauline traditions for the historical and eschatological life of Christians). And this option for the hare also means that we must try to expose critically the idealistic guarantee of the threatened identity of Christianity. This guarantee leaves out of account the power of praxis to save the historical identity of Christianity and acts as a kind of theological hedgehog trick which aims to safeguard the identity and triumph of Chris-

161

tianity without the experience of the race (that is, without the experience of being threatened and possibly of being defeated).

5. The exposure of the hedgehog trick or a criticism of the transcendental and idealistic versions of the guarantee of identity

There are two versions of this hedgehog trick, both of which can be used to explain both the universally historical and the transcendental attempt to undermine history.

The first version of the hedgehog trick stands for the universally historical and idealistic approaches. Like the two hedgehogs, those who suggest these approaches have the course of history in view. Because they view it from both ends, however, there is no need to enter it. The hare runs and the hedgehog stands in a trick situation of duplication at the relay points of history as a whole. In this way, history is made into a movement of the so-called objective spirit which we have already seen through. And theology is made a kind of information service for world history, but one that is consulted less and less by the public.

The ultimately promised saving meaning of history is not disclosed as it were while the course of that history is being run. It is not evoked, remembered and narrated (for all men) as a practical experience of meaning in the middle of our historical life. It is, so to speak, rigidified into a definition for reflection that cannot be affected by collective historical fears or threats of catastrophe and is therefore not in need of any hope provided with expectation. The present state of meaning has had all its wrinkles ironed out and is free of all contradictions. It is, as it were, 'hopelessly' total. There is only a very weak eschatological and apocalyptical sense of danger and of the needs of the age. This eschatological consciousness has been successfully removed from the theologies of history and transferred to the realm of individual history.

The second version of the hedgehog trick stands for the transcendental and idealistic approach, the idea of a transcendental Christianity. The hare runs and the two hedgehogs are 'always already' there. In the North German fairy-story, the hedgehog husband and wife alternate with each other, calling: 'I am already here'. By means of their transcendental omnipresence, they harass the hare to death. In this second version, is not the threatened historical identity of Christianity guaranteed for too high a price: the price of confusing identity with tautology? The two hedgehogs—the hedgehog's wife is exactly the same in appearance as her husband—stand for this tautology and the running hare stands for the possibility at least of historical identity. The running itself, during which it is also possible to remain motionless, belongs, together with its danger, to the guarantee of identity. Nothing can compensate for it transcendentally. In my opinion, everything else leads in the end to tautology—one hedgehog is exactly the same as the other, the beginning is like the end, paradise is like the end of time, creation is like the fulfilment and at the end the beginning repeats itself. History itself—with its forms of identity that are constantly threatened and in danger of being overcome—cannot intervene. The transcendental magic circle is complete and, like the two hedgehogs, it cannot be overcome.[14] One therefore suspects that the process of transcendentalization of the Christian subject may have been guided by a tendency to unburden and immunize. Should this process of transcendentalization not give Christianity a kind of imnipresence which would ultimately remove it from every radical threat in the sphere of history? Is the vanguard of the historical and apocalyptical attack made by Christianity and its identity not destroyed by this process of transcendentalization of the Christian subject and is the battle therefore not prematurely broken off?

6. A plea for a narrative and practical Christianity

In this section, I consider one of the most decisive questions, perhaps the most decisive of all: Can there be another point of departure for Christian theology apart from the one that insists that the universal meaning of history and the historical identity of Christianity is already established? How could universally historical meaning continue to be called into question for theology? Has history not been saved a long time ago in the definitive eschatological action of God in Jesus Christ? Is it not essential for theology to argue as both the approaches that are criticized here do, that is, transcendentally or universally historically? Is Christian theology in this sense not necessarily idealistic? And should it therefore, for its own sake, not accept the criticism that it does not take history, with all its contradictions, antagonisms, struggles and sufferings, seriously and that it makes an 'as if' problem of it? Does not every other attempt lead to a contradictory idea of a conditioned salvation or to a confusion of salvation and Utopia?

That is why attempts are made (in these approaches and generally) to save history by transferring man's experience of contradictions, non-identity and possible failure and the experience of the absence of salvation to the sphere of individual history. This individual history is all that matters. The individual can apply the eschatologically definitive history of salvation to himself. He can also dissociate himself from it. The history of salvation subsists to some extent without reference to history. It is only historical as a history of application or renunciation.

How, then, can these 'solutions' avoid the danger of regarding history as a history of salvation considered as a totality without reference to the subject, in other words, of looking over the heads of the people who are bowed down under their own histories of suffering? Does this one, universal history of salvation that is founded in Christ not take place in the histories of salvation? But how does this take place? And how is it possible to speak about it if, in the case of the history of salvation, the idea of a history without reference to the subject is denied? Finally, should the salvation of the whole of history that has been promised at the end of time be reduced to a harmless, teleological history of meaning in which it is no longer possible to consider seriously, let alone provide a conscious theological assessment of the catastrophic element that is present in that history?[15]

It is because of the existence of these questions that I make a plea for a narrative and practical structure of Christianity, its historical identity and its idea of eschatological salvation. Has narrative not, after all, to do with (individual) histories? And does the emphasis on the narrative identification of the Christian identity not point clearly in the direction of individual histories in which individuals apply the universal history of salvation to themselves or deny themselves that history?

In this context, it is important to point to one very decisive factor. As distinct from pure discourse or argument, narrative makes it possible to discuss the whole of history and the universal meaning of history in such a way that the idea of this universal meaning is not transferred to a logical compulsion of totality or a kind of transcendental necessity, as a result of which the mystical-political histories of individuals would be of secondary importance in comparison with the saving meaning of history as a whole and could only be incorporated subsequently into the framework of a definitive history dissociated from the subject. In the narrative conception of Christian salvation, history and histories—the one history of salvation and the many histories of salvation and the absence of salvation of individuals—merge together without diminishing each other.[16] The individual histories do not take place without regard to the previously narrated history of salvation and the history of salvation is able to assimilate the individual histories. The narrated (and remembered) universality and definitiveness of the meaning of history mean that the historical praxis of opposition to meaninglessness and the absence of salvation is not superfluous, because it is transcendental or universally historical, but indispensable.

The universality of the offer of salvation in Christianity does not have the character of a transcendental or universally historical concept of universality. It has rather the character of an 'invitation'. The inviting logos of Christianity does not in any sense compel. It has a narrative structure with a practical and liberating intention. If this is expressed in Christological terms, it means that the salvation that is founded 'for all men' in Christ does not become universal via an idea, but via the intelligible power of a praxis, the praxis of following Christ. This intelligibility of Christianity cannot be transmitted theologically in a purely speculative way. It can only be transmitted in narrative—as a narrative and practical Christianity.[17]

It is also clear from this that the so-called historical crisis of identity of Christianity is not a crisis of the contents of faith, but rather a crisis of the Christian subjects and institutions which deny themselves the practical meaning of those contents, the imitation of Christ.

The imitation of Christ is a question of decisive importance for the version of the crisis of identity that is served up every day in many varieties of the criticism of religion and ideology and which has become popular, within Christianity, in the catch phrase: "Yes to Jesus, no to the Church'. What we have here is a deep suspicion, rooted in the pre-rational Christian consciousness, that the living identity of the Christian body with Jesus has become lost in later Christianity, that Christianity cast off its conformity to Christ a long time ago and that many of Jesus' intentions were long ago successfully taken over by other historical movements. This suspicion cannot be reduced simply by interpreting more subtly the historical attitude of Christianity, in other words, by a more scholarly form of hermeneutics and a more critical reconstruction of the history of Christianity. It can only be diminished by providing evidence of the spirit and power of Christianity in consistent imitation of Christ, in other words, by practical conformity to Christ. Our memories of the failure of Christianity and the deeply rooted disappointments felt by individuals and whole groups and classes of people cannot be overcome and eliminated from the world simply by means of rational explanation. For even if we were to keep strictly to the details of history in opposition to the collective memories of suffering, we would not be regarded as in any sense justified in the presence of those memories. It is clear, then, that this version of the crisis of identity of Christianity also compels us to accept the praxis of the imitation of Christ and points at the same time to the urgent need for a narrative and practical Christianity.

I have already dealt with a series of fundamental questions that are related to the version of a narrative and practical form of Christianity that I have briefly outlined here as post-idealistic. I have done this above all in Chapters 7 and 8 and shall be considering such questions again in Chapters 11 and 12 below. All that I have said in connection with these problems must lead to a reduction and even a complete suppression of the suspicion that this narrative and practical identification of Christianity is basically a form of regression or evasion in defining historical identity. The idealistic misunderstanding both of the intelligible status of praxis and of the practical status of narrative (and memory) as categories that are capable of saving identity that is present in this suspicion ultimately redounds on the critics themselves.

Notes

1. In this case, religion is certainly not excessively privatized, as it is in middle-class societies, but it is radically secularized. I at least find it very difficult to see how it can in this way preserve its identity. What is more, this identity is not, from the purely historical and social point of view, simply available to us. Two indispensable aspects of its identity are, for example, prayer and mysticism. It is a form of semantic deception to continue to speak affirmatively about religion while at the same time not accepting it as valid and dismissing it as a false form of consciousness. It is better in this case to speak of a utopia, which is the object of nobody's prayers. It is important to say this explicitly because we should not, while criticizing the excessive privatization of religion in middle-class societies, become blind to the danger that is inherent in the neo-Marxist secularization of religion.

2. See, for example, C. Seyfarth and W. Sprondel, eds., *Seminar: Religion und Entwicklung* (Frankfurt, 1973).

3. See the relevant works by H. Blumenberg.

4. Habermas has insisted on this in various statements that he has made recently. These comments are, however, sporadic and Habermas has not gathered them together to form a theme.

5. P. L. Berger, 'Zur Soziologie kognitiver Minderheiten', *IDZ* (1969), Heft 2.

6. For these other symptoms of the crisis and the reaction of the Church to them, see J. B. Metz, *Followers of Christ*, p. 30 ff.

7. The term 'theory' is used here in the wider sense in which it is employed as a means of characterizing theological concepts.

8. See J. Moltmann, 'Die Revolution der Freiheit', *Perspektiven der Theologie* (Munich, 1968), pp. 189–211.

9. In this context, the most important of Rahner's volumes in his *Schriften zur Theologie* to be consulted are VIII to X (E.T.: *Theological Investigations* 9, 11, 12, 14). See also, for discussion of this theory, E. Klinger, ed., *Christentum innerhalb und ausserhalb der Kirche* (Freiburg, 1976).

10. See the relevant statements in Rahner's *Schriften zur Theologie* IX (1970), p. 192 (*Theo. Inves.* 11:180).

11. *Op. cit.*, p. 190 (E.T.: p. 179).

12. In this particular question, the difference in the theological theory of knowledge between tanscendental theology and a practical fundamental theology breaks through.

13. It is only in this way that it is possible to avoid the danger of making a full knowledge of faith, in other words, orthodoxy, an élite form of orthodoxy that could never be an affective form of popular orthodoxy. It might perhaps be an orthodoxy based on a feudalistic dependence in a 'Church for the people', but it could never be the orthodoxy of a 'Church of the people', in which the people themselves have come of age and have become the subject of their religious identity.

14. I am, of course, not of the opinion that Rahner's theology is in any way tautological (just as Barth's theology is not tautological).

15. We are bound to question the frequently loose employment of the term

'meaning' (especially in the context of the 'meaning of history') in theology. The term has undeniably become the darling of theologians and, like all favourite children has quickly become spoilt and overestimated. It is, of course, true that theologians cannot dispense with this category (even in its general sense), but they should not forget that this meaning is not entirely without danger, an article that can be taken unthinkingly out of the bronze treasure-houses of ontology whenever it ought really to be introduced and defined by the intelligible power of Christian action itself. There is no way of making sure of meaning, either transcendentally or in the universally historical sense. In their discussion of the question of meaning, theologians should therefore not let themselves be tempted by the desire to objectivize meaning or to ignore and therefore, in a spirit of apocalyptical unconsciousness, to forget that the one towards whom Christians direct their expectation of meaning will come again not only as the one who will complete the kingdom of God, but also as the one who will overcome the antichrist. This implies that Christians have also to bear in mind what Ernst Bloch has said, in his well-known adaptation of Hölderlin's saying: 'When salvation approaches, the danger increases'.

16. This narrative mediation is, in my opinion, of great importance in a Christian theology of religions. Narrative and practical Christianity can, in its encounter with these other religions, keep hold of its eschatological and universal history of meaning without at the same time having to accept the histories of the other religions in a totality of meaning.

17. For a more exhaustive treatment of the narrative and practical structure of Christology, see J. B. Metz, *Followers of Christ,* p. 50 ff.

10. Hope as imminent expectation or the struggle for forgotten time

Noncontemporaneous theses on the apocalyptic view

The thirty-five theses that follow in this chapter—some of them can be read as comments and suggestions—are intended above all as corrections. Because their aim is to clarify what is perceived as a danger or a need, such corrections are often exaggerated. This should be borne in mind when the theses are critically examined. The apocalyptic element is used in them to give expression to the time factor in theology and Christianity. The aspect of expectation in Christian hope is stressed in order to bring Christian praxis—the imitation of Christ—within the scope of time. I would like to emphasize that my observations are based on the fact that the crisis in Christianity is not really a crisis of its message and the content of faith, but rather a crisis of its subjects and institutions, in that these are too remote from the practical meaning of the Christian message.

These theses also constitute my own special tribute to the late Ernst Bloch and his apocalyptic wisdom, a vision that he inherited from the Jewish traditions that have for too long been closed to Christianity. In the last letter that he wrote to me, Bloch spoke about the difficulty of living 'with a real belief in the momentary expectation of the last things . . . presence as such, even though it may be treacherously ironed out, is the opposite of an apocalyptically conscientous presence'. Christian theologians can learn from Bloch even if they have to contradict him.

Symptoms of timelessness

I

The age of timelessness. No one has time. No one takes time. May it be that the demands made on everyone are an expression of defeatism, a special form of resignation that is produced by our experience of timeless time?

II

The age of the inflation of time: 'Twins travel to eternity'. On 19 August 1977, it was reported that the space flight of Voyager I and Voyager II would, as far as could be predicted, never end. Both had left the solar system. In 40,000 years at the earliest, they would fly past another star. (The enlightened King of Prussia, Frederick the Great, believed, no doubt in accordance with the teaching of the Bible, that the world was 5,000 years old!)

III

There is a cult today of the makeable—everything can be made. There is also a new cult of fate—everything can be replaced. The will to make is undermined by resignation. The cult of the omnipotent control of man's destiny on the one hand and the cult of apathy and unpolitical life (which will be brought to light by the perfection of technology) on the other belong together like two sides of the same coin. Man's understanding of reality, which guides his scientific and technical control of nature and from which the cult of the makeable draws its strength, is marked by an idea of time as a continuous process which is empty and evolving towards infinity and within which everything is enclosed without grace. This understanding of reality excludes all expectation and therefore produces that fatalism that eats away man's soul. Man therefore is already resigned even before society has been able to introduce him successfully to this resignation as a form of pragmatic rationality.

IV

Samuel Beckett's *Waiting for Godot* is not a play that can be easily twisted into an eschatological drama about man's waiting for God. It may, however, be a play about waiting or, more accurately, a play about man's catastrophic inability to wait.

V

Catastrophes are reported on the radio in between pieces of music. The music continues to play, like the audible passage of time that moves forward inexorably and can be held back by nothing. As Brecht has said, 'When crime is committed, just as the rain falls, no one cries: Halt!'

VI
The shortest definition of religion: interruption.

VII
The first categories of interruption: love, solidarity, which, as M. Theunissen has said, takes time, memory, which remembers not only what has succeeded, but also what has been destroyed, not only what has been achieved, but also what has been lost and in this way is turned against the victory of what has become and already exists. This is a dangerous memory. It saves the Christian continuum.

Timelessness as a system
VIII
There is a new form of metaphysics, called evolutionary logic. In it, time has been made indifferent and has come systematically to control man's universal consciousness. Everything is timelessly and continually reconstructed on the basis of this philosophy. This includes the religious consciousness and the dialectical criticism of religion.

IX
This evolutionary logic has not developed in any sense meaningfully. It has become an acceptance of technical rationality which can no longer be justified and within which structures, tendencies and forms of greater or lesser complexity can be distinguished and selected, but which can never be made more clear. This evolutionary logic works functionally with the help of different symbols and is also guided by the fundamental symbol of evolution itself. This symbol, however, is no more rational than the time-symbols of religion and is far more difficult to penetrate than they are. As Nietzsche pointed out, 'evolution does not aim at happiness; it is only concerned with evolution'.

X

We are not concerned here with the use of evolution in the empirical natural sciences or in politics, but with its ideological application, that is, with the generalization of the symbol of an undirected evolution that is almost mythical. Criticism of evolutionary logic can help directly to delimit and clarify the theoretical status of evolution.

XI

The symbols used to enable us to understand the concept of time have changed. The apocalyptic symbolism of discontinuity and the end of time has given way to the pseudo-religious symbol of evolution which, in its impenetrable way, has penetrated to the depths of everyone's consciousness, to such an extent that its irrational control and its quasi-religious totality have become almost imperceptible. The extensive use of the word 'evolution' in all spheres of life is a sign of this irrational position of influence.

XII

Revolutionary consciousness in the grip of evolutionary timelessness: Marx, who praised revolutions as the locomotives of world history. Walter Benjamin has suggested that it may be quite different from this and that revolutions are really the hand of the human race, travelling in this train, on the emergency brake.

XIII

The modern world, with its scientific and technical civilization, is not simply a rational universe. Its myth is evolution. The silent interest of its rationality is the fiction of time as an empty infinity, which is free of surprises and within which everyone and everything is enclosed without grace. The social signs are easy to discern—on the one hand, widespread apathy and, on the other, unreflecting hatred; on the one hand, fatalism and, on the other, fanaticism.

Theology in the grip of timelessness

XIV

The theme of imminent expectation, which is central in the New Testament, is again and again discussed in Christian theology, yet

172

it strikes modern man, who has for so long thought of time as an empty, evolutionary continuum stretching into eternity, as an enormous claim, a myth dating from ancient times. Nonetheless, the theological re-interpretation of the idea of imminent expectation as 'constant expectation' or 'constant readiness' (in other words, as a timeless existential experience) is really a semantic deception and misleading to the temporal structure of Christianity, since the latter has not a timeless, but a temporal essence. This re-interpretation is an indirect confirmation of the extent to which theology has submitted to the anonymous pressure of an evolutionary consciousness of time or rather an evolutionary disintegration of time. This applies even more to those who, with radical honesty, believe that the problem of imminent expectation has already been solved because the parousia has not come, but time has, as any rational person can see, continued. Any theology, however, which accepts the idea of time that is current in an evolutionary view of history, in which time is seen as a continuous process, will lose everything else (together with the idea of imminent expectation).

XV

Rudolf Bultmann maintained that the problem of mythical eschatology had been solved by the simple fact that Christ's parousia had not, as the New Testament expected, taken place, but that world history had continued and would—as every person of sound judgment knew—continue on its course. Afraid of unsound judgment, theology long ago fled into the gentle arms of evolutionism and especially historical evolutionism. This embrace will, however, prove fatal. The logic of evolution is the rule of death over history—in the end, everything makes as little difference to it as death. Nothing that has ever been can be spared its continuity, that is indifferent and without grace. This evolutionary logic is not innocent, nor is it (in the sense of a methodological atheism) agnostic. In evolutionary logic, God—the God of the living and the dead, the God who does not let the past, the dead, rest in peace—is simply unthinkable. It is, far more than any form of emphatic atheism, which remains rooted in negation, a real absence of God.

XVI

Theology in the grip of timelessness: even with its concentration on time, it has not been possible for Christianity to break this grip;

173

this concentration has led to the idea of the paradox of time and eternity. This eternity, however, as the opposite of human time, is not God, but nature or rather *Deus sive natura*. In the Bible, God is not the opposite of time, but the end of time, its delimitation and discontinuity—and therefore its possibility.

XVII

All the prevailing versions of modern eschatology—both present- and future-oriented versions—seem to have been successfully adapted to an evolutionary understanding of time that is alien to them. This understanding has compelled the Christian imminent expectation (if it has not already been dropped in advance) to become extremely privatized—to the death of the individual—and has induced it either to think of the future of God as strictly timeless or to project that future on to an evolutionary scheme with the help of a transcendental or universally historical teleology.

XVIII

The deep error of theology, our unawareness of the problem of time, is strikingly evident in the distinction that is made between horizontal and vertical in theology and Christianity in general. As a criterion for eschatological consciousness—cross-wires in the sight, to focus on one's opponent!

XIX

The evolutionary ideal of time is so dominant nowadays that the kingdom of God is sometimes deprived of all sense of time. (The kingdom of God is contrasted with the kingdom of this world and transcendence is contrasted with immanence.) Sometimes, however, it is made to fit into a pattern of evolution in which the category of fulfilment is regarded as an evolutionary process and the kingdom of God is seen as a pure utopia that is achieved by means of human progress. Neither of these approaches does justice to the essential element of time in the Christian message of the kingdom of God.

XX

Taking everything into consideration, is it possible to look forward to the end of time? Or has the expectation of an end of time become no more than the expression of a mythical eschatology, because time itself has become a homogeneous continuum that is without surprises, a bad infinity in which anything can happen? Anything, that is, except one thing: that moment which becomes the 'gate through which the Messiah enters history' (W. Benjamin on the Jewish idea of the Messiah) and because of this surprising moment would time be found for time?

XXI
'It is time for it to be time; it is time' (Paul Celan).

Against the grip of timelessness: memory of the apocalyptical vision

XXII
It is not utopias that can break the grip of timelessness, but the eschatological consciousness that does not let its apocalyptical sting be drawn by evolution. Utopias would prove to be the ultimate trick of evolution if only they existed and no God (in whose presence the past is not secure).

XXIII
The apocalyptical vision in the history of religion: whenever it has become exhausted in number games and idealistic calculations forecasting the progress of the history of salvation, it is clear that it was already exhausted and degenerate. It used to be a mystical analogy with an experienced political reality. We can learn the nature of this political reality by examining the history of religion and the New Testament. They were times of crisis, persecution, large-scale injustice and hatred.

XXIV
The Jewish-Christian apocalyptical vision has correctly been described by Ernst Käsemann as the 'mother of Christian theology'. It came to be regarded not as a mythical expulsion of time into a rigid world pattern, but rather as a process by which time could be restored to the world. In that case, we can see man's consciousness of catastrophe as expressed in the apocalyptical vision basically as a consciousness of time, not a consciousness of the time of catastro-

175

phe, but a consciousness of the catastrophic nature of time itself, of the character of discontinuity and the end of time. This catastrophic nature of time calls the future into question. It is, however, precisely for this reason that it becomes authentic future, acquires a temporal structure and loses its character of timeless infinity into which the presence can be projected and extrapolated at will. (The catastrophic images of the apocalyptical vision are above all prohibitions with the future in mind, in other words, prohibitions against thinking of the future simply as an empty screen on which images can be projected.)

XXV

Christology without an apocalyptical vision becomes no more than an ideology of conquest and triumph. Surely those whose apocalyptical tradition was so triumphantly suppressed by Christianity—the Jews—must have experienced this most painfully.

XXVI

The Christian idea of imitation and the apocalyptical idea of imminent expectation belong together. It is not possible to imitate Jesus radically, that is, at the level of the roots of life, if 'the time is not shortened'. Jesus' call: 'Follow me!' and the call of Christians: 'Come, Lord Jesus!' are inseparable.

XXVII

Imitation in imminent expectation: this is an apocalyptical consciousness that does not cause, but rather accepts suffering—defying apathy and hatred.

XXVIII

A passionate expectation of the day of the Lord does not lead to a pseudo-apocalyptical dream-dance in which all the claims made by the imitation of Christ are obscured and forgotten, nor does it lead to an unreflecting radicalism, for which prayers of longing and expectation can only be perceived forms of refusal or self-deception. Imminent expectation does not allow the imitation of Christ to be postponed. We are not made apathetic by the apocalyptical feeling for life, but by the evolutionary idea. It is the evolutionary symbol of time that paralyzes the imitation of Christ. Imminent expectation, on the other hand, provides hope, which has been pacified and led astray by the evolutionary idea, with perspectives of time and expectation. It introduces the pressure of time and activity into Christian life. It does not deprive responsibility of its power, but rather provides it with motivation. Our apocalyptical consciousness is not threatened with a paralyzing fear of catastrophe. It is, on the contrary, called upon to display a practical solidarity with the least of the brethren; this is clear from the apocalyptical chapters at the end of the gospel of St Matthew.

XXIX

Apocalyptical consciousness of this kind calls the timeless understanding of time that has become so firmly established in theology into question. This understanding of time enables theology to regard itself as a kind of constant reflection that is institutionally protected and cannot be interrupted by any imminent expectation, without pressure of activity or surprises and experienced in rendering harmless expectations that are open to disappointment, but are nonetheless genuine.

Against wrong choices in Christian eschatology

XXX

It is not primarily a question of the relationship between eschatology in the present and eschatology in the future (or a question of a balanced mixture of both), but rather of the relationship between an eschatological and an evolutionary consciousness of time, in which the idea of evolution is still misunderstood by many theologians, who think of it as pointing to a meaningful teleology.

XXXI

It is also not primarily a question of the (presumably specifically Christian) problem as to how much we have already been saved and to what extent we have not yet been saved. (In what sphere of time do we in fact encounter this difference between 'already' and 'not yet', in other words, between the present and the future?) No, the question is: How much time do we (still) have? That is the question of eschatological time that corresponds to the non-evolutionary nature of time.

177

XXXII

It is also not a question of distinction between time in this world and existential time, made so that the apocalyptical and temporal expectation can be kept firmly on the time of the individual's death. Time as such must be interpreted differently from evolution if the time of the individual's death is not to be seen in a purely evolutionary way, that is, as being overwhelmed by the anonymous waves of evolution. If the catastrophic and continuous nature of time is not understood, the experience of catastrophe on the part of the individual confronted with death will be even more catastrophic and death will be even more deadly. A society and a church without a Christian apocalyptical vision has, in other words, made death more deadly.

XXXIII

It is therefore not a question of a choice between eschatological and apocalyptical time. The reduction of eschatological time that is usually connected with this distinction has reinforced a process in Christian theology in which universal eschatology, which is orientated towards time in this world, has receded further and further and has become almost completely overshadowed by an individual eschatology that is almost exclusively orientated towards existential time. The questions that concern the apocalyptic vision most deeply—to whom does the world belong? to whom do its suffering and its time belong?—have, it would seem, been more effectively suppressed in theology than anywhere else.

XXXIV

The choice between faith-time and rational time is also extremely dubious. This fiducial reduction of our understanding of time has to be seriously called into question. Heinrich Schlier has posed a number of pertinent questions in this context: Is the elimination of concrete eschatology, in which the ultimate future and, with it, future as such not only revealed in faith and anticipated in the mode of faith, but also recaptured and cancelled out, because it only exists as future in faith? Time, Schlier has pointed out, has become submerged, extensiveness has been lost and distance has been obliterated in the ideal but isolated event of faith. Are these phenomena not analogous, he has asked, to the conviction of the pneumatic

Christians of Corinth, who believed that there was no resurrection of the dead?

XXXV

It is not only necessary to be careful about the overworked specifically Christian element, the Christian identity that, at every opportunity, insists on the salvation that has already been given in Christ. There may also be a special kind of weariness with regard to this identity, with the result that all the safety signals are put out because the danger of old age and the dictatorship of what has already been experienced is preferred to the way of hope and expectation. As Teilhard de Chardin observed, 'We go on asserting that we are awake and are waiting for the master. But, if we were honest, we would have to admit that we expect nothing at all'.

PART III

Categories

THE categories that are discussed in this part of the book (the word category is used here in the widest sense) are closely connected with each other. It is only if they are taken together that memory, narrative and solidarity can be regarded as the basic categories of a practical fundamental theology. Memory and narrative only have a practical character when they are considered together with solidarity and solidarity has no specifically cognitive status without memory and narrative.

It is important to keep the systematic roots of these categories that are to be found in the first part of the book ('Concept') constantly in mind. It will then be clear why such concepts as subject, praxis, society and history, cannot be regarded as categories in my theological approach. This is because they are axiologically present and effective in that approach. In the second part of the book ('Themes'), the categories that are discussed more fully in the present part are given sliding functions and are applied in a variety of contexts. In this part of the book, they are described in some detail and, at the same time, I go beyond individual description to make it possible to survey my approach to theology as a whole.

It is, of course, true that the three basic categories presented here each cover a number of further categories that occur in practical fundamental theology. These include such categories as love, interaction, work, suffering, struggle, sorrow, reason, language, time and so on. These further categories have already been mentioned in individual passages throughout the book. In this part, which can be described as 'Memory-narrative-solidarity', I deal mainly with these three major categories in an as yet not fully elaborated attempt to systematize them.

11. Memory [1]

Before I begin to clarify memory as a basic category of practical critical reason, I should like to recapitulate briefly and consider, at least in part, the theological status and significance of memory within this approach to a political theology as a practical fundamental theology.

It should be clear from what has been said so far in previous chapters that memory should not be regarded as a concept of resignation or tradition in contrast to that of hope. It should above all, in the sense of a dangerous memory, be thought of as the expression of eschatological hope, elaborated in its social and historical mediation. [2]

In this context, then, memory has a fundamental theological importance as what may be termed anamnetic solidarity or solidarity in memory with the dead and the conquered which breaks the grip of history as a history of triumph and conquest interpreted dialectically or as evolution. [3]

Going beyond its local application, memory can have a very decisive ecclesiological importance in defining the Church as the public vehicle transmitting a dangerous memory in the systems of social life.

As the excursus that follows will show, memory is also of importance in our dynamic understanding of dogmatic faith. With its help, dogmas can be seen as formulae of dangerous memory.

In this approach to a fundamental theology, too, memory, as the memory of suffering, is the basic concept in a theological theory of history and society as such [4] and at the same time the basic concept of a theology in the 'age of criticism'. [5]

In this connection, memory is of fundamental importance in our theological understanding of man as a subject. It can therefore be called memory as a category of the salvation of identity.

Finally, memory is also of central importance in any theory of history and society as a category of resistance to the passage of time (interpreted as evolution) and, in this sense, as the organon of an apocalyptical consciousness.

It will be clear from this brief résumé of the status and application of memory in a practical fundamental theology that there is an urgent need to discuss at greater length its origin and development as well as present function outside theology. In the sections that follow, then, I shall attempt to provide a historical and systematic outline of memory as a fundamental concept in a philosophy based on the primacy of practical critical reason.

1. An outline of the scope of the problem: memory as a fundamental concept?

It is possible for memory to be expressed in two ways as a fundamental concept by a philosophy for which the consideration of historical relationships of foundation and reference do not belong simply to the perceived prehistory of rational knowledge. In the first place, it can be expressed philosophically in so far as this relationship mediating between history and reason is articulated in the title 'memory'. In the second place, it is expressed if both fundamental aspects of Greek philosophy and the tradition of Jewish-Christian thought are articulated in the category 'memory'. The connection to which we are referring here is that between the Platonic doctrine of *anamnesis* as the foundation of rational knowledge on the basis of previously known truth and the Jewish-Christian emphasis on history and freedom. This relationship can be presented in such a way that both elements seek the categorial form of their specifically contemporary mediation (between *a priori* rational truth and the history of freedom) in the concept of memory.

Other developments and applications of the concept of memory—for example, in the anthropological and psychological question of the distinctive quality of human perception in which ideas are stored in a temporal relationship—simply set the same fundamental questions in motion, though with different priorities of knowledge. In contrast to this, a distinction such as that between memory and recollection is of secondary importance and it is clearly hardly possible to deal with the theme of memory by selecting and distinguishing concepts. It is not possible to prove beyond all doubt, either on the basis of linguistic usage or on the basis of the history of concepts, that the distinction between memory and recollection is valid.[6] It has, for example, been suggested that recollection is a psychological capacity and that memory is a historical organon and that the two can be separated in this way. Gadamer, however, has postulated that recollection should be 'liberated from its status as a psychological capacity and recognized as an essential element of man's ultimate historical being'.[7] At the same time, it is clear that the scope of the problem of defining such a concept as memory is very great—this is indicated by the existence of such concepts as apriority, truth, tradition, authority, history, theory and praxis and freedom, as well as many others. All this suggests that a contemporary elaboration of this concept should be based primarily, although not exclusively, on the traditions of practical philosophy, the philosophy of history and hermeneutics.

Finally, we have to ask whether and to what extent memory—in our world of science and technology that has placed itself outside history—can be regarded as a fundamental philosophical concept. Can it, in other words, claim not only a regional and derived significance, but also a radical importance? This question is dependent on the extent to which philosophy is able to deal with the theme that is disclosed by the concept of memory in such a way—based on the primacy of practical reason—that the old question of previously known natural truth arises again in a new form in the discussion of the question of reason becoming practical as freedom. In that case, memory would be an indispensable fundamental concept in a philosophy that regards itself as the theoretical form of reason that aims to become practical as freedom (in the medium of history).

2. Two traditions in the understanding of memory and the form of their mediation

Any discussion of the concept 'memory' in an attempt to reduce to a theme the relationship between reason and history has to follow a broadly historical course. I have therefore divided this section into three parts. In the first (a), I consider Plato's doctrine of *anamnesis*. In the second (b), the eschatological *memoria* of Christianity is presented and, in the third (c), both these teachings are brought together in Hegel's philosophy in a mediation that has had a lasting effect on every elaboration of this concept that has followed.

(a) *Anamnesis,* memory, is a key concept in Plato's philosophy. It is introduced, in the *Meno,* as a gnoseological term, analogous to the doctrine of the idea in the *Phaedo. Anamnesis* is a fundamental concept in Plato's teaching. He regarded it as the basis of formal rational knowledge and treated it as the constitutive problem of reason. A foundation of rational knowledge based on previously known truth—previously known in the mode of forgetfulness and therefore remembered with the help of the maieutic process[8]—introduces the *a priori* metaphysics of reason and knowledge. As Picht has pointed out, however, 'remembering *a priori* knowledge is incomplete if it forgets that it originated in the inspiration of the Homeric poet by the muses'.[9]

A part is played in the *Meno* by the myth of the existence of the soul before birth and the Orphic idea of drinking from the source of memory in the other world. The basis of *anamnesis* is therefore attributed by Plato to divine inspiration and he does this moreover in narrative form. He continues throughout his argument to insist that rational knowledge is based on previously known divine truth.

Aristotle, on the other hand, dealt with the theme of memory within the context of his teaching about abstraction and ability. In this teaching, he set in motion a psychologically and empirically orientated tendency in which memory is seen above all as a question of perception and the unity of man's consciousness in time.[10] The Platonic doctrine of *anamnesis* persisted, although it underwent certain changes, through neo-Platonism (for example, in Plotinus, who tried to connect the traditional teaching more closely with Aristotle's theory and therefore made the soul the basis of memory[11]) and Thomas Aquinas (in his theory of the *a priori* light of reason that, according to the *De Veritate,*[12] can be disclosed in the *memoria* knowledge) down to Descartes and Leibniz. Descartes regarded the innate idea of God in the form of a knowledge based on memory at least as a *modus cogitandi.*[13] Leibniz brought the Platonic doctrine of *anamnesis* up to date in his defence of *a priori* knowledge against the sensualism of the Anglo-Saxon thinkers of the period, who favoured the Aristotelian tradition of memory. Finally, Kant did away with the function of apriority as the foundation of knowledge, so that only what is produced by reason in accordance with its own plan can be encountered in apriority. We are bound to ask, however, whether Kant's successful destruction of apriority can be reconciled with the basic structures in his practical and historical teaching. He accepts, after all, a tradition of memory—the Christian tradition—which preserves, in a somewhat changed form, the Platonic doctrine of *anamnesis*.

(b) The history of Christianity is decisive in determining the central meaning of the concept of memory. Christianity has penetrated the space of the Greek logos and its metaphysics as a community of memory and narrative. It is aware that its memories are related to a single historical event in which man has been irrevocably redeemed and set free in the eschatological sense by God. From the formal point of view, memory has thus been taken into the context of faith and freedom. At the same time, it has also ceased to be a purely archaeological repetition backwards, as Kierkegaard described Plato's *anamnesis*. In Christianity, memory is, in its eschatological orientation, a repetitive memory forwards.[14]

Augustine was deeply influenced by Plato's doctrine of memory and developed this theory of memory in the central passages of Book X of his *Confessions*.[15] He rejected the Greek cyclic way of thinking and the transmigration of souls and replaced the theory of remembering previously known ideas and previously known divine truth by that of a *memoria*, in which the soul sees through itself in the light of divine illumination and perceives itself in its own way of life. In Augustine's teaching, memory acquired the status of a hermeneutical category, able to interpret history in the presence of God. Augustine was followed in this tradition of memory by Bonaventure (the *Itinerarium mentis in Deum*) and Pascal (the *Memorial*).

Paul, of course, declared that he was indebted both to the Greeks and to the non-Greeks.[16] All Christian theology is also similarly indebted. The result has been that, in the course of history, there has been a creative antithesis at various levels of philosophical thought between Greek metaphysics and the Christian tradition. The consequent contribution to the theme of memory has led to an important mediation of reason and history. This has found its clearest expression in the work of Hegel in this sphere.

(c) Hegel's explicit statements about memory can be found in various contexts and assessed in different ways. (There are references in secondary, 'anthropological' passages in his work. He deals more exhaustively with the question, as an expression of the movement of objective spirit, at the end of his *Phänomenologie*.)

However his references are interpreted, it is certain that his philosophical work as a whole demonstrates, perhaps more fully than
that of any other modern thinker, his concern with memory in
which the previously known—that is, *a priori*—truth of classical
metaphysics is mediated with the history of freedom of the human
spirit. This memory is, according to Hegel's intention, opposed to a
purely representational attitude towards history in the historical
consciousness. It is, however, taken out of the grip of Plato's
anamnesis. In it, what is particular in history does not become a
pure example or a mere case of a general phenomenon that is
previously known. It does not recall truth as an abstraction from
historical relationships. It compels philosophy to consider truth at
the historical level of its mediation and to understand its general,
universal nature to some extent on the basis of historical apriority.
In this way, it becomes a memory that is critical (of the present
time), at least as what has been called a 'sensitivity to every form
of inferiority of the status achieved'.[17] It also functions as a protest
against subjection to previously existing conditions. In this sense, it
may well be true that this memory incorporates within itself metaphysics and history, archaeology and eschatology[18] and that it aims
to be practical, as a liberating form of criticism. In its praxis, it neither precedes nor goes against the praxis of the Enlightenment, with
the result that it attempts to set in motion a form of Enlightenment
that is not trivial.

3. Memory in the sphere of hermeneutics and criticism

Memory, as the systematic expression of the relationship between
reason and history, can be found above all in two post-Hegelian
philosophical movements. Although Hegel's thought has had a different effect on each of these tendencies, both are to a greater or
lesser degree explicitly influenced by it and both have come to
function, in their different ways, as criticisms of historical reason.

(a) The first is the movement of hermeneutical philosophy. This
is directed against historism and its destruction of the relationship
between life and history and its abstract tendency to contrast history
as memory and history as science. As a result of this historical contrast, the science of history is not in a position to become, in its ex-

tension, memory, nor does the historical memory possess the factual and logical pre-conditions at its disposal to enable it to realize itself.[19] The purely historical relationship with the past not only presupposes that the past is past; it also works actively to strengthen the fact that what has been is not present. History has replaced tradition, in other words, it occupies the place that should be occupied by tradition.[20]

The contemporary hermeneutical tendency in philosophy, then, developed as a reaction against a world dominated by science and deprived of memory and tradition, the theoretical basis of which is to be found in historism. Its immediate predecessor was the so-called philosophy of life, one of the leading exponents of which was Wilhelm Dilthey. Dilthey's reflections about the structure of the historical world based on the 'cultural sciences' were an extension of Droysen's view that memory functioned as a condition governing the possibility of historical investigation and that history could not be objectivized to an unlimited degree. Because he tried to base the concept of memory on the category of experience, Dilthey was, however, unable to free it from the suspicion of historical psychologism.

Nietzsche's criticism of the contrast between life and history also forms part of this general philosophical tendency. This criticism resulted in a plea against memory and for forgetfulness as the factor that made life possible. He added memory as a fitting in and interlocking process[21] to the isolated historical consciousness, to which he accredited 'a degree of sleeplessness, rumination and historical sense, in which what is living is harmed'.[22] Since he overlooked the critical function of the memory of suffering in the same way as he underestimated the calming effect or 'submissiveness' of forgetfulness, he rejected as 'masochistic' the formula that was offered to him in the statement: 'only what does not cease to hurt remains in the memory' as a means of understanding the continuity of history in the sense of a 'remembered history of suffering'.[23]

Bergson's idea of memory also belongs to this philosophy of life. He made a clear distinction between memory as the dynamic basis of the unity and continuity of the spiritual life of the person, and perception. His ideas were in turn developed at the level of social history and social psychology by Halbwachs.[24] Finally, Scheler's attempt to free memory from psychological conceptions and to understand it as the foundation of a free, critical relationship with regard to the 'historical determination' that is active in a pre-rational and natural way in the person's experience also forms part of this philosophical movement.[25]

It is also clear from the fact that many of these varieties of the pholosophy of life function as encoded philosophies of history, life appearing in them as the subject and sphere of meaning of history as a whole, in the same way as nature appears in several forms of the natural philosophy as the subject of the historical processes of becoming, that these philosophies of life are very close to the hermeneutical problem of memory. In various ways, memory is always central in all these philosophical processes. In the case of Schelling, for example, 'all philosophy consists of a process of remembering the state in which we were at one with nature'.[26] In the case of Bloch, on the other hand (and in some of the less frequently discussed representatives of the Frankfurt school[27]), memory accompanies all utopian philosophies of history and functions as a 'mole in the ground', pointing to a universal 'resurrection of fallen nature' and 'going forward as a movement back into the ground'.[28]

I am also bound to point in this context to the impulses that are active in this understanding of memory in the criticism of historical reason that is current in contemporary hermeneutical philosophy. These impulses have been developed above all with the problem of being in mind, a question that has been discussed at length in existential and ontological hermeneutics. Heidegger, for example, regarded remembering as 'the foundation of metaphysics in so far as it is the fundamental ontological act of the metaphysics of being'. Since, however, 'authentic memory . . . always has to interiorize what is remembered, that is, re-encounter it more and more in its inner possibility',[29] the idea of being must also go forward, remembering, to meet what memory preserves in the word 'being' as something that is still outstanding and belongs to the future. History mediated in the memory thus remains 'fate'. This also applies to the way in which memory presents history as a making present of the past. As Picht has said, 'we expereince the present effect of the past and are quite upset. History takes place by our being upset. It is experienced, but we are for the most part not aware of this experience. The presence of the past is therefore different from memory. It is memory in the mode of forgetfulness'.[30]

(b) The second of the two philosophical movements which can be contrasted with this first movement of the philosophy of life and existential and ontological hermenuetics, in which memory plays a leading part, is connected with the critical use of memory in those philosophies that attempt to continue the process that began in the Enlightenment to emphasize the practical aspect of reason. They do not, however, want to neglect the relationship between reason and history, between criticism and tradition and so on in favour of an abstract form of reason that is divorced from history or abandon it as erroneous, as wrongly ideological or as a threat to praxis. What we have here are above all forms of a practical and critical philosophy of history and society that have been inspired by Kant's philosophy of practical reason and the Marxist and psychoanalytical criticism of ideology.

These forms of philosophy can be seen—especially in the context of the introduction and use of memory—as debates with historical criticism and the criticism of ideology. (Historical criticism has proved and still proves its value as a criticism of ideology in its criticism of authorities, institutions and unenlightened traditions.) Confronted with the directness of this criticism, these philosophies also investigate its interests and motives and raise the question (that has been asked since the time of Kant) of the so-called criticism of criticism, which in turn questions the abstract will to criticism and exposes it as an ideology that unquestioningly accepts a gradual progression in the forward movement of the critical consciousness. In this process, the criticism of criticism is not regarded as a formal metacriticism—in the sense of analytical systems or theories—which continues to discuss this problem and delegate it to a purely theoretical level (with a tendentious *regressus in infinitum*), but as a problem of theory and praxis in the context of practical reason that is, in its realization, always situated within certain social and historical relationships of foundation and reference. In this sense, history—as a structure of tradition that normalizes action—is always immanent in reason which becomes practical in its liberating task of criticism. This view of the irreplaceable relationship between reason and history, which is close to the hermeneutical standpoint, was not subsequently imputed to the Enlightenment. However well-founded, justified and necessary the criticism of traditions and their authorities that began during the Enlightenment was, this process that took place in the Enlightenment compelled man to recognize that memory was not simply an object, but an inner aspect of all critical consciousness which was seeking self-enlightenment. In this sense, critical enlightenment realizes itself in opposition to the tendency to denounce as superstition everything in the consciousness that is directed towards memory and tradition and that does not obey the calculation of scientific and technical reason, leaving it to private choice and individual lack of obligation or exposing it to the suspicion of a subjectivity without theory. This understanding of critical enlightenment is confirmed in the contemporary Enlightenment theories that are not primarily indebted to the tradition of the hermeneutical philosophy of history, in other words, in the relevant theories of the Frankfurt school. What we find in the teaching of this school, then, is similar to what is found in other positions in the tradition of practical philosophy,[31] a critical use of memory in the constitutive problem of practical reason.

This is already apparent in Walter Benjamin's theses on the philosophy of history. For Benjamin, memory, and especially the memory of the history of suffering in the world, is the medium of a realization of reason and freedom that is critically opposed to an unreflected and banal idea of a non-dialectical progress of reason.[32] Herbert Marcuse has suggested, within the referential framework of psychoanalysis, that critical measures are provided by the rediscovery of the past, that the restoration of the capacity to remember goes hand in hand with the restoration of the knowing content of the imagination and that in this way the *recherche du temps perdu* becomes a vehicle of liberation.[33] This insight is suggested as a fundamental postulate, that the restoration of memory to its rightful place as a means of liberation is one of the noblest tasks of philosophy.[34] Marcuse has elsewhere expressed this idea in terms of the theory of history and society, claiming that our memory of the past can give rise to dangerous insights and that established society seems to fear the subversive contents of memory. Remembering, Marcuse believes, is a way of relieving oneself from the given facts, a way of mediation that can momentarily at least break through the omnipresent power of the given facts. Memory recalls past fears and past hope and, in the personal events that arise again and again in the individual memory, the fears and longings of mankind are perpetuated. This, Marcuse suggests, is an example of the general in the particular.[35]

Theodor Adorno stressed the intention in the theory of knowledge and insisted that 'the tradition of knowledge is itself immanent as the mediating aspect of its objects. Knowledge changes the form of these objects as soon as it makes *tabula rasa* with them by virtue of objectivization. In itself, it shares, in its form that has become independent with regard to the content, tradition as an unconscious memory. No question could be asked in which knowledge of the past was not preserved and did not obtrude'.[36] If rational knowledge critically repudiates the directly normative compulsion of remembered contents, how can it then preserve memory in a changed form and eventually not let it sink down—as a vague and unconscious memory—to the level of an epiphenomenon of reason divorced from history? Adorno answered this question by referring to an aporia: 'Tradition is confronted by an insoluble contradiction. No tradition is present to be called upon. If all tradition is extinguished, however, the advance to inhumanity will begin'.[37]

Habermas has attempted to develop a practical philosophy of history and, in the interest of emancipation, to interpret the history of man and to orientate action in the present. He too has stressed the importance of memory in this process: 'The experience of reflection . . . recalls the thresholds of emancipation in the generic history of man'.[38] The continued elaboration of the problem of memory in the concepts of reconstruction and self-reflection in fact conceals the connection that is revealed in memory between communicative action and historical frames of reference. It would seem that the interests of knowledge (emancipation and coming of age) are naturalized to such a degree as linguistic structures that are remote from history that the process of memory has ceased to take place in them.

The critical treatment of memory has therefore clearly run into some of the unsolved problems of hermeneutics. At the point where both intersect, certain characteristics of memory as a philosophical concept can be formulated in a manner that also expresses a number of previously unregarded aspects of the various philosophies of memory.

4. Memory as the medium by which reason becomes practical as freedom: characterization and consequences

In my outline of the extent of the problem of the concept of memory, I indicated that the process could be regarded as the means by which reason could become practical as freedom. In what follows, I shall deal with memory basically as the memory of freedom that, as a memory of suffering, acts as an orientation for action that is related to freedom, under the heading (a). I shall then discuss how its narrative structure (b) leads it to criticize historical technology that is dissociated from memory and to encounter the traditions of *anamnesis* and the Christian *memoria* (c).

(a) The form of memory that is immanent in critical reason is the memory of freedom. It is from this form of memory that reason acquires the interest that guides the process by which it becomes practical. The memory of freedom is a definite memory. In contrast to a vague use of freedom, which makes it possible to reproduce the concept of freedom indiscriminately and on the basis of contradictory presuppositions, the definite memory of freedom is related to the traditions in which the interest in freedom arose. These traditions are, in the narrative characteristics, that is, as the narrated history of freedom, not the object, but the presupposition of any critical reconstruction of history by argumentative reason.

In its practical intention, the memory of freedom is primarily a *memoria passionis,* a memory of suffering. As such, it mediates a praxis of freedom in a form that resists being identified, either openly or in secret, with a praxis that is expressed as a progressive control of nature. In its practical intention, a philosophy of history that is orientated towards the memory of suffering is therefore prevented from explaining history as the history of freedom simply in the categories of a history of domination, even if this domination is that of an abstract and banal coming of age. It is prevented from this by the introduction of a concept of the whole (of history) that is indispensable in any practical philosophy of history and by avoiding a concept of totality (of the praxis of control and domination) in that concept of the whole of history.

Respect for the suffering that has accumulated in history makes reason perceptive in a way which—in the abstract contrast between authority and knowledge within which the problem of the autonomy

195

of reason is usually discussed and to which our understanding of emancipation as the *a priori* interest of reason is apparently fixed—cannot be expressed. In this perception, history—as the remembered history of suffering—has the form of a dangerous tradition. This dangerous tradition cannot be done away with or rendered harmless either in a purely submissive attitude towards the past—as it is in many approaches to hermeneutical theories of reason—or in an attitude towards the past that is based purely on the criticism of ideology, as it is in many approaches to critical theories of reason. It is, in any case, mediated in a practical way. It takes place in dangerous stories in which the interest in freedom is introduced, identified and presented in narrative form.

(b) This memory has an essentially narrative structure. It functions as a criticism of a concept of memory that is derived from an idea of the abstract identity of the consciousness that has determined all teaching about the memory since Kant's concept of the transcendental synthesis of apperception. Husserl's phenomenology has been particularly influential in this context.[39] Wittgenstein's *Philosophical Investigations*[40] and Schapp's later phenomenological studies[41] were directed against this memory. Schapp taught that a consciousness that was 'involved in stories' formed the basis of the abstract unity of the phenomenological subject and that this consciousness was made explicit in narrative form and pointed to a cognitive primacy of narrated memory in the connection between the historical nature of consciousness and what Lübbe called a 'consciousness in stories'.[42]

(c) This cognitive primacy of narrated memory has a number of consequences. I shall discuss the most important of them here. Because of this primacy, philosophy is obliged to make a link between narrative and argument. In addition to Danto's analytical theory of narrative,[43] for example, there is also a need for a hermeneutical and critical theory in which the relationship between philosophy and, on the one hand, literature and, on the other, the antihistory of suffering that is narrated in it could be developed. The practical reason of philosophy cannot be expressed by the technology of the control of nature, in which science is made practical by application. The cognitive primacy of narrated memory would seem rather to point in the direction of a criticism of those forms of historical reason that become a technology turning backwards, after the magisterium of history has been dethroned, after what has been called *historia magistra vitae*[44] has been ruled out as the basis of argument and after the art of narrative has been forgotten in the science of history.[45] That particular process is distinguished by a purely cybernetic use of memory.[46] It is also increasingly orientated towards a history that has been classified rationally and purposefully in a data bank and a computor memory that cannot forget and therefore cannot remember. There is a clear tendency in this process towards a total objectivization of history and man living in history—the stigma of the post-historical. As opposed to an abstract criticism, however, the cognitive primacy of narrated memory compels philosophy, which cannot be persuaded by universal criticism to abandon the question of truth or to reduce it to the level of a preliminary historical stage of emancipative total reflection, to consider carefully one of Nietzsche's hypotheses. According to Nietzsche, then, 'we who know today, we who are godless and opposed to metaphysics, take *our* fire from the blaze that was set alight by a faith that is centuries old, the Christian faith that was also the faith of Plato—faith that God is the truth and that the truth is divine'.[47] This cognitive primacy of narrated memory and therefore of a 'consciousness that is involved in stories' is therefore valid in contrast with the abstract unity of the consciousness and the various forms of doubt and criticism which are without presuppositions and which arise in that abstract unity. What is more, it also means that the theological use of memory is not relegated in advance to a special zone that is inaccessible. Theology may at the same time also regard memory or its social counterpart, tradition, as the mediation between God's absolute revelation and the recipient of that revelation.[48] It is not purely by chance that Christian faith is categorially described as the *memoria passionis, mortis et resurrectionis Jesu Christi* and that attempts are made (for example, above in Chapter 6) to justify that faith in the narrative and argumentative form of a liberating memory as a definite form of hope.

Notes

1. This chapter is an adapted version, rewritten to fit into the whole concept of the book, of a text first published as an article in *Handbuch philosophischer Grundbegriffe*, II, ed. H. Krings, H. M. Baumgartner and C. Wild (Munich, 1973).

2. See 'Politische Theologie in der Diskussion', H. Peukert, ed., *Diskussion zur politischen Theologie, op. cit.*

3. The idea of solidarity in memory with the dead is also at the basis of the argument used in the publication, *Unsere Hoffnung*, of the synod of German bishops; see especially I, 3('Auferweckung der Toten').

4. See my contribution in Metz, Moltmann and Oelmüller, *Kirche in Prozess der Aufklä*rung.

5. See my contribution, 'La théologie à l'âge de la critique', *Le Service théologique dans l'église*. Mélanges Congar (Paris, 1974), pp. 134–148.

6. See, for *anamnesis,* L. Oeing-Hanhoff, 'Zur Wirkungsgeschichte der Platonischen Anamnesislehre', *Collegium philosophicum. Festschrift für J. Ritter* (Basle, 1965), pp. 240–271. For 'memory', see C. von Bormann, *Historisches Wörterbuch der Philosophie,* ed. J. Ritter, II, p. 636 ff.

7. H. Gadamer, *Truth and Method* (New York & London, 1976–7), p. 17.

8. See Meno 81 d; see also 86 b.

9. G. Picht, *Wahrheit—Vernunft—Verantwortung, op. cit.*, p. 42.

10. See 'Memory' in the *Encyclopaedia Britannica.*

11. Enneads IV, 6.

12. *De ver.* 10, 2 and ad 5.

13. *Medit.* III 13.

14. *Die Wiederholung,* ed. E. Hirsch (= *Samlede Vaerker* III, p. 173): 'Repetition is a decisive expression for what was known as "memory" among the Greeks. Just as the latter taught that all knowledge was remembering, so too will modern philosophy teach that the whole of life is repetition. Repetition and memory are the same movement, although they move in opposite directions. What is remembered is repeated backwards and the repetition remembers the matter forwards'.

15. X 6–27.

16. See Rom 1. 14.

17. O. Marquard, 'Hegel und das Sollen', *Philosophisches Jahrbuch* 72 (1964), p. 118.

18. M. Theunissen, *Hegels Lehre vom absoluten Geist als theologisch-politischer Traktat* (Berlin, 1970), p. 325 ff.

19. A. Heuss, *Verlust der Geschichte* (Göttingen, 1959), p. 68.

20. G. Krüger, 'Die Bedeutung der Tradition für die philosophische Forschung', *Studium Generale* 4 (1951), p. 322 ff.

21. Edition Schlechta, III, p. 829.

22. Edition Schlechta, I, p. 213.

23. Edition Schlechta, II, p. 802.

24. M. Halbwachs, *Das Gedächtnis und seine sozialen Bedingungen* (Berlin and Neuwied, 1966).

25. See 'Reue und Wiedergeburt', *Gesammelte Werke* V, p. 35.

26. *Werke,* ed. K. F. A. Schelling, IV, p. 77.

27. See M. Theunissen, *Gesellschaft und Geschichte.*

28. E. Bloch, 'Subjekt—Objekt', *Gesamtausgabe* VIII, pp. 476, 474.

29. *Kant und das Problem der Metaphysik* (Frankfurt, ²1951), p. 211.

30. G. Picht, *Wahrheit—Vernunft—Verantwortung, op. cit.,* p. 288.

31. See, for example, W. Oelmüller, *Die unbefriedigte Aufklärung* (Frankfurt, 1969).

32. *Zur Kritik der Gewalt und andere Aufsätze* (Frankfurt, 1965), pp. 78–94.

33. H. Marcuse, *Triebstruktur und Gesellschaft* (Frankfurt, 1968), p. 24 f.

34. H. Marcuse, *op. cit.,* p. 228.

35. *One-dimensional Man.*

36. *Negative Dialectics.*

37. T. W. Adorno, 'Thesen über Tradition', *Ohne Leitbild* (Frankfurt, 1967), p. 34 f.

38. J. Habermas, *Erkenntnis und Interesse* (Frankfurt, 1968), p. 31.

39. See Husserl's fundamental work, 'Vorlesungen zur Phänomenologie des inneren Zeitbewusstseins', *Husserliana* IV (The Hague, 1952); see also his 'Cartesianische Meditationen', *Husserliana* I (The Hague, 1950).

40. Oxford, 1958.

41. *In Geschichten verstrickt* (Hamburg, 1953); *ibid., Philosophie der Geschichten* (Leer, 1959); for Schapp, see J. Habermas, *Logik der Sozialwissenschaften* (Tübingen, 1967) and H. Lübbe, ' "Sprachspiele" und "Geschichten". Neopositivismus und Phänomenologie im Spätstadium', *Bewusstsein in Geschichten* (Freiburg, 1972).

42. See above, note 41, for the book of this name.

43. *Analytical Philosophy of History* (Cambridge, 1965).

44. See R. Koselleck, *Natur und Geschichte. Festschrift für K. Löwith* (Stuttgart, 1967).

45. See H. Weinrich, *Literatur für Leser* (Stuttgart, 1972).

46. See K. W. Deutsch, *Politische Kybernetik* (Freiburg, 1967).

47. Edition Schlechta II, p. 208.

48. See J. Pieper, *Überlieferung* (Munich, 1970); G. Scholem, 'Offenbarung und Tradition als religiöse Kategorien im Judentum', *Über einige Grundbegriffe des Judentums* (Frankfurt, 1970), pp. 90–120.

Excursus: Dogma as a dangerous memory [1]

Christian faith can be understood as an attitude according to which man remembers promises that have been made and hopes that are experienced as a result of those promises and commits himself to those memories. Neither the intellectual model of consent to certain articles of faith nor the existential model of a decision made in man's existence is in the foreground of this interpretation of faith. What is important here is the figure of eschatological memory. [2]

What is meant here is a phenomenon that has been mentioned before in this book: not the memory that sees the past in a transfiguring light, nor the memory that sets a seal on the past by being reconciled with all that is dangerous and challenging in that past. It is also not the memory in which past happiness and salvation are applied merely individually. [3] What is meant in this context is that dangerous memory that threatens the present and calls it into question because it remembers a future that is still outstanding.

This memory breaks through the grip of the prevailing consciousness. It claims unresolved conflicts that have been thrust into the background and unfulfilled hopes. It maintains earlier experiences in contrast to the prevailing insights and in this way makes the present unsafe.

As *memoria*, faith is able to provide an answer to the question that is so frequently discussed by theologians—that of a mediation between the already and the not yet of the eschatological salvation made possible in Jesus Christ. The common theological discussion of the tension between the already and the not yet is ultimately meaningless. If our understanding of salvation is not to be stripped of its historical content and reduced to the level of a mere idea, it is obviously essential for the 'already' to be accepted and understood in the 'not yet', that is, for the datum of salvation to be accepted in the hope. The already is, after all, a determining modality of the not yet, in so far as the 'not yet' claims to be more than and different from a 'not' or a 'nothing'.

Various attempts have been made in contemporary theology to define Christian faith in its relevance to the world and history. These attempted definitions all have one thing more or less in common with each other—they all interpret faith above all as an act of faith, as *fides qua creditur,* as far as possible without any content, as a figure of man's free non-objective decision. Interpreted in this way, faith can certainly be contemporary. At the same time, however, an interpretation of this kind is always in danger of obscuring the power of Christian faith, which is derived from its content and conviction, to criticise society and devalue it to the level of a symbolic paraphrase of modern consciousness, without in fact contributing in any way towards changing that consciousness.[4]

On the other hand, as *memoria,* faith makes it clear that Christian faith is a dogmatic faith which is tied to a certain content, a *fides quae creditur.* It also shows how it is able, because of this, to achieve the critical freedom which is related to the history of social freedom. In the perspective of the eschatological message, the Christian is called upon in faith to bring about this freedom. The biblical traditions and the doctrinal and confessional formulae that are derived from those traditions appear in the light of this interpretation as formulae of *memoria.* In other words, they are interpreted as formulae in which the claim of promises made and past hopes and fears that have been experienced are recollected in the memory in order to break the grip of the prevailing consciousness, to obtain release from the compulsions and restrictions of the world of today and to break through the banality of the present and the immediate future.

This interpretation of the meaning of the Christian formulae and confessions of faith is perhaps an unusual one, but it may seem more convincing if the particular situation in which modern society finds itself and in which Christian faith has to be handed on is considered. Modern society is, after all, becoming increasingly divorced from history and memory. In it, it is more and more apparent that traditions can only be preserved and kept alive in the present if they have to do with institutions and the formulae by which those institutions understand themselves. The individual is bound to be increasingly exposed to a loss of memory. A Christian may be able to live completely independent of the institution today and continue in his own generation to be nourished by the substance of Christian faith. The succeeding generation will, however, have no point of contact with that faith. It will be more than ever exposed to the danger of the prevailing loss of memory and history.

The process of remembering, in other words, the process by which a memory is made present and the present is overcome, cannot exclusively or even primarily take place in the individual. As formulations of the collective memory, dogmas may therefore have an entirely new part to play here. They can, as it were, compel me to recollect in the present something that I cannot grasp or realize on the narrow basis of my own personal experience. In other words, dogmas prevent me from letting my own religious experience operate simply as the function of a prevailing consciousness.

Dogmatic or confessed faith is being bound to doctrinal statements which can and must be understood as formulae of mankind's memory that is subversive and dangerous and that has been repressed and misunderstood. The criterion of the genuine Christianity of that memory is the critical and liberating dangerous quality which can redeem man and with which it is able to introduce the remembered message to the present age, with the result that men are, as Bonhoeffer has suggested, astonished and frightened by it and overcome by its force.[5] These dogmatic formulae and confessions of faith are dead, meaningless and empty—they are, in other words, unsuited to the task of saving Christian identity and tradition in the collective memory—when there is no sign of their danger—to society and the Church—in their remembered contents, when this dangerous quality is extinguished by the mechanisms of its institutional mediation and when the formulae have the exclusive function of preserving the religion that transmits them and of reproducing an authoritarian Church institution that is no longer, as the body responsible for publicly handing down the Christian memory, subject to the dangerous claim of that memory.

This can in fact be demonstrated on the basis of the classical formulae of faith.[6] An attempt has been made by Erik Peterson, for example, within the framework of his writings about the political implications of monotheism,[7] to criticize the doctrine of the Trinity and in this way to make its redeeming and liberating quality of danger visible. Peterson did this by considering the monarchical concept of domination that is criticized in the Trinitarian formula, but failed to apply that criticism to the structure of the Church itself. We can also say in this context that our understanding of the memory of Jesus Christ as the memory of the coming of the kingdom (or domination) of God in Jesus' love for the oppressed and rejected can also be used as a dangerous and liberating force to change the direction of the classical Christological formulae. This is a task which theology could undertake and which would, in my opinion, be extremely fruitful.

If the Christian formulae were to be interpreted as formulae of mankind's dangerous memory, this would lead to a corresponding growth in our understanding of faith itself. Faith would in that case not continue to be dead, authoritarian faith or the opium of the people, a people not yet come of age. Faith, then, should, by being interpreted as memory, be made comprehensible as the hermeneutical expression of man's freedom and as the memory that functions within the contradictions present in a history of human freedom which is interpreted as linear and moving in one direction (and which believes that it can overcome past sufferings and hopes, obliterate the challenge of the dead or, without any sacrifice of freedom, ignore the past). If we are to avoid the error of making the inheritance of the modern history of freedom harmless by the application of romantic or restorative methods or of sacrificing that inheritance to a middle-class or totalitarian idea of progress, we must harness the strength of dogmatic memory.

This dogmatic or definite (defined) memory can never empty itself so entirely of the content of memory that all that it preserves of that content is what can be mediated exclusively by means of critical reflection. (This has been stressed again and again in this book). As a definite (or defined) memory, it always has certain aspects of a consenting but critical appropriation of the kind that is also encountered in the historically mediated form of Christian faith. It is true that this definite memory affects only part of modern society, but, especially when it is a memory of Christian faith, it is directed towards all men in their threatened freedom and hopes.

The critical and liberating strength of Christian dogmatic memory—as a definite memory—therefore never has a purely intellectual or theoretical attitude. Its critical power is characterized by the definite nature of the memory itself. In this memory, it is conscious of the deadly conflict between God's promises and a history that is dominated by man's alienated desires and interests. Its criticism is not a total criticism. It is characterized by the renunciation of self and the persistence, the impatience and the patience that are required by the Christian memory as the imitation of Christ. In this sense, then, dogmatic faith and the praxis of imitation are indissolubly connected to each other.[8] Dogma can be seen in this light as practical memory.

Notes

1. This excursus is an adapted version, rewritten to fit into the whole concept of the book, of a text originally written in 1968 and first published as part of my contribution, 'Politische Theologie in der Diskussion', to H. Peukert, ed., *Diskussion zur 'Politischen Theologie', op. cit.*

2. It would be interesting to investigate how it was possible for the memory to change so much in sacramental theology and, to the detriment of the memory and the sacrament, to be isolated and frequently given a wrong ritualistic interpretation, devoid of the subject.

3. See J. B. Metz, 'Technik—Politik—Religion', W. Heinen and J. Schreiner, eds., *Erwartung—Verheissung—Erfüllung* (Würzburg, 1969); *id., Reform und Gegenreform heute* (Mainz and Munich, 1969).

4. I tried, in my *Reform und Gegenreform heute,* to clarify the meaning of dogmas as formulae of a dangerous memory.

5. D. Bonhoeffer, *Widerstand und Ergebung* (Munich, new ed., 1970), p. 328; E. T. *Letters and Papers from Prison* (London, ³1967).

6. The document published by the Synod of German bishops, *Unsere Hoffnung,* can be regarded as an attempt to set out the central statements of the Christian confession of faith in their social character and as dangerous pronouncements. I am preparing a full explanation of this document, which will, I hope, go further in this direction. It will be published as *The Faith of Christians.*

7. E. Peterson, 'Der Monotheismus als politisches Problem', *Theologische Traktate* (Munich, 1951), pp. 45–147.

8. For the constitutive significance of imitation and its implications for Christology, see J. B. Metz, *Followers of Christ, op. cit.*

12. Narrative[1]

In this part of the book, I have often referred to the narrative and practical structure of theology, especially, for example, in connection with its eschatological and apocalyptical teaching (in Chapter 10 above) and its soteriological concern with salvation and redemption (Chapter 7). Christology too should have a narrative and practical structure.[2] In Chapter 9, we also considered the need for a narrative and practical (or mystical and political) form of Christianity rather than a transcendental and idealistic form in view of the problems of identity confronting theology today. The short apology for narrative that follows in this chapter is undertaken as an attempt to make good the almost complete absence, in the German-speaking countries at least, of the idea of narrative in any of the more recent theological and philosophical works of reference. Lexicons are very revealing, especially in what they leave out. In this short apology for narrative, I am particularly indebted to the work of the specialist in the field of the science of literature, Harald Weinrich.[3] In it, I stress above all the narrative structure of the category of dangerous memory that I discussed in the preceding chapter.

I cannot hope to deal systematically or fully here with the theological theme of narrative, but can only mention a number of different and significant points. I have not attempted a linguistic analysis, partly because I am simply not competent to do so. Another reason is because it is not theologically relevant to incorporate the narrative potential of Christianity into a linguistic theory (in order to close it as a form of pre-scientific communication). An even more important reason is that narrative processes have to be protected, interrupted in order to justify them critically and even guided in the direction of a competent narrative without which the experience of faith, like every original experience, would be silenced!

1. Narrative and experience

However familiar we may be with the name, the narrator is not present for us, alive and active. Not only is he remote from us—he is always becoming more remote. It is as though an apparently inalienable and assured ability had been taken away from us. This is the ability to exchange experiences.[4] The atrophy of narrative is particularly dangerous in theology. If the category of narrative is lost or outlawed by theology as pre-critical, then real or original experiences of faith may come to lack objectivity and become silenced and all linguistic expressions of faith may therefore be seen as categorical objectivizations or as changing symbols of what cannot be said. In this way, the experience of faith will become vague and its content will be preserved only in ritual and dogmatic language, without the narrative form showing any power to exchange experience.

Theology is concerned with irreducible original experiences which, when they are articulated in language, reveal unmistakably narrative features. This applies particularly to its consideration of the statements made by the Old Testament prophets about a God who overthrows all that is old and makes everything new and who makes this new reality felt painfully in opposition to all that is familiar and taken for granted. It applies equally to the totally new experience of the resurrection of the crucified Jesus as narrated in the New Testament. This narrative structure is clear throughout the whole of Scripture, from the beginning, the story of creation, to the end, where a vision of the new heaven and the new earth is revealed. All this is disclosed in narrative. The world created from nothing, man made from the dust, the new kingdom proclaimed by Jesus, himself the new man, resurrection as a passage through death to life, the end as a new beginning, the life of future glory— all these show that reasoning is not the original form of theological expression, which is above all that of narrative. The logos of theology, so long as it conceals its own narrative form, is as embarrassed by them as reason is by questions concerning the beginning and the end and the destiny of what is new and has never yet been. The question about the beginning, the *archē,* which enabled the Greeks with their logos to break the spell of pure narrative in myth, leads thought straight back to narrative. The beginning and the end can only be discussed in narrative form—Kant was aware of this when he spoke of the 'rhapsodic beginning of thought' which was not open to argumentative reconstruction. Above all, what is new and has never yet been can only be introduced in narrative. As Adorno has observed in the closing passages of his *Minima Moralia*, if reason is closed to the narrative exchange of experiences of what is new and completely breaks off that exchange for the sake of its own critical nature and its autonomy, it will inevitably exhaust itself in reconstructions and become no more than a technique. This question will be discussed more fully below.

2. The practical and performative aspect of narrative

There are examples of narrative traditions which resist the influence of our supposedly post-narrative age—for instance, the Hassidic stories, Johann Peter Hebbel's or Bertolt Brecht's 'calendar' stories or the 'traces' of Ernst Bloch, whose main work, *Das Prinzip Hoffnung*, reads like a great encyclopedia of 'hope' stories. They all illustrate the practical character of such narratives, their communication of an experience and close involvement of the narrator and the listener in the experience narrated.

'Most born storytellers pursue a practical interest. . . . This is indicative of the distinctive nature of all true stories, all of which have an overt or hidden use—a moral, a practical instruction, a rule of life. In every case, the storyteller is a man who knows what to do with the listener. . . . His stories are based on experience, either his own or other people's, which he transforms into the experience of those who listen to his stories'.[5]

Martin Buber has reaffirmed this characteristic in his introduction to the Hassidic stories and has also drawn attention to other important features of the narrative form: 'The story is itself an event and has the quality of a sacred action. . . . It is more than a reflection—the sacred essence to which it bears witness continues to live in it. The wonder that is narrated becomes powerful once more. . . . A rabbi, whose grandfather had been a pupil of Baal Shem Tov, was once asked to tell a story. 'A story ought to be told', he said, 'so that it is itself a help', and his story was this. 'My grandfather was paralyzed. Once he was asked to tell a story about his teacher and he told how the holy Baal Shem Tov used to jump and dance when he was praying. My grandfather stood up while he was telling the story and the story carried him away so much that he had to jump and dance to show how the master had done it. From that moment, he was healed. This is how stories ought to be told'.[6]

This text is remarkable for two reasons. In the first place, it is a successful example in a critical, post-narrative age of how narrative teaching can be linked with narrative self-enlightenment about the very interest which underlies the narrative process. In this case, the story is not ideologically unconscious of the interest that governs it. It presents this interest and tries it out in the narrative process. It verifies or falsifies itself and does not simply leave this to discussion about the story which lies outside the narrative process. This is, in my opinion, a very important aspect of the narrative form which cannot, unfortunately, be pursued further here.

In the second place, Buber's text points to an inner relationship between the story and sacrament, in other words, to the story as an effective sign and to the narrative aspect of the sacrament as a sign. The sacramental sign can easily be characterized as a linguistic action in which the unity of the story as an effective word and as practical effect is expressed in the same process. The aspect of ceremony and ritual may perhaps mean that the sacrament is not clearly recognized as a saving narrative. On closer inspection, however, it is evident firstly that the linguistic formulae used in the administration of the sacraments are typical examples of what are known as performative expressions,[7] and secondly that they narrate something. The story form occurs, for instance, in the eucharistic prayer ('on the night that he was betrayed . . .') and the formula of the sacrament of penance is incorporated within the framework of a narrative action.

I am convinced that it is very important to bring out this narrative aspect of the sacrament more clearly. If this is done, the relationship between word and sacrament may be more fully elaborated theologically. Above all, it should also be possible to relate the sacramental action more closely to stories of life and suffering and to reveal it as a saving narrative.

3. The pastoral and social aspect of narrative

Marginal groups and religious sects are always active in society and it would be wrong for the churches *a priori* to silence or reject their disturbing message. Although the underlying ambiguity of these groups prevents us from accepting them uncritically as providing the best chance of Christian renewal, they have one very positive merit—they and others employ, not argument and reasoning, but narrative. They tell the story of their conversion and retell biblical stories, sometimes in a patently helpless way that is open to manipulation. Is this simply a sign of spiritual regression, of the danger of archaism, of infantilism in the religious life, of emotional, pseudo-religious enthusiasm or of an arbitrary and contemptuous rejection of serious theological reasoning? Or is it rather the visible appearance of something that is usually repressed in the public and official life of the Churches? Are these marginal groups not in fact drawing on something that has for too long been hidden and neglected in Christianity, its narrative potential? Are they not remembering that Christians do not primarily form an argumentative and reasoning community, but a story-telling community and that the exchange of experiences of faith, like that of any 'new' experience, takes a narrative form?

This is important in the question of pastoral care and the proclamation of faith, which are, I believe, in a critical situation because we are no longer able to narrate with a practical and socially critical effect and with a dangerous and liberating intention. For too long, we have tried to suppress the narrative potential of Christianity and have confined it to credulous children and old people, although it is these who are especially sensitive to false or substitute stories or to an illusory exchange of experiences. This is why, in giving renewed emphasis to narrative, it is important to avoid the possible misunderstanding that story-telling preachers and teachers will be justified in their narration of anecdotes, when what is required are arguments and reasoning. After all, there is a time for story-telling and a time for argument. There is a difference between the two which has to be recognized.

A second misunderstanding has also to be avoided, that of believing that to stress the narrative element in pastoral care, preaching and teaching is to withdraw into the purely private sphere or the aesthetic sphere of good taste. If they give this impression, our stories will only reveal the extent to which we have forgotten how to tell them. It is true that there are many different kinds of narrative—stories which pacify, those which relieve feelings, like political jokes made under a dictatorship, and those which include a quest for freedom and stir the listener to imitation. Stories are told by very wise men who have, as Heinrich von Kleist observed, 'eaten a second time of the tree of knowledge' and by little people who are oppressed or have not yet come of age. These, however, tell not only stories which tempt them to celebrate their immature dependence or their oppressed state, but also stories which are dangerous and which seek freedom.

Freedom and enlightenment, the transition from dependence to coming of age, are not achieved simply by giving up narrative language in favour of the art of reasoning possessed by those who are enlightened and those who claim it as their privilege. (The old problem of the relationship between intellectuals and the working class has, I believe, its origins primarily in a misunderstanding among intellectuals of the emancipatory character of narrative language, just as the value of the narrative form which is at the basis of Christianity is so often underestimated by theologians.)

There can, of course, be no *a priori* proof of the critical and liberating effect of such stories, which have to be encountered, listened to and told again. But surely there are, in our post-narrative age, story-tellers who can demonstrate what stories might be today—not just artificial, private constructions, but narratives with a stimulating effect and aiming at social criticism, dangerous stories in other words. Can we perhaps retell the Jesus stories nowadays in this way?

4. The theological aspect of narrative—narrative as the medium of salvation and history

The emphasis given in the preceding section to the pastoral aspect of the story form might give the impression that narrative is above all useful in teaching and catechesis as an indispensable aid to applied theology, but that it does not affect the structure of theology itself in any way. This is, of course, not the intention at all—to say that the narrative form characterizes the proclamation of faith and rational-argument theology is too superficial a distinction, suppressing the underlying structure of theology itself. In this section, then, the theological aspect of narrative and the inseparable connection between narrative and argument (explanation, analysis, and so

210

on) will be discussed. This means, of course, that there is an arbitrary element in the discussion of this question.

The question as to how history and salvation can be related without each being diminished may be regarded as of central importance in contemporary theology. History is the experience of reality in conflict and contradiction, whereas salvation is, theologically speaking, their reconciliation by the act of God in Jesus Christ. An integral part of history is the suffering experience of non-identity through violence and oppression, injustice and inequality, guilt, finiteness and death. In this sense, history is always a history of suffering. (When all men will once enjoy equal opportunities in a classless society, it should not be difficult to regard history as a history of suffering, since it is precisely in such a period that man's self-destructive nihilism, his despair and boredom—what Ernst Bloch has called the 'melancholy of fulfilment'—often becomes so apparent.[8]) A narrative memory of salvation would in no sense lead to a regressive confusion of the distinction that dominates our problem. On the contrary, it would enable salvation in history, which is, of course, a history of suffering, to be expressed without either salvation or history being diminished. The category of narrative memory prevents salvation and redemption from becoming paradoxically unhistorical and does not subordinate them to the logical identity of argumentational mediation.

Narrative is unpretentious in its effect. It does not have, even from God, the dialectical key which will open every door and throw light on the dark passages of history before they have been trodden. It is not, however, without light itself. Pascal drew attention to this light in distinguishing, in his *Memorial,* between the narrated 'God of Abraham, Isaac and Jacob' and the God of rational argument, the 'God of the philosophers'.

Every attempt to present the connections between the history of salvation and the history of suffering in a purely argumentative way in the end proves to be hidden stories. This is in itself a strong plea for theology to have a narrative structure. A few examples can be quoted from contemporary theology. One is the transcendental theology of Karl Rahner, which only avoids tautology by narrating again and again the connections between the history of salvation and the history of suffering within the framework of an existential biography. There are also those theologies that stress the paradox-

211

ical unity that exists in the histories of salvation and suffering. It is only when these paradoxes keep to the narrative unity of what cannot be reconciled in a purely argumentative way and express that unity cognitively that they can avoid a contradiction. The same applies to all universally historical approaches, which can only avoid a dangerous totalitarianism of meaning in their attempt to reconcile the histories of salvation and suffering when they keep to a meaning of the end of history that can be narrated in advance. The same can also be said of the recent attempts to connect the history of suffering back to the history of God within the Trinity. These attempts can also only avoid the danger of a speculative gnosis by being deciphered as argumentative narratives. If theology deliberately neglects its narrative character, both the argumentative and the narrative aspects of theology are bound to suffer.

The introduction of narrative memory and the accentuation of its cognitive primacy in theology is therefore not an *ad hoc* construction. It goes further than this, making present the mediation of the history of salvation and the history of man's suffering as encountered in the witnesses and the testimonies of Christian faith.

Christianity as a community of those who believe in Jesus Christ has, from the very beginning, not been primarily a community interpreting and arguing, but a community remembering and narrating with a practical intention—a narrative and evocative memory of the passion, death and resurrection of Jesus. The logos of the cross and resurrection has a narrative structure. Faith in the redemption of history and in the new man can, because of the history of human suffering, be translated into dangerously liberating stories, the hearer who is affected by them becoming not simply a hearer, but a doer of the word.

If this narrative memory is reduced by theology to a preliminary mythological stage in the Christian logos, then theology is clearly functioning uncritically with regard to the possibilities and the limits of expressing the Christian message positively in the experience of the non-identity of history.

It is often forgotten, in the theological criticism of mythology, that the narration of critical argument is inherent in theology as a mediating aspect of its content. This also has to be borne in mind in connection with historical criticism in theology. It is important to point out here that there is a difference between regarding the historical question and the historical truth that is related to it as a problem that has been forced on Christianity in modern times and is therefore in this sense inevitable and as a medium in which the truth of Christianity and its saving message are originally expressed and identified.

A purely argumentative theology which conceals its origin and does not make this present again and again in narrative memory inevitably leads, in the history of human suffering, to those many modifications in reasoning which result in the extinction of the identifiable content of Christian salvation. I do not intend this to be regarded as a reason for excluding argument from theology. There is no question of regressively obscuring the distinction between narrative memory and theological argument. It is much more a question of acknowledging the relative value of rational argument, the primary function of which is to protect the narrative memory of salvation in a scientific world, to allow it to be at stake and to prepare the way for a renewal of this narrative, without which the experience of salvation is silenced

5. The narrative structure of practical and critical reason

Does what I have suggested so far in this chapter not amount ultimately to an uncritical blurring of differences in view of the modern emphasis on critical reason? Is the idea of a history of human suffering not made arbitrary and unsuitable by modern historical criticism? How can narrative and criticism be reconciled with each other?

As a result of the triumph of historicism, all tradition, including the narrative and memorative tradition of Christianity, has been transformed into history, that is, into the object of a critical reconstruction of historical reason. In the meantime, a criticism of this historical reasoning has been developed, which does not accept without question the absence of memory and of tradiiton in the scientific world of today, the absence which has resulted from our preoccupation with historicism. This criticism has above all been developed in the context of modern hermeneutics and also of a practical and critical philosophy of history and society.

This criticism, which is based on the distinction between knowledge and interest, is concerned with the fundamental themes of historical reason. It is not a purely formal meta-criticism which transposes the problem on to a purely theoretical plane. It deals rather with the problem as one of practical reason which occurs within certain historical traditions of memory and narrative. The theme of narrative and memory inevitably occurs again and again in this context and, what is more, it is in this case critical with regard to historical reason, which is without any narrative element and therefore recognizes neither memory nor forgetfulness as a cognitive principle. As Theodor Adorno observed, 'Forgetting is inhuman because man's accumulated suffering is forgotten—the historical trace of things, words, colours and sounds is always the trace of past suffering.'[9]

This compels a renewed respect for the history of suffering in our critical consciousness. History acquires for reason the form of a 'dangerous tradition', which is passed on not in a purely argumentative manner, but as narrative, that is, in 'dangerous stories'.

These stories break through the spell of a total reconstruction based on abstract resaon. They show that man's consciousness is a consciousness which is entwined in stories, which always has to rely on narrative identification and which, when the relative importance of the magisterium of history has been recognized, cannot entirely do without the magisterium of stories. In his film *Fahrenheit 451,* François Truffaut presented in a most vivid form this consciousness in stories, which is nourished by the accumulated narrative potential that is derived from books, as a refuge of resistance, the only alternative to a world of total manipulation and absence of freedom.

6. Questions and perspectives

This apology of narrative naturally gives rise to a number of questions. In my opinion, the following are the most important. They open up several interesting perspectives for future theological study.

Among other questions, there is that of the historical Jesus—how are the history of Jesus and the stories of Jesus related? Has the canon of the Old and New Testaments not caused a 'ban' to be imposed on narrative, preventing a retelling or further telling of stories in accordance with the contemporary situation? And should the meaning of the distinction between canonical and apocryphal stories not be re-examined? Would it not be possible for a narrative theology to provide a suitable basis for the distinction between the historical Jesus and the kerygmatic Christ which has in recent years resulted in an almost insoluble dilemma?

How is it otherwise possible for Christology to express verbally what is new and distinctive in its object (Christ)—an object that cannot be mediated by any external model (of a metaphysical or quasi-metaphysical nature)—unless it does so in narrative form? Is narrative not the language of the interruption of the system[10]—in other words, the language of everything that eludes interpretation by our complex and metatheoretical systems of knowledge? Does not Christianity itself—necessarily—seem to be the only departure from the system and to be, in this sense, subversive with regard to all the models of understanding and all the systems of interpretation that are offered to it or forced upon it? If this subversive element is not simply to become incapable of expressing itself and a question of random choice, surely it is bound to be articulated in narrative?

I have already discussed elsewhere the inevitably narrative character of a Christology, the constitutive element of which is the praxis and experience of the imitation of Christ.[11] How, for example, can the term narrative or story be defined more precisely? It cannot, after all, be regarded as synonymous with the term 'historical account', since non-historical forms of knowledge or communication, such as the saga, fairy-tale or legend, have a narrative structure. What is the relationship between fiction and authenticity in narrative texts? What does it mean when we say that a story is 'true' and in what sense can we speak of a narrative disclosure of truth?[12] What relationship is there between narrated time and physical time?[13] How are the story and the story-teller related to each other and how does the difference between the story and the story-teller prevent us from regarding narration as a pure textual problem?

In connection with the undoubted presence of narrative aspects in the individual sciences, we are bound to ask whether these are of merely secondary importance and of purely heuristic value. Does the 'logic of research' not use patterns of the narrative if it is to explain change, continuity and discontinuity in the sciences? Does our insistence on the narrative structure of theology not give rise to renewed questions about the scientific nature of theology and the cognitive character and the binding force of theological propositions?

Should the point of departure chosen by theology not always be the narrative language of the people with its worlds of religious and social symbols, in contrast to the metalanguage of linguistic specialists and sociologists which has the narrative language of the people outside and before it? And should theology not give more careful attention to its closeness to poetry?[14] Should it also not take care not to give way unthinkingly to a standardized ideal of knowledge (which would outlaw narrative)?

Finally, I am bound to point out emphatically that Christianity is not only a community engaged in interpretation and argument, but also a community with a practical intention of memory and narrative. The verbal content of Christianity should therefore be seen primarily as a major narrative which contains argumentative structures and elements and produces such structures. It is important to bear in mind that this process does not take place the other way round, which would mean that narrative would only serve as an illustration and a clarification of an exalted idea 'for the people'!

A theology that takes all these questions into account does not in any way exclude itself in advance from all scientific and social debate. On the contrary, it is possible for it to be active in an interdisciplinary manner and in criticizing society. It could (and ought to) claim as a right its need to draw attention to the subject and the danger of a praxis without reference to the subject as opposed to a scientific consciousness that is always threatening to lose sight of the subject and to emphasize the so-called 'death of man'. It should also make its claim as opposed, for example, to a science of history which represses the intelligibility of its narrative elements and in this way becomes a science of structures, processes and systems. In the same way, this theology ought also to insist on its right to exist in contrast with purely analytical linguistic science in which narrative has, as a process, been paralyzed (and even pinned and classified like a butterfly in a collector's case) and in which too the narrator (as a subject) only occurs in his 'characteristics'. It ought finally to be possible to elaborate, in an interdisciplinary debate of this kind (in which theology would be able and would indeed have to learn a great deal), a practical and critical theory in which—within the framework of a theory of innovatory linguistic ac-

216

tions [15]—the distinctive quality of narrative would be taken seriously into account.[16]

Notes

1. This chapter is an adapted version, rewritten to fit into the whole concept of this book, of a paper written in 1972, originally entitled 'Gnadengesuch für eine narrative Theologie bzw. Christologie' (see *Evangelische Theologie*, 1973, p. 340 ff) and read at the publisher's conference of the journal *Evangelische Theologie* at Grafrath in October 1972. It was first published in its original translation in *Concilium* 9 (1973), pp. 84–96, as 'A Short Apology of Narrative'.

2. See the Christological passages in J. B. Metz, *Followers of Christ, op. cit.*

3. See H. Weinrich, 'Narrative Theology', *Concilium* 9 (1973), pp. 46–56.

4. W. Benjamin, 'Der Erzähler', *Illuminationen* (Frankfurt, 1961), p. 409.

5. W. Benjamin, *op. cit.*, p. 412 ff.

6. See M. Buber, *Werke* III (Munich, 1963), p. 71. G. Scholem has reproduced a Jewish story in his *Jüdische Mystik* which also speaks of narrative as an effective sign, although it points in a different direction from Buber's story: 'Whenever Baal Shem Tov had something difficult to do, some secret work that would benefit God's creatures, he used to go into the forest, to a particular place, light a fire and pray, sunk in meditation. This all took place as he had planned. A generation later, when the Maggid of Meseritz had to do the same, he also went to the same place in the forest and said: "We cannot make the fire, but we can say the prayers" and everything went according to his plan. A generation later, Rabbi Moses Leib of Sassov wanted to do the same. He also went into the forest and said: "We cannot light the fire and we no longer know the secret meditations, which animated the prayer, but we know the place in the forest where it was done and that must be enough for us". And it was enough. A generation later, however, when Rabbi Israel of Rishin had to do the same, he sat down on his golden chair in his castle and said: "We cannot light a fire, we can no longer say the prayers and we do not know the place, but we can tell the story". The story-teller adds that the story alone had the same effect as the actions performed by the other three'.

7. See J. L. Austin, *How to do Things with Words* (Cambridge, Mass., 1962), for the theory of performative expressions.

8. I have no need here to clarify further the extent to which the history of salvation and the history of suffering are able and indeed have to be mediated verbally by means of narrative. Nor have I to show how attempts to produce this mediation by argument either of a transcendental and existential kind, dialectical and pardoxical kind or a universally historical kind are bound to fail. I have already done this in some detail above in Chapter 7 in the course of outlining an approach to a memorative and narrative soteriolgy and for this reason do not need to repeat it here.

9. T. W. Adorno, 'Thesen über Tradition', *Ohne Leitbild,* p. 34 ff.

10. If its authenticity is to be brought out, religious narrative must be clearly distinguished from stories that can be integrated rationally into a system.

11. See the Christological passages in my *Followers of Christ, op. cit.*

12. For the narrative structure of our *a priori* knowledge of the truth, see above, Chapter 11.

13. For 'time' as a basic problem in theology, see above, Chapter 10.

14. See the excursus that follows this chapter ('Theology as biography?') and D. Sölle, *Realisation* (Darmstadt and Neuwied, 1973).

15. See H. Peukert, *Wissenschaftstheorie—Handlungstheorie—fundamentale Theologie, op. cit.*

16. For the interdisciplinary orientation of theological studies today, see J. B. Metz and T. Rendtorff, *Theologie in der interdisziplinären Forschung* (Gütersloh, 1971).

Excursus: Theology as biography? [1]

1. The thesis

One of the most striking aspects of modern Catholic theology is the deep division in it between theology as a system and religious experience, doxography and biography and dogmatism and mysticism. This does not mean, of course, that the individual theologian today is not—or has not been in recent centuries—deeply religious and even mystical. It is not this private, individual reconciliation between doctrine and personal history that I am discussing here, but rather the fact that this reconciliation has not itself become theology and that it has not become public, communicable and historically important within the main stream of theology. For as long as society as a whole had a religious aim and theological reason was universally accepted as the key form of reason, the crisis of identity that existed in theology and had indeed been brought about by this division was able to continue in a hidden form. As time passed, however, the separation became more and more visible.

Religious experience, the articulation of Christian history in the presence of God and the idea of mystical biography became more and more overshadowed by doxography, with the result that the contents of that experience were interpreted in a more and more subjective and impressionistic way and theology thus became less and less capable of making those contents the public property of the Church and society. Dogmatic theology on the other hand became an increasingly objectively atrophied form of teaching and often functioned as a systematized fear of contagion from life that was not understood.

I am referring, of course, to the prevailing system of neo-scholastic theology which, with a number of individual exceptions, was universally accepted in the Church. Recent attempts to bridge the gulf between doxography and religious experience give the impression that the gulf continues to exist and is as wide as it ever was. There are many questions being asked, for example, about the relevance of dogma, the context within which it should be considered, its value with regard to religiosity and its practical and pastoral significance. There is also an indirect suggestion that dogmatic theology has in itself hardly anything at all to do with Christian praxis and therefore cannot have any deep effect on it or change it in any way.

What form, then, should theology take if it is to succeed in putting an end to this division between dogma and personal history or biography? What type of theology would be able to bring about a reconciliation between what has been divided for so long and act as a creative mediator? I would tentatively suggest that the intention of such a theology would be indicated in the name 'biographical dogmatic theology' or 'theological biography'. By 'biography' in this context I do not mean a literary reflection of subjectivity with the purpose of finding a symbol for the interpretation of the world and life as such. (This was Goethe's definition of biography.) Theology is biographical when the mystical biography of religious experience in the concealed presence of God is written into the doxography of faith. It is also biographical if it is not a derived theology that is exclusively preoccupied with one concern and ultimately tautological in its search for irrefutability, but is rather a concentrated and shortened narrative of biography in the presence of God.

Biographical theology introduces the subject into the dogmatic consciousness of theology. It does not in any sense propagate a new form of theological subjectivism. 'Subject' is not a term that can be exchanged at will in this context for any other. It is man involved in his experiences and history and capable of identifying himself again and again in the light of those experiences. Introducing the subject into dogmatic theology therefore means raising man in his religious experience and biography to the level at which he becomes the objective theme of dogmatic theology. In other words, it means that dogmatic theology and biography can be reconciled with each other and that theological doxography and mystical biography can be brought together.

This is not suggested in the interest of any precious or esoteric theology, but rather in the interest of systematic scholastic theology on the one hand and in the interest of the biographical dogmatism of the average Christian believer on the other. Theological reflection can be expressed in the biographical mediation of theory and praxis as the mystical biography of a life led on the basis of faith or as the history of the witness borne every day by that life. This can be done without recourse to great changes or special coversions and elucidations. The biography of a whole people, the average, everyday collective routine religious experience of the Catholic people could be spelt out in that mediation. No special gifts or events and no exceptional mystical experience would be presupposed in it, apart, of course, from the mystical experience without which faith can never exist. This means that the biographical theology that I am proposing would be a mystagogy for all without any fear of popularization or contagion from dull, ordinary everyday life and its religious experiences that can hardly be deciphered.

Who, after all, is in greater need of a biographical form of dogmatic theology than the Christian who finds it very difficult to feel part of theological teaching as a whole, to be affected by it or involved in it and to identify himself or his own experience with the mysticism of that theology because it is so often concealed from itself? And where would he find greater need of it than in modern society, in which his identity is called into question, the death of the subject and the end of the individual are proclaimed, the experiences of the individual can no longer keep pace with the advances of technology in a world that is based on unfeeling reason and those same experiences are increasingly enclosed within a world that has a stabilizing effect on expectations that conform to the system and at the same time banishes or reduces to nothing all hopes and dreams that call society into question? Modern society after all prefabricates man's pattern of life and produces a weariness with human identity that eats at man's soul.

One question that has to be raised by a biographical theology is whether or not theology is scientific. What is meant by 'scientific' in theology? It has to be borne in mind in this context that the most important achievements in theology and the history of the Church are—and for the most part always have been—derived from an impure kind of science in which many factors are involved. Biography, imagination, accumulated human experience, conversions, visions and prayer have all been compounded into a theological system.

Theology today is also not simply a professional affair conducted

221

by university teachers. A biographical theology should therefore not let itself be forced into the pattern of an exact science. The experienced conviction and instructed experience of faith cannot be satisfactorily justified by the metalogical rules of analytical argument. Theology has therefore to prevent itself from submitting unconditionally to the rules of the exact sciences and accepting their vocabulary. It can never be a natural science of the divine.

This unity between theological teaching and life, theoretical dogmatic theology and practical biography, is bound to strike a theology that has long ago accepted a standardized scientific language and pattern of thought and is therefore no longer sure of its own identity as regressive, out of date and even archaic. This, however, is as though theology could banish the direct and naïve conviction of experience without sacrificing its identity! Does the language of a theology which takes all this into account not have the effect of being too poetical, lyrical, invented or emphatic to be able to derive universal intelligibility and consent from theology as a whole?

On the other hand, however, we are also bound to ask why biographical theology should deny itself to such an extent and be so critical of its own language that it loses confidence in itself and lacks the courage to insist firmly on a distinctive and relevant language.

Whoever refuses to believe Heinrich Böll or Peter Handke, for example, can go to Klopstock, who said in the eighteenth century: 'There are ideas that can only be expressed poetically or rather it is in accordance with the nature of certain objects to think of them poetically and to say that they would lose too much if they were expressed differently. Reflections about the omnipresence of God are, in my opinion, of this kind'.[2]

In the German-speaking countries, we find statements of this kind difficult to accept because of our German ideology that can only recognize a scientific manner of expression. Yet 'science' covers more in the German speaking countries than it does anywhere else in the world. If our culture was more like that of the English-speaking, Romance or Slav countries, where greater public recognition is given to poetry, we would be less inclined to use the word 'amateur'. 'Amateur', however, would seem to describe quite well the unsuspecting attitude of those who happily and unscrupulously subject theology to a standardized scientific language.

I describe Karl Rahner's theological work in the following section as biographical dogmatic theology or the mystical biography of a Christian believer today and ascribe to it the significance of a paradigm with regard to the narrative and biographical theology that I have been discussing here. I do not, however, do this because Rahner's thought bears striking and easily identifiable traces of this particular theological approach. There are certainly many other clearer examples of biographical theology than Rahner's! No, I regard his transcendental theology as a paradigm because it can only be understood as a nontautological theology of the subject, that is, in its theological evidence and uniqueness, by its appearance as an existential biography that introduces itself as a narrative and as a discussion of religious experience. To that extent, Rahner's apparently strictly dogmatic theology has succeeded in putting an end to the division between dogmatic theology and biography to which I referred at the beginning of this excursus. It has, moreover, done this with a creative strength and mediatory capacity that is reminiscent of the great mediations in the history of western theology.

2. The paradigm

Rahner himself has described his extraordinary, immense and incomparable theological work as a continuation of the traditional scholastic theology of the Church, a revelation of its partly buried and suppressed intuitions and intentions and a release of its inner dynamic power. He has also declared that he does this by means of transcendental reflection. Bearing this in mind, it is not too difficult for the specialist in the field of theology to take preliminary bearings of this great work, classify it and evaluate it.

What, then, does Rahner mean by 'transcendental theology'? His theological approach has, on the one hand, made the system of scholastic theology open to the subject and, on the other, has liberated the subject from the rock of a scholastic objectivism in which it had been held captive. Rahner does not treat this subject as a purely reflective definition that can be made objective again at will. His subject is man in the history of his own experience, which cannot be identified or communicated without elements of narrative. In this sense, Rahner has raised the religious history of man to the level of an objective theme of dogmatic theology.

The most striking and frequently quoted aspect of Rahner's work is that he deals with so many themes. A random glance at any of the pages in a bibliography of his work will show how varied these themes are. It will at the same time show the variety of ways in which he deals with so many different questions in theology, the Church and public life. His work is quite simply a theologically substantial report about life in the light of contemporary Christianity. It is not just a classical canon of questions. It does not deal simply with questions that arise within the system. Rahner's canon is life itself—not life as selected by the theological canon, but life as it imposes itself and often uncomfortable life.

Rahner has always done more than simply be interested in what is interesting. He has also been concerned in an unprecedented way with the needs and questions of others. The great variety of his theological work is therefore not just the result of a random choice, possibly based on fashion. It is systematic. The great movement of reduction that characterizes his work is not, as has often been suggested, because of an attempt on his part to trace one theological doctrine back to another. It is rather because he has always tried to bring doctrine and life together within the context of the modern world. This is why science becomes theology for him. It is not, as is so often the case, a question of theology becoming science in a previously defined way. It is also why everyday questions become theological questions for him. (To the horror of those who for the sake of the supposedly sicentific character of dogmatic theology refuse to consider all these questions concerned with everyday life and confine themselves to the classical questions of theology, although the latter are the everyday questions of a previous period— dogmatic theologians did not confine themselves in the past to the formulation of concepts based on earlier experiences, but again and again communicated and handed down new experiences with those concepts!) We may also add that Rahner has always done this in season and out of season and scientifically or in an 'amateur' fashion, as he himself has often described the excessive number of claims made on him by life's questions and experiences. But who are the amateurs in this case?

Rahner's theology is a narrative, biographical dogmatic theology which is at the same time more objectively instructive than any other theology today. He himself claims that his theology has as its prototypes and sources Thomism and transcendental philosophy, but there are certainly others as well. I would mention, for example, Augustine, Bonaventure, Newman, possibly Pascal, Kierkegaard and possibly also Bonhoeffer. It is not, of course, a question here of demonstrable dependences (though we should not forget that Rahner made important contributions to the patristic tradition, that he regards Thomas Aquinas as closer to Augustine than to the Thomists and that he has always cared more for Tauler than for Suarez and Molina). It is rather a question of presumed affinities in the structure, status and quality of his theological work. It is certain that many different and often quite divergent theologies can claim quite rightly to be the offspring of Rahner's theology. In the same way, his theological ancestors have also been very many and very different, even mutually contradictory. Like most classical theologians, he is in no sense of pedigree stock. Nor are his descendants pure-bred. His theology, which can, as a religious biography, be regarded as theological doxography (both of these aspects being fused into a single whole and each of them complete in itself), is very close indeed to a type of theological writing with which it has hardly ever been compared—theology based on the history of human life.

It is true of dogmatic theology based on the history of man's life that its unity is a crystallization of its great multiplicity. Anyone who confined himself, in reading Rahner's theology, to pure principles would possibly derive only exalted tautologies from it. The basic theme of his work can only really be heard if one listens to all the variations. His system is not without stories, his doctrine is not without communicated experiences and his doxography is not without mystical biography—none of the first can be understood without reference to the second.

It is neither possible nor even necessary to try to establish the passage of biographical dogmatic theology in the individual theological themes with which Rahner deals in his work, although it would not be difficult to distinguish, for example, the narrative, mystical biographical element in his essays dealing with Christology, soteriology, eschatology and historical theology.

The strongest suspicion against a biographical way of dealing with theology is raised by the theology of the Trinity. It is therefore worth while considering what Rahner has said about this branch of theology in his introduction to a treatise that he wrote on the triune

225

God as the transcendental ground of the history of salvation. He claimed that the mystery of the Trinity was the ultimate mystery of our own reality and that it could also be experienced in that human reality. This experience provided us with a methodological principle that could be applied to the Trinity. The Trinity, Rahner insisted, was a mystery with a paradoxical character that had an echo in man's existence. This meant that it would be meaningless to avoid considering that character or to try to conceal it by a violent but subtle use of concepts and conceptual distinctions, applied with the aim of throwing light on the mystery, but in fact only providing verbalisms that would have the effect of analgesics and simply deaden the pain suffered by those naively perspicacious spirits who have to revere the mystery without understanding it.[3]

'Mystery' is a key-word of fundamental importance in Rahner's biographical dogmatic theology. The concept of the incomprehensible God and man's experience as withdrawn from himself into that incomprehensibility are both contained within it. The Ignatian mysticism of the omnipresence of God—God in the world—can also be felt in Rahner's work. Doxography and mystical biography are merged into one another. This unity is reinforced by Rahner's distinctive understanding of theology as study, initiation, mystagogy and the induction of life into the experience of mystery.

In one respect, however, Rahner's biographical theology is radically different from its prototypes. It is above all a biographical dogmatic account of the simple, one might even venture to say the average, Christian, the mystical biography of an undramatic life. It is the biographical dogmatic theology of a markedly anti-biographical type. In this respect, then, it is quite different from the comparable theological work of Augustine, Newman or Bonhoeffer, whom I included among his ancestors. This difference is not, however, simply a disadvantage—it is, on the contrary, an aspect of the distinctive quality and one of the great advantages of Rahner's theological work. It makes his theology present and contemporary in a very specific way and very relevant to the sociology of religion.

Rahner's passionate attempt to write scholastic theology—ordinary theology—for all men and to do not more than this is counterbalanced by his intention to involve the story of the ordinary Christian's religious life and indeed the history of the Christian people's life in dogmatic theology. A great deal of what he has written has been termed élitist and has been excluded by some scholars from the main body of his work—his extension of the doctrine of *fides implicita,* for example, his application of the principle of *bona fides* and the related theory of anonymous Christianity. But these so-called élitist theologoumena have been determined by precisely the opposite intention. Rahner himself has a distinctly proletarian aversion to everything élitist or esoteric. He has never tried to imitate the arcanum of religion with an air of autocratic affectation. This is why he has succeeded, despite his undeniably difficult language, in coming close to very many people and not simply Church members or practising theologians, in other words, the élite. It is also why he has been able to deal in his writings with many different needs without adapting his themes.

It is, of course, possible to question Rahner's biographical theology critically. The questions that arise in particular in this context are those which confront the directly theological orientation towards the subject and are therefore also present in any biographical theology and which cannot accept uncritically as valid the predominance of anthropology in theology as opposed to history and society. It would be valuable, in any total approach to a practical fundamental theology, to break through this biographical conception of dogmatic theology and move in the direction of a theological biography of Christianity in which the twofold mystical and political structure of that theology, in other words, the social pattern of Christian faith, was more consistently taken into account and made the moving force of theological reflection.[4]

What should by now be clear, then, from this consideration of Rahner's theological approach as a paradigm, is the type of theology to which the narrative structure of Christian faith most closely corresponds. In struggling with the neoscholastic tradition and evolving a dogmatic theology that is basically a concentrated and shortened biography of human history in the presence of God, Rahner has contributed to the history of the identity of modern theology that can no longer be ignored. He has, in brief, produced a mystical biography with a dogmatic intention.

Notes

1. This chapter is an adapted version, rewritten to fit into the whole concept of this book, of a paper written in 1974 as a tribute to Karl Rahner on the occasion of his seventieth birthday. It was entitled 'Karl Rahner—ein theologisches Leben. Theologie als mystiche Biographie eines Christenmenschen heute' and was published in *Stimmen der Zeit,* May 1974, and in a shorter version entitled 'Theologie als Biographie' in *Concilium,* May 1976.

2. Dorothee Sölle, *Realisation, op. cit.,* Foreword.

3. See *Mysterium Salutis* II (Einsiedeln, 1967), p. 346.

4. I have written in greater detail about the twofold structure of Christian and theological existence in my *Followers of Christ, op. cit.* For an attempt to discuss a historical theology and the hermeneutical problems connected with this theology, see T. R. Peters, *Die Präsenz des Politischen in der Theologie D. Bonhoeffers.*

13. Solidarity

1. A general definition in connection with a practical fundamental theology

In the first part of this book, 'solidarity' was a central concept in the definition of a practical fundamental theology as a political theology of the subject, a theology based on the idea of the possibility of all men becoming subjects in the presence of God. In the form of a solidarity based on the memory of the dead and those who have been overcome—a solidarity with those who have died based on the dangerous memory not only of the successful, but also the defeated, not only of the victorious, but also the lost—the idea of solidarity also plays an important part in 'Themes' (Part II). There it functions not only as historical solidarity looking forward to future generations, but also as solidarity backwards. In the second sense, it gives emphasis to the specific character of human destiny and the human reserves of Christianity and theology and is able to join, with that specific character, in discussion about human history and society.[1]

As a category of practical fundamental theology, solidarity is above all a category of help, support and togetherness, by which the subject, suffering acutely and threatened, can be raised up. Like memory and narrative, it is one of the fundamental definitions of a theology and a Church which aims to express its redeeming and liberating force in the history of human suffering, not above men's heads and ignoring the problem of their painful non-identity. Although Christians believe that the suffering caused by guilt and death has been overcome in Christ, this does not exonerate them from the task of committing themselves in solidarity to the overcoming of suffering caused by oppression and injustice, the suffering of not yet or no longer being able to be subjects. It is in this solidarity that memory and narrative (of salvation) acquire their specific mystical and political praxis. Without solidarity, memory and narrative cannot become practical categories of theology. In the same way, without memory and narrative, solidarity cannot express its practical humanizing form. It is only when they co-exist that memory, narrative and solidarity can effectively be categories of a practical fundamental theology.

It is especially in the systems of personalistic or existential theology that solidarity would appear to have theological validity. This is not necessarily so explicitly within this kind of theology, but it can certainly be found in a concealed and implied way in the I-Thou relationship and at the interpersonal level.[2]

I criticized this approach in my first published reflections about a political theology and showed it to be, in the light of a practical fundamental theology, a form of privatized theology for which all the phenomena of the interpersonal are expressed only in their private and depoliticized form, as I-Thou relationships, interpersonal relationships or neighbourhood relationships.[3] In this interpersonal, I-Thou syndrome in theology, political theology would criticize a predominance of rustic romanticism in which solidarity (if this occurs at all) appears either in the form of natural sympathy or as a life led in direct personal encounter. This hardly touches the reality of complex communications and great isolation that prevails in the typical city community of today. Political theology also recognizes in the predominance of the private aspect the theologically reproduced private character that distinguishes the late middle-class society based on exchange and the satisfaction of needs and bisects in advance the idea of Christian solidarity.[4] Within a society that is characterized by exchange, solidarity—if it occurs at all—appears only as a solidarity based on an alliance between equal partners (men who are either already partners or who are attempting to become partners). The principle on which this partnership is based is: 'I will look after your interests if you look after mine'. The fundamental interest of each of the two partners in the alliance is in exchange and the purpose of the partnership is mutual success and progress. In such a partnership, the partners are competent because they are equal in value and compensate each other equally. But the fact that commitment in solidarity is not simply futile, but can mean loss, that there are usually no shared equal values in this commitment in solidarity, that this solidarity is qualitatively more than a merely purposeful alliance between equal partners and that humanism is more than a purely purposeful human action and commitment can be without self-interest—these are Christian concepts that are often obscured in the partnership of shared interests that exists in the society of exchange.

As Max Weber and others have clearly shown in their sociological analyses and as writings about the 'ban on love' in our society of exchange have emphasized,[5] it is very difficult if not impossible to unite the process of rationalization based on the theory of evolution that is taking place in the modern world with the Christian religion that is based on the commandment of love. A form of solidarity not only with men of reason, but also, even more radically, with those in need would seem to have little chance of survival in a rationalized society based on exchange.

If this opposition between the principle of exchange in society and solidarity is taken into account, it becomes obvious that no practical fundamental theology can accept uncritically an idyllic application of the idea of solidarity, but is bound to do what it does with regard to the ideas of memory and narrative, that is point to the challenging aspect of that idea. It will moreover stress that challenge not only for the sake of those who want to accept the principle of solidarity, but also for the sake of those who systematically reject it. In the case of those who achieve a solidarity that is no more than a sympathetic contact between allies or partners or else an altruistic alliance based on mutual protectionism, the logic of the Christian idea of solidarity will eventually result in a counter-alliance that is expressed in the partisanship of the imitation of Christ. It is worth remembering in this context what we have stressed again and again in this book, namely that the Church will only become a Church in solidarity when it ceases to be a protectionist 'Church for the people' and becomes a real 'Church of the people'.

Nonetheless, solidarity is strictly universal in its application to practical fundamental theology. It extends to those who have been overcome and left behind in the march of progress. It includes the dead. Indeed, the theological category of solidarity reveals its mystical and universal aspect above all in its memory of solidarity with the dead. In the context of practical fundamental theology, solidarity provides an apocalyptical stimulus.

The tension between mystical and universal solidarity and partisan solidarity cannot be released simply by theological argument. We cannot therefore place any faith in the many attempts that have been made to reduce the partisan aspect of Christian solidarity by providing pseudo-universal syntheses and balanced forms of proportional representation (and thus excluding concrete solidarity). We also distrust those arguments which regard solidarity as something that is in itself already limited and are therefore not stimulated by the factual impossibility of universal solidarity.

In a practical fundamental theology, the essentially twofold structure of solidarity is preserved. In other words, solidarity is seen on the one hand as mystical and universal and on the other as political and particular. This double structure protects the universal aspect of solidarity from apathy and its partisan nature from hatred and forgetfulness. It raises again and again the question: With whom should there be solidarity? What form should solidarity take?

Christian solidarity in memory with the dead is not determined by an abstract interest, nor is it primarily motivated by care or anxiety of the kind that provokes the question: What will happen to me in death? On the contrary, its guiding question is: What happens to others, especially those who suffer? (This is connected with care about one's own identity in death.) In its twofold mystical and political structure, solidarity can be seen as a category by means of which the subject is saved when he is threatened, for example, by forgetfulness, oppression or death. It is therefore a category of commitment to man to enable him to become and remain a subject.

I would like to give this idea of solidarity a rather more precise form. For this reason, I shall in the following two sections consider two types of solidarity and relate them to the concept of a practical fundamental theology. The first is the kind of solidarity that is found in the contemporary theories of science and action and the second kind of solidarity is world-wide.

2. Solidarity only among the rational?

It is possible to mention many different kinds of solidarity in this context. There is a risk of doing injustice to these scholarly theories within the rigorous limits of space imposed on us here, but it is important to draw attention to them because they have a place within the framework of critical examination of solidarity on the basis of a practical fundamental theology.[6]

Hegel's idealism is certainly behind the approaches mentioned here. This idealism is transcendentally based on the rationality of the subject and it provides a re-evaluation of and a compensation for the inequalities that it observes among those who come into contact with each other. Hegelian idealism thus effects a transcendental simulation of the equal status of the partners! In these contemporary approaches, moreover, this idealism is also frequently combined with a subtle form of evolutionary logic. Both Habermas' universal pragmatism and Apel's community of communication seem to me to imply this idealism, especially in the manner in which they both presuppose the mutual recognition of the subjects envisaged in their universal rules. All the relationships developed in these and other similar theories of communicative action—both the unlimited community of communication postulated by Apel and the universal solidarity suggested by Habermas—have, at least tendentiously, the character of a relationship based on exchange.

Any practical fundamental theology is bound to criticize a discussion of the rational and those with equal rights, with whom all the relevant theories of science and action that have emerged in recent years seem to be concerned, a discourse that is, in other words, directed towards universal freedom in solidarity. It is critical because of the objective history of human suffering that has from the beginning accompanied action undertaken in solidarity. As Peukert has observed, 'The normative implications of a theory of communicative action for the identity of subjects and the structure of society become insuperable difficulties as soon as an attempt is made to think out the historical constitution of a human society united in solidarity'.[7]

Practical fundamental theology opposes this reciprocal form of solidarity by enlisting the support of a Christian solidarity that is accompanied by the categories of dangerous memory and narrative. It does not stress the history of triumph and conquest which is proclaimed in a concentrated form in Hegel's idea and even more emphatically in the contemporary theories of evolution as the proper sphere that governs and corrects human speaking and action. On the contrary, it is concerned with the history of man's suffering and regards this as the best possible corrective. Practical fundamental theology functions as a practical criticism of science and attempts to break through the élitist circle of argumentative competence. Its logic, which is the result of the Christological idea of

233

imitation, stresses that not only rationality but also and above all indigence (need) is the decisive presupposition for recognizing the subjectivity of others.[8]

3. World-wide solidarity?

In Chapter 1 of this book, the world situation was analyzed and the global structures determining man's concrete fate today were examined. In Chapter 4, the fundamental theological pronouncement—the Word of the God who calls all men to be subjects in his presence—was discussed. Both of these questions open up world-wide perspectives to theology. (It may be observed in parenthesis that theology today ought to be more pleased with criticism of its all-inclusiveness and arrogance than with criticism based on its presumed tendency to an abstraction, in which a concrete overall survey can only be acquired by ignoring these structures. But can the danger of arrogance, vagueness and a reluctance to learn from experience not be traced more satisfactorily back to those theologies which reject a world-wide perspective and continue to regard their special point of view—which is often a central European one—as the only valid theological and Christian one?)

It is only in this world-wide perspective that the theological category of solidarity can acquire its full dimensions. For this reason, it is also only now, when men are more fully present to each other as men (not simply intellectually, but in their interdependence, suffering and need), that the full extent of the commitment that is implied in the apparently obvious statement that all men are equal as God's creatures can be really understood. We have already considered the implications of the theological truth that all men are created in the image of God in the first part of this book and therefore cannot accept this concept isolated from the deep inequalities which exist today in the world and make it impossible for so many men to become subjects. Our reflections on man's state as a creature made in God's image and its implications also provide theology with the means to criticize all ideologies of equality in which only private interests are pursued, in a concealed way, in an unprofitable discussion of the question of the equality of all men.

A theology that is no longer able to remain separate from these points of view is clearly confronted with the challenge of the fundamental socialist notion of international solidarity with the working class and with the demand to achieve world-wide solidarity in this way. It is not possible to go into the dangers and tensions involved in this idea here, except to say in passing that they are often revealed in the conflict over who is the real political representative of this solidarity and that Christians do not have simply to copy this form of solidarity or to reaffirm it in those places where it is or appears to be in force. The Christian praxis of solidarity will always be directed towards the imitation of Christ. This imitation has always betrayed its own special form of mysticism whenever it has avoided the partisan nature of political action or has given a merely spiritualized value to the process of imitation.[9] Christianity is therefore not able to remain neutral in the struggle for world-wide solidarity for the sake of the needy and the underprivileged. It is compelled, with its emblem proclaiming that all men should become subjects in solidarity in the presence of God and its refusal to regard the already existing subject in society simply as the only valid religious subject, to take part in that struggle.

These problems and tasks can no longer be regarded as marginal or thought of as typical of the ideas held by scattered groups of left-wing Christians. As I have emphasized frequently throughout this book, the world situation in which the Church finds itself places these problems very high on the Christian and theological agenda. One particularly urgent question in this context is, for example, how the one world Church should react to its own class problem, that is, the great contrast between the Church of the North and that of the South? How should it reconcile this antithesis with its own understanding of itself as the one community at the Lord's table and the sign of eschatological unity?[10] Whenever the Church has remained unmoved by questions of this kind, however, and has passively accepted the fact that it simply reflects within itself the social contrasts of the outside world, it has irresponsibly furthered the conviction that religion and the Church are pure superstructures of that society.[11]

Whether or not the German Church, for instance, can surmount its failure in the nineteenth century to deal with these problems (a failure of which it accused itself in the German bishops' publication of the Church and the working class) and whether it will succeed in 'growing into the working-class world' now that the working class 'instead of growing into the Church has only for the most part grown away from it' [12] depends above all on whether and to what extent that Church is prepared to accept the challenge made by the workers in the world Church and the world itself. No attempt to 'grow into' the world of the working class will succeed in the German Church if it remains one-sidedly preoccupied with theory and reality in the Church in northern Europe alone.

When Christianity takes its place in the movement towards the development of world-wide community it will be able to express, in and for that great community, its understanding of a solidarity that is free from violence and hatred. Love of one's enemies and opposition to violence and hatred do not, however, dispense Christianity from the need to struggle for the state when all men will be subjects. If it does not do this, it will fail in its task to be the home of hope in the God of the living and the dead who calls on all men to be subjects in his presence.

Notes

1. In the discussion about political theology, this extended form of historical solidarity struck me for the first time as important when I was debating this approch in 1969 with critics. I have dealt with it systematically as a matter of increasing significance in this book from Chapter 5 onwards (See especially the emphasis on this universal historical solidarity as the foundation of a criticism of abstract and total emancipation in Chapter 7).

2. My reflections about a political theology began therefore with a criticism of transcendental theology based on intersubjectivity. See, for example, 'Unglaube als theologisches Problem', *Concilium* 6/7 (1965).

3. See my *Theology of the World, op. cit.,* pp. 109–110.

4. Criticism of this (middle-class) bisection corresponds to the criticism of the bisection of history and justice made by a political theology of the subject of the post-middle-class form of socialism that clings to the idea of universal solidarity and justice, but believes that it is possible to abandon the idea of justice for the dead which has to qualify this universality and to do this without any human loss.

5. See M. Horkheimer and T. W. Adorno, *Dialectics of Enlightenment, op. cit.,* p. 101.

6. See H. Peukert, *Wissenschaftstheorie—Handlungstheorie—fundamentale Theologie, op. cit.*

7. H. Peukert, *op. cit.,* p. 283.

8. K. Füssel, 'Das praktische Fundament der Glaubenssätze', *Ordnung und Konflikt* (Dokumente der Alpbacher Hochschulwochen, 1977), (Vienna, 1978). If the

theological concept of solidarity is indissolubly connected with the concepts of memory and narrative—and if these are the categories that prevent us from defining history as a history of conquest—then this connection impels us to look for a theological form of hermeneutics which would attempt to save the forgotten subject (in opposition to an evolutionary theory based on the death of the subject and a Utopia as a paradise of the conquerors. This would provide at least one important point of departure for a debate between representatives of political theology and the protagonists of materialistic hermeneutics.

9. For the theme of the imitation of Christ, see my *Followers of Christ, op. cit.*

10. The fact that this problem has to be considered by theologians and the Church means that the latter would not be able to avoid theorizing, especially in their discussion of the theory of dependence.

11. See the publication of the German bishops: *Unsere Hoffnung,* IV, 3.

12. See especially Part I of the publication of the Synod of German bishops: *Kirche und Arbeiterschaft.*